1983

January 29, 2005
To Jenae from your cousin
Sherry Brunette

THE
PYRAMIDS

THE
PYRAMIDS

By AHMED FAKHRY

THE UNIVERSITY OF CHICAGO PRESS
CHICAGO AND LONDON

The University of Chicago Press, Chicago 60637
The University of Chicago Press, Ltd., London

© *1961 by The University of Chicago. All rights reserved*
First Published 1961. Second Edition 1969

Printed in the United States of America

81 80 79 78   9 8 7 6

International Standard Book Number: 0–226–23471–1 (clothbound)
Library of Congress Catalog Card Number: 61–8645

Contents

Illustrations

Publisher's Note to
Second Edition

Dr. Fakhry's study was originally published in 1961. Since then, important developments have occurred in the use of cosmic ray muons as "X-rays" to study the pyramids. These developments have been reviewed by the author in a new chapter, "Recent Investigations," which has occasioned the publication of this second edition. Dr. Fakhry has also seized the occasion to correct a number of minor errors in the main text.

I

Introduction

If you ask a world traveler which famous monuments made the strongest impression on him, he will probably reply, "the pyramids of Giza." The reasons differ; one visitor may admire their colossal scale, another, their architectural perfection, a third, their antiquity, a fourth, their romantic situation, a fifth, their history. I have lived from time to time in excavation houses near the pyramids, and for the past ten years in a house in the desert less than a quarter of a mile west of the Great Pyramid of Khufu. I find that there is no limit to their inspiring beauty. On very dark nights those huge, black, triangular shapes loom up against the sky to connect heaven and earth. People are gay and noisy when they visit the pyramids by day, but at night the romantic beauty of the site and the realization of its antiquity turn the frivolous visitor into a quiet and serious admirer.

Whenever the pyramids are mentioned, that of Khufu—the Great Pyramid of Giza—springs to mind. But visitors to Egypt see many others at the edge of the plateau west of Cairo, and there are others as far south as the Sudan. Altogether, there are more than seventy known pyramids in Egypt, and no one can estimate how many lie hidden under the sands of the desert.

The pyramids can be grouped in several geographic areas, from north to south. There are ten groups in the Memphite necropolis. The north-ernmost is that of Abu Rawwash, where Rededef, Khufu's successor, built his pyramid. Here also stood an unidentified pyramid, the ruins of which can still be seen. Apparently there used to be a still more northerly pyramid at Athribis (the modern Tell Atrib), near Benha in the Delta. A French expedition saw this brick pyramid in 1800, but its superstruc-ture has since entirely disappeared.[1] A Liverpool expedition identified the position of this pyramid as recently as 1938. Today the place is marked by a small pile of bricks, which has neither the shape of a pyramid nor any identification of age. The second group of pyramids south of Abu Rawwash is that of Giza, where we find the Great Pyramid and nine others surrounding it. A third group is at Zawiet el Aryan, about three miles south of the Giza group. Three more miles to the south bring us to the fourth group, the famous pyramids of Abusir. Below these is the extensive field of Saqqara, which is divided into Saqqara North and Saqqara South. Then comes the seventh group at Dahshur, where we find the two stone pyramids of Sneferu, and several others of the Middle Kingdom. The eighth group is that of Mazghuna; the ninth, that of Lisht. The pyramid of Meydum makes up the tenth group. It is considered the last pyramid field in the necropolis of Mem-phis. In addition, there are the famous Twelfth Dynasty pyramids of the Faiyum; a few scattered pyramids in Upper Egypt, which have not been thoroughly excavated and whose dates are not known; and the pyra-mids of the "Ethiopian" type in northern Sudan.

The pyramids were originally built as tombs for kings. (In later times the right was extended to queens as well.) The earliest attempt to build a tomb in pyramidal form is represented by the Step Pyramid at Saqqara, constructed about 2780 B.C.; the first true pyramid dates from the reign of Sneferu at the beginning of the Fourth Dynasty, about 100 years later. Thus the Great Pyramid of Giza is not the oldest pyramid. When it was planned, more than 4,600 years ago, there were others standing not far from it. The great architects who worked on it were trained less than fifteen miles to the south at the pyramids of Khufu's father, King Sneferu.

---

[1] *Description de l'Égypte*, Vol. V, Plate 27; also A. Rowe, in *Annales du Service*, XXXVIII, 524.

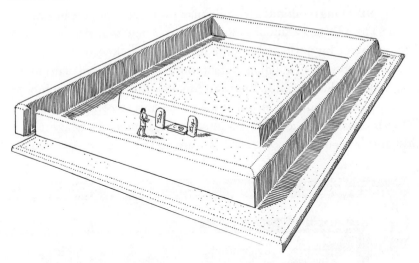

1. *A typical royal mastaba of the Early Archaic Period. A reconstruction of the mastaba of Queen Mer-Neith. (After Ricke,* Bemerkungen, *II, 17.)*

The concept of a pyramidal tomb is in fact the result of centuries of development and experiment. The earliest royal tombs are of considerable interest, because they show the development of funerary architecture prior to the pyramids.

The tombs of the earliest historical kings of Egypt have been found at Abydos in Upper Egypt, 360 miles south of Cairo. Abydos was the royal necropolis of the southern capital, This. The tombs date from about 3200 B.C. At about the same time, the necropolis of Saqqara arose on a desert plateau west of the northern capital, Memphis. One of the difficult problems facing the Egyptologist is the existence of two tombs for the same king, one in the south at Abydos, and one in the north at Saqqara. The dead king could have been buried in only one. Probably the most reasonable solution to this problem is that the Abydos tomb was a cenotaph, an empty tomb in honor of the king. Both sites have revealed royal tombs, and, although they differ in detail, their main features are the same. All are built of mud brick in the form of a huge rectangle. Archeologists call them *mastabas* because they resemble in shape the brick benches of this name outside the houses in Egyptian villages. Under each mastaba lay a burial chamber surrounded by many other chambers and storerooms.

Egyptian kings continued to build mastaba tombs until the beginning of the Third Dynasty, about 2780 B.C., when a new page was written in the history of Egyptian architecture. King Zoser followed the tradition of his predecessors in building his first tomb, a mud-brick mastaba in the south at Beit Khallaf, not far from Abydos. But his second tomb, at Saqqara, was an important milestone in the history of Egypt. Among Zoser's officials was a young architect named Imhotep, whose father had also been an architect. Imhotep's rare abilities were recognized by

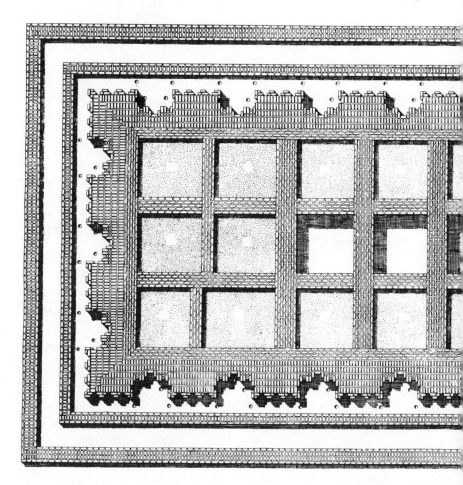

2. *Plan of the mastaba of King Ḥor-aḥa, at Saqqara. (After Emery,* The Tomb of Ḥor-aḥa.)

his master, who gave him a free hand to plan his tomb. One important innovation was the use of stone, which had been used sparingly in previous times. Imhotep built Zoser's mastaba at Saqqara, including the inclosure wall entirely of blocks of stone. The mastaba itself underwent several fundamental changes. Imhotep superimposed one mastaba upon another, each smaller than the last, until they totaled six. The completed structure had more or less the form of a pyramid with large steps.

Zoser's Step Pyramid dominated the necropolis. A successor copied

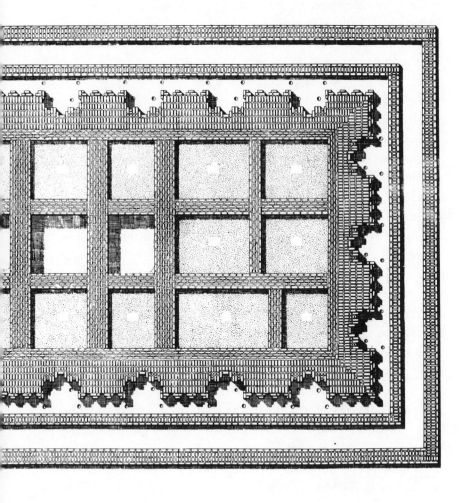

it, and it became the prototype for later royal burials until the end of the Third Dynasty. King Sneferu, the founder of the Fourth Dynasty (about 2680 B.C.), tried to build his royal tomb in the form of a true pyramid at Dahshur, about seven miles south of Zoser's Step Pyramid. The result was the famous Bent Pyramid, so called because it has two angles. It is unique among Egyptian pyramids, and was certainly not intended to have this form. The builders finished it in haste, and had to diminish the angle. But, in constructing the small pyramid at the southern side (part of the pyramid complex), they kept the sides at a single angle. King Sneferu built still another great pyramid about one mile north of the Bent Pyramid. Its angle was smaller, so that its sides were not as steep. Both monuments stand on the western plateau, dwarfing the pyramids which were built east of them in later times.

It was at Dahshur that the ancient masons were confronted with new problems and had to find solutions for them. The names of some of the overseers and masons are known, and it is noteworthy that the leading men among them belonged to the royal family. These men respected and developed the great traditions of Imhotep. The results were appreciated when Sneferu's son and successor, Khufu, built his pyramid.

The pyramids can be understood only in the context of the religious and social background of the Old Kingdom. From the beginning of Egyptian history, the people believed in life after death. They could not imagine their future life as essentially different from life on earth, although they thought it would be more elaborate and comfortable. They did their utmost to preserve their bodies, believing that these were necessary to the well-being of the *Ka*.

Ka is an ancient Egyptian word which is very hard to translate into a single word of any modern language. Alan Gardiner has remarked, after a detailed study of this point: "The term appears to embrace the entire 'self' of a person regarded as an entity to some extent separable from the person." He adds that "this Ka corresponds occasionally to 'personality,' 'soul,' 'individuality,' 'temperament' or even can mean a man's 'fortune' or 'position.'" The Egyptian wanted his Ka to be able to recognize its body after death and to be united with it; for this reason he felt that it was very important to have his body preserved. This is why the Egyptians mummified their bodies and excelled in embalming them.

Other measures were also necessary. Offerings and prayers in a chapel were essential. Representations of utensils and food provisions were carved in relief on blocks of stone, so that they would act as substitutes if the offerings ran short or failed. The Egyptians also made statues and placed them in tombs and temples to act as substitutes for the body if it should perish. By the time of the Fifth Dynasty, it was also considered necessary to have inscriptions of the Pyramid Texts on the walls of interior passages and chambers. These texts, used in the priests' liturgy, contain archaic forms in both ideas and language constructions, indicating that the texts were much older than the inscriptions themselves, and probably date back to the earliest Egyptian civilization.

Egyptian tombs thus grew more and more elaborate with time. As to why they became pyramidal, scholars have offered various explanations. Some Egyptologists believe that the development of the pyramid represented simply an architectural evolution. Others have seen in it the triumph of one religious cult over another.

Conflicting religious beliefs existed from earliest times. The texts show that the individual, after his death, wished to avoid the horrors of darkness. Because the sun made its journey in a boat, model boats were, in later periods, placed in the tomb for this solar journey. According to other beliefs, the Ka mingled with the fixed stars in the northern half of the sky. The life after death also had close connections with the cult of the god Osiris.[2] During the earliest period, sun worship had the strongest appeal, and the kings considered themselves representatives of the sun-god on earth. There must have been a connection between the pyramid form and the sun cult.

From the beginning of Egyptian history, a symbol of the sun-god in the form of a pillar stood in the temple of Heliopolis. In the Archaic period, it was replaced by a symbol of a phoenix perching on the *benben*, an object of pyramidal shape. We can readily imagine a link between the

---

[2] Osiris was a god who died at the hands of his brother Seth and was avenged by his son Horus. The kings of Egypt and eventually all Egyptians were identified with Osiris after death. The Osiris cult appealed to the imagination of the people more than the sun cult and fulfilled their religious needs as the sun cult never did.

benben and the pyramid, but it is difficult to understand the relation between the *benben* itself and sun worship. Egyptologists offer as an explanation the appearance of the sun's rays shining through a break in the clouds, which look like gigantic pyramids connecting heaven with earth. In several statements in the Pyramid Texts, the dead king is described as using the rays of the sun as a ramp by which to ascend to the heavens. The texts say that the heavens strengthened the rays of the sun to enable the king to accomplish his ascent. In view of this, it is a reasonable hypothesis that the change from the step pyramid to the true pyramid was accompanied by a development in the cult of pyramid builders, and that the true pyramid was a colossal *benben*, which could also be a substitute for the rays of the sun and thus enable the dead king to rise to the heavens.

3. *The phoenix perching on the* benben. (*Papyrus of Anhai, British Museum, London.*)

2

Building and

Administering a Pyramid

Of the problems concerning the pyramids, their construction is the most puzzling. Even the Roman writer Pliny, who condemned the pyramids as an "idle and foolish exhibition of royal wealth," found much to wonder at. "The most curious question," he wrote, "is how the stones were raised to so great a height." Probably every visitor since that time has stared up at these colossal monuments and wondered how they were built. In the Great Pyramid alone, there are over two and a quarter million stone blocks, some of them weighing seven and a half tons. The imagination is staggered by the amount of work involved, even if done with modern equipment. And one must always bear in mind that the ancient Egyptians built these masterpieces with the simplest methods; even the pulley was unknown in Egypt before the Roman period. Both in quarrying and building, workmen used copper chisels and possibly iron tools, as well as flint, quartz, and diorite pounders.[1] The only additional aids were large wooden crowbars and, for transportation, wooden sledges and rollers. If any special skill has disappeared, it is that of the overseers who supervised the timing of the various operations.

However, moving blocks that weighed between eight and ten tons

[1] Dunham and Young, in *Journal of Egyptian Archaeology*, XXVIII, 57 f.

(and some as much as twenty-five) was not considered difficult by people who later transported the colossus of Rameses II to the Ramesseum at western Thebes. (This giant statue, made from one block of stone, weighed not less than 1,000 tons.) Another such feat involved the granite obelisks which still stand in the temple of Karnak at Luxor, at Mataria near Cairo, at Tanis in the eastern Delta, and in many countries outside Egypt. Some of them weigh not less than 300 tons. They had to be brought from the quarries far to the south of Aswan, unloaded from barges, and set upright upon their bases in confined spaces among already existing buildings.

Indeed, the process of quarrying, transporting, and erecting these monuments was such an ordinary matter that the Egyptians did not always consider it worthy of record. Most of the information we have is based on the study of the monuments themselves, especially those left unfinished when their builders died.

In the early years of his reign, each new king was occupied with several important matters. First, there were lengthy and complex coronation ceremonies and the smoothing-out of administrative difficulties occasioned by a change in rulers. He may also have supervised construction required by his obligation to give his predecessor a good burial. Eventually, however, the king decided to build a tomb for himself and gave orders to his architects and overseers to carry out such a project. The choice of a place for a new pyramid depended on many circumstances. The king might choose a site near the monuments of his ancestors, or he might prefer a new location. But it had to be on the western bank of the Nile overlooking the valley. This location was preferred for two reasons: the Egyptians believed that the realm of the dead lay in the west, where the sun sets; the western plateau, especially near the ancient capital of Memphis, suits the purpose much better than other areas. It is near the cultivated land; it rises precipitously to a height of about 200 feet; and its surface is almost flat, with very few natural defects. Moreover, the plateau can be reached by valleys, which in ancient times were used by the laborers as ramps for moving materials. The site also had to be composed of a solid mass of rock to support the enormous weight of the projected monument. There had to be enough space around it for the various parts of the pyramid complex and for the tombs of the courtiers, whose ideal it was to be buried by special favor near the king they had served during life. Another necessity was a sufficient supply of good stone in easily accessible places.

Preparations began on the day the site was chosen. The king's highest officials directly supervised the building of his pyramid, and the ruler himself came to see the progress of the work from time to time. The builders left nothing to chance. Architects worked from a plan, which usually included all the interior passages and chambers, although some were hewn out afterward from the solid mass of masonry. The overseers calculated exactly what they needed; gangs of stonecutters (each with its own name) began to cut stone to measure. Most of the stone used in the pyramids was limestone from the immediate vicinity. Certain parts, such as the lining for the passages and chambers, required a better kind of limestone, also quarried near Memphis. The casing was almost invariably of fine white limestone from quarries at Tura, on the eastern bank of the Nile, a little south of modern Cairo. Expeditions also went to Aswan for granite, and to other specially selected quarries.

Meanwhile, architects fixed the exact position of the pyramid. A pyramid was generally built with the sides facing the four cardinal points, possibly so that the entrance, on the north, would be toward the North Star. This orientation would not have been difficult, because the Egyptians had enough knowledge of astronomy to evolve a workable calendar at an early stage of their civilization. Next came the task of leveling the site. It has been suggested that this could easily have been done by erecting dikes around the proposed area and filling it with water. However, all the elevated parts did not have to be removed, because some could be included in the building itself.

Workers would then begin cutting the substructure of the pyramid. The best example of this stage of the work is the unfinished monument of King Neb-ka at Zawiet el Aryan, between Giza and Abusir, where one can see the descending passage, the excavation for the burial chamber with its floor of granite blocks, and the granite sarcophagus. (It is significant that the sarcophagus was put in place at this early stage.)

Meanwhile, workers had built ramps from the valley, where the quarries lay, to the plateau. Stones quarried across the river or in remote regions had been carried on barges along the Nile and deposited on the

4. *The transportation of stone blocks in a quarry at Tura.*

shore nearest the pyramid. Now the actual transportation could begin. There is a scene showing the transport of blocks of stone from the quarries of Tura, in which we see oxen dragging the sledges. This was not usual. Power for most hauling was supplied by a large number of men, who dragged the sledges with ropes. According to another scene and the inscriptions accompanying it, 172 men worked to drag an alabaster colossus of the Twelfth Dynasty nomarch, Dhutihotep, from the quarries of Hatnub to nearby El Bersheh, in Middle Egypt. This statue measured over 6.5 meters high, and must have weighed more than sixty tons. The scene also shows men carrying crowbars, and others pouring liquid from pots in order to prevent the wooden runners of the sledges from catching fire as a result of friction. It is generally thought that this liquid was water, but if we examine the copies of the scene, especially those made at the beginning of the nineteenth century, when the colors were fresh, we see that it could be also another material. The Egyptian text mentions a word which means "liquid"; some time ago I suggested that it was probably milk but I prefer to leave it as an open question. The number of men working for this provincial governor was considered remarkable. The author of the text took pride in referring to their strong arms, and said that every one had the valor of a thousand men.[2]

It was the custom when transporting especially large or important monuments to set out offerings upon them and to burn incense, presumably in order that the gods should look kindly upon the operation and bring it to a successful ending.

Workmen smoothed the sides of the stone blocks very carefully and laid them in place with a thin layer of mortar. After the workmen had laid the first few courses of masonry, it would have been impossible to

[2] The principal publication of this scene is P. E. Newberry, *El Bersheh*, Part I, pp. 19–26, Plate 15.

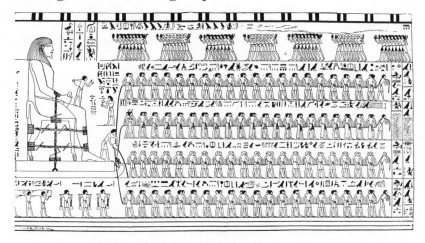

5. *Transporting a colossal statue. From the tomb of Dhutihotep, El Bersheh.*
(*Newberry*, El Bersheh, *Part I, Plate 15.*)

proceed on the work without a new arrangement—something to enable
the builders to reach the higher courses. From the monuments which
have been left unfinished, we are quite certain that ramps of earth and
rubble served this purpose. Brick retaining walls held the rubble in
place, and the whole structure was removed when the work was finished. The recent discoveries at Saqqara show that such ramps were built
around the Unfinished Step Pyramid, and, because it was not completed, they are still there. We may presume that the Egyptians also used
this method of construction in building the true pyramids. Building the
ramps was almost as great a task as building the pyramid itself. Special-
ists have discussed the problem in great detail; they offer various sugges-
tions, but most agree that no pyramid was ever built without ramps.[3]

The pyramid may have been cased from the bottom upward as the
work proceeded, or from the top downward, when the monument was
completed and the ramps were being removed. Both methods are pos-

[3] W. M. F. Petrie, *The Pyramids and Temples of Giza* (London, 1883), pp. 163 ff.;
and more recently his article, "The Building of a Pyramid," *Ancient Egypt* (1930), Part
II, pp. 33 ff.; L. Borchardt, *Die Entstehung der Pyramide, an der Baugeschichte der Pyramide
bei Mejdum nachgewiesen* (Berlin, 1928), p. 37; S. Clarke and R. Engelbach, *Ancient
Egyptian Masonry: The Building Craft* (London, 1930), pp. 117 ff.; and J.-P. Lauer, *Le
Problème des pyramides d'Égypte* (Paris, 1948), pp. 161 ff.

sible. Judging from the construction of some of the mastabas, it is more reasonable to suppose that workmen put the casing in place as they went along, and dressed the surfaces down when demolishing the ramps.

Additional problems involved feeding and housing the men working on the pyramids, and obtaining water for drinking and building. The barren, rocky plateau is waterless, and no wells can be dug there. The answer to these problems again lies in the Egyptians' splendid powers of organization. They built primitive barracks; in every room lived a gang of not more than ten workmen. A special group prepared food and carried water for drinking and washing. Clothes and tools were distributed from the royal storehouses.

Such work could never be done in a few years. The only record of the time necessary to build a pyramid is that left by Herodotus. He mentions that it took thirty years to construct the pyramid of Khufu, of which ten were spent in building the causeway and cutting the substructures. Herodotus gives the number of workmen as 100,000, and says that they were changed every three months. When we examine the pyramid, and if we accept his figure for laborers, we must conclude that the completion of such a monument by ancient methods can hardly have taken less time or effort.

Because of the elaborate ceremonies connected with the cult of the dead, pyramids were surrounded by several other structures. The whole made up what is called the *pyramid complex*. In the mastaba tombs of the

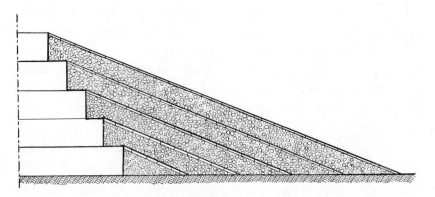

6. *A section of the type of ramp used in building a pyramid.* (*After Croon.*)

First and Second Dynasties, storerooms for offerings surrounded the burial chamber of the owner and members of his family and household. All were hidden for eternity, and the entrance to the tomb, on the north, was blocked and sealed. Outside the eastern side of the tomb stood a simple chapel, the main elements of which were a *stela*, or gravestone, and an offering table. The royal tombs of Abydos were robbed and have been destroyed, and much has been lost forever. We should not forget that the methods of excavating in the last century were less careful than those used now, and archeologists may have over-looked details which would seem significant to us. For example, in the more recent excavations of the tombs of this period at Saqqara and Helwan, archeologists have found pits for boats. These were dug at the sides of the mastabas, regardless of whether they belonged to royalty or private individuals. Perhaps they also existed at the Abydene tombs, but escaped the notice of nineteenth-century excavators.

As we have seen, a great change in the construction of a royal tomb took place at the beginning of the Third Dynasty. A new form, the Step Pyramid, had a temple at its northern side and a large tomb for the king at the south. Actually, the latter must have been used for a purpose other than burial, because Zoser was buried under his Step Pyramid. No remains of a chapel at the eastern side have been found, and to this date no boats have been located.

The reign of Sneferu, the founder of the Fourth Dynasty, marked a new era in Egyptian architecture. The first true pyramid and pyramid complex date from this time and became the accepted models for later pyramid builders. The complex consisted of the following parts:

The pyramid in its stone inclosure (sometimes called a *temenos*).

A mortuary temple in front of the eastern face of the pyramid.

A chapel in front of the entrance, on the north.[4]

A small ritual pyramid in its own inclosure outside the southern inclosure wall of the parent pyramid. This pyramid also had a small chapel with two stelae in front of its eastern face, and per-

---

[4] The remains of a mud-brick chapel, or rather an offering place, were found in front of the entrance of the pyramid and the remains of a stone chapel in front of the small ritual pyramid at its southern side.

haps a chapel in front of the entrance on the north side. It was never used for burial, and its small interior chamber contained only vases of pottery.

Rock-cut, boat-shaped pits around the pyramid. These have not yet been found around the pyramids of Sneferu, as the places where they are likely to exist are still incompletely excavated, but they occur at the pyramid of Sneferu's son Khufu, as well as at Abu Rawwash, at the Second Pyramid of Giza, and elsewhere. Long before the discovery of the large wooden boats to the south of the Great Pyramid, pieces of gilded wood and rope were found in one of the other boat-pits belonging to the same complex.[5]

A long ramp, called a causeway, connecting the upper pyramid inclosure with the Valley Temple near the edge of the cultivated land.

The Valley Temple at the lower end of the causeway, which served as an entrance to the entire complex. In it stood many statues and stelae.

The body of the dead king was brought to the Valley Temple in order to be washed and purified and to undergo the various processes of mummification. Scholars have shown that, at the time of the Fourth Dynasty, three important ceremonies took place in the Valley Temple.[6] The first of these was the washing and purifying of the body, a ritual which took only a short time. The second, mummification, lasted much longer. (It is recorded in a queen's tomb at Giza that 272 days elapsed between her death and her burial.) The third ceremony, called "The Opening of the Mouth," was performed after the mummification was complete, on the day of the burial. It was a magic rite designed to enable the body to speak once more and to enjoy the offerings in the second and more important life which he was about to begin.

The washing of the body may have been done in the first hall of the Valley Temple, or possibly on the roof. It is not known where the em-

[5] Selim Hassan, *Excavations at Giza*, Vol. VI, Part I, pp. 41 ff.

[6] B. Grdseloff, *Das Ägyptische Reinigungszelt* (Cairo, 1941). See also E. Drioton, in *Annales du Service*, XL, 1007–14, and Selim Hassan, *Excavations at Giza*, IV, 69 ff.

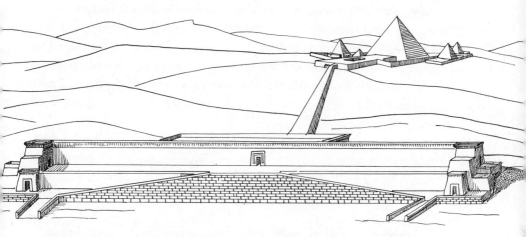

7. *The pyramid complex of Pepi II at Saqqara South.* (*After a restoration by Jéquier,* Le Monument funéraire de Pepi II.)

balming was carried out. All authorities agree, however, that "The Opening of the Mouth" ceremony was performed in front of the statues in the great hall of the Valley Temple. In later times these ceremonies took place in the Mortuary Temple east of the pyramid.

After the mummy had been placed in its tomb, the pyramid entrance was closed forever and hidden behind one of the casing stones, and priests began the services that were to last for eternity. The services for a dead king in the pyramid temples consisted mainly of presenting daily offerings, each item of which was accompanied by a special prayer or

8. *A* hem-neter *priest.*
From a tomb in the Giza necropolis.

other ritual. This presentation of offerings resembled the serving of an earthly meal. It was preceded by the purification ceremony, in which incense, natron pellets, and pure water played a part. Libations and a final purification followed the serving. There were also special duties and ceremonies on the official feast days, of which the Egyptian calendar had many. The public probably took part and had access to parts of the temples.

The son of the deceased king had to prepare for his father's burial, take part in some ceremonies, and complete the unfinished parts of the tomb. Some did this thoroughly and others only partially, if at all. The political situation at the time of the change was no doubt an important factor.

Priests who served gods, kings, and queens were called *hem-neter* priests (God's servants). Those in the cults of non-royal persons were called *hem-ka* (Ka servants). The cults of both royal and private persons also demanded the services of the *we'b* priests (purificators). *We'b* priests served the king during his lifetime, and the title was common among physicians. Both *hem-neters* and *we'bs* had different grades. Some were novices; others were inspectors and overseers. Priests recited the prayers and incantations in a special way, with specific gestures and postures. If they were not performed according to ritual tradition, the ceremony was considered ineffective.[7] Every pyramid required a great number of priests attached to its cult, because they were divided into shifts which were on duty for certain hours of the day and for certain days of the month. Most priests also held secular posts. Women could hold certain offices in the priesthood of the pyramid cult, and the highest rank of all, that of *hem-neter*, was not barred to them.[8] Some of the priestly posts were hereditary in certain families for many generations. This explains the occurrence of the same name among priests of different periods. For example, we may find a man of the Old Kingdom named Sneferu-hotep, who held the title of "Inspector of the Priests of

[7] For a study of the priests and officials of the pyramid cult, see H. Junker, *Giza*, VI, 6–25.

[8] See, for example, the rock-cut tomb of Queen Bu-nefer at Giza; Selim Hassan, *Excavations at Giza*, III, 176, and the numerous examples of women who were *hem-neters* to certain goddesses, such as Hathor and Neith.

Sneferu," and a man of the Middle Kingdom bearing the same name and title. He may have been a descendant of the older man. Persons devoted to a cult of a god or king often bore names compounded with that of the god or king they served.

Kings endowed their monuments with large estates, so that the priests could present the offerings forever. The endowments were permanent, and the cults of kings buried during the Old Kingdom continued to exist for thousands of years. It is known that priests for Sneferu, Khufu, Rededef, and Khafre were still officiating in the ruins of their respective temples in Ptolemaic times. A great number of secular officials looked after the estates. There were guards, scribes, masters of secrets (secretaries), overseers, and men who looked after the temple property. In addition, there were tenant farmers, who worked the lands of the pyramid endowments and in return supplied the temples with produce. The administrative buildings of these properties usually stood near the temples, and near them the houses for the priests.

The now silent ruins of the pyramids and their temples were thus once crowded with priests bringing offerings to the dead kings. Today we see nothing but stone, debris, and occasional walls. But once the pyramids, with their dazzling white casings, illuminated the whole neighborhood, the splendid temples were complete, and their halls resounded to the hymns and prayers of the venerable priests, grave and dignified in their white robes. The altars were heaped with offerings and covered with flowers, and the perfume of incense added to the sacred atmosphere. But, even though the prayers are no longer heard and the walls no longer echo to the chanting of the priests, paintings and inscriptions buried deep within the tombs and temples bear witness to the bustling activity silenced by the centuries.

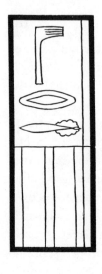

3

The Step Pyramid

of Saqqara

The famous cemetery of Saqqara is fifteen miles from the center of modern Cairo. It is one of the most important sites in Egypt, with its tombs of unrivaled beauty, its temples, and the Serapeum (a subterranean cemetery of the sacred bull, Apis). All these, however, are eclipsed by the Step Pyramid and its subsidiary monuments.

As we have seen in a previous chapter, the kings who reigned before Zoser built their royal tombs in the form of a large mastaba of mud brick. Egyptian tradition attributes to Imhotep, Zoser's architect and vizier, the first use of stone in building. The ancient Egyptians had used stone for parts of monuments long before, and the use of stone was not a royal privilege; it appeared in the private tombs of the First and Second Dynasties at Helwan, across the river from Saqqara. But there is no doubt that the Step Pyramid, which dates from about 2780 B.C., was the first great free-standing monument built of stone and that this was the first royal tomb with a superstructure built entirely of stone blocks.

Modern knowledge of this pyramid dates from the early nineteenth century. Travelers and explorers had visited Saqqara before this time and left various accounts and sketches. But none of them tried to

9. *The Step Pyramid of Saqqara.*

excavate the interior of the Step Pyramid, and none left a description of any lasting value.[1]

The earliest record of excavations is that of the Prussian Consul-General von Minutoli, in 1821. He penetrated the subterranean galleries and made several discoveries there, the most important of which was one of the blue-tiled chambers. Von Minutoli described his work in *Reise zum Tempel des Jupiter Ammon*, with several excellent drawings made by the Italian artist Valeriani. He in his turn left a record of his work in *Atlante del Basso ad Alto Egitto Illustrato*. Von Minutoli found inside the Step Pyramid parts of a mummy and a few inscriptions with the name of Zoser. He sent these to Europe, but they were lost at sea during a storm. The mummy is often discussed, and is generally attributed to the Third Dynasty. Many years later, archeologists found part of the same mummy in the same place. Dr. Derry, who examined

[1] The Arabs knew Saqqara under the name Abusir. For references to this site in the manuscripts of the early travelers and explorers, see Porter and Moss, *Topographical Bibliography*, III, 85–89.

this latter fragment, says that the methods of its wrapping and preservation strongly suggest those of the Old Kingdom.[2] Thus it may be part of the mummy of Zoser himself.

Colonel Howard Vyse of England came to Egypt in 1837 to conduct archeological research and enter the pyramids. He needed an efficient manager for the work, and by good fortune acquired the services of a fellow countryman, J. S. Perring. Perring's work in and around the pyramids of Giza, Saqqara, Dahshur, and other important sites was the earliest strictly scientific research. Most of his measurements were accurate, and it is astonishing to see the work he accomplished in less than three years. That on the construction and substructure of the Step Pyramid is the first of which we have a detailed report.[3] Perring rediscovered the galleries described by Von Minutoli, found the room with the blue faience tiles, and made a drawing of the inscriptions. He excavated further, found other galleries and a heap of mummies, and reached a chamber bearing the name of King Zoser. The result of Vyse and Perring's work, *Operations Carried on at the Pyramids of Gizeh*, as well as their atlas of plans and drawings, is indispensable to archeologists.

Perring's work was followed by that of the German Karl Lepsius. The Lepsius expedition arrived in the autumn of 1843 and stayed until the winter of 1845. Although the expedition was engaged chiefly in copying inscriptions in Egypt and Nubia, it also conducted excavations. The Step Pyramid was a chief point of interest for Lepsius. He was the first to recognize that it had originally been built as a single mastaba, to which others had been added.[4] The expedition entered the pyramid and removed part of the blue-tiled walls and the inscribed blocks bearing the name of Zoser which framed them. Lepsius and his assistants published the results of their efforts in twelve large folios, the first of which appeared in 1849.

After the work of Lepsius, the substructure of the Step Pyramid was visited repeatedly by Mariette, Maspero, Petrie, and Borchardt, among others. They discussed the galleries but never investigated the mounds

[2] *Annales du Service*, XXXV (1935), 25–27.

[3] Howard Vyse, *Operations Carried On at the Pyramids of Gizeh in 1837* (3 vols.; London, 1840–42), III, Plates A–D, between pp. 42–43, 44–45, and 46–47.

[4] R. Lepsius, *Denkmäler* (Text), I, 189–95.

surrounding the pyramid. Most of these archeologists, especially Maspero, were more interested in opening the pyramids than in excavating around them.

Only after the end of World War I did the Antiquities Department of Egypt decide to begin excavating around the pyramids of Saqqara. From 1920 until his death in 1931, C. M. Firth was in charge of the work which continued, both inside and out, to produce sensational results. His work on the Step Pyramid itself began in 1924. New tiled galleries were found underneath the pyramid, as well as subterranean galleries packed with vases. The latter, estimated to be not fewer than 30,000 in number, are of alabaster, granite, diorite, breccia, schist, and many other kinds of stone. In 1927 Firth was joined by J.-P. Lauer as architect. After Firth's death, J. E. Quibell joined Lauer, and they continued together until 1936. Lauer is still engaged in this work, but the substructure of the pyramid has not been completely investigated.[5]

We do not know much about Zoser. His father and predecessor was King Khasekhemwy, whose reign is noted for the use of stone in building and for the manufacture of many stone vases. The name Zoser does not occur on any monument before the Twelfth Dynasty. On his contemporary monuments, he is called Iry-khet-Neter.

Zoser's name was closely associated with the region south of Aswan, known in Greek times as the Dodekaschoinos. The names of Zoser and his architect, Imhotep, are recorded on the well-known "Famine Stela" of the Ptolemaic period, more than 2,700 years after Zoser's death. The stela is carved on a rock on the Island of Sehel, south of Aswan. According to the inscription, there was a great famine during the reign of Zoser because for seven years the Nile had failed to rise. When Zoser asked Imhotep for advice, he replied that to stop the famine it was necessary to gain the favor of the god Khnum, the god of the First Cataract, the

[5] The monuments of Zoser are perhaps the most frequently discussed of those of the Old Kingdom. The principal publications are: C. M. Firth and J. E. Quibell; *The Step Pyramid* (Cairo, 1935–36), in two volumes, and the work of J.-P. Lauer, *La pyramide à degrés* (Cairo, 1936–39), in three volumes. Ricke, in his *Bemerkungen zur Ägyptischen Baukunst des alten Reiches* (Zürich, 1944), I, has expressed theories which differ from Lauer's interpretation. Lauer has answered these criticisms in a short book, *Étude complémentaires sur les monuments du roi Zoser à Saqqarah* (Cairo, 1948).

birthplace of the Nile. It was only Khnum who could fill the granaries of Egypt. Zoser went south to the First Cataract and conferred great riches upon the temple of Khnum. Soon afterwards the Nile rose to its proper height, and Egypt was saved.

This text was written in a late period when the priests of Khnum were struggling against the increasing influence of the priests of Isis and is therefore a propagandistic forgery. A study by Paul Barguet has shown that the Zoser of this text is actually Ptolemy V Epiphanes, and that it dates from 187 B.C.[6] But it shows that the name of Zoser had lingered in the memory of Egyptians, and that his cult continued until the end of ancient Egyptian history.

The stela also indicates the great reputation attained by Imhotep, the master architect of the Step Pyramid and its complex. Whether Imhotep began his career under Zoser or under Zoser's father is still unknown. An inscription on the pedestal of one of Zoser's statues,[7] a contemporary work, gave Imhotep's titles as the Chancellor of the King of Lower Egypt, the First One under the King, the Administrator of the Great Mansion, the Hereditary Noble, the High Priest of Heliopolis, The Chief Sculptor, and the Chief Carpenter. Later documents refer to Imhotep as Vizier, Overseer of Works of Upper and Lower Egypt, Overseer of the (pyramid) City, Chief Ritualist of King Zoser, and Scribe of the God's Book. These titles may have been conferred upon him at a later date.[8]

Imhotep's titles indicate that he did not belong to the royal family but was a self-made man. We do not know where he was born, but a vague and brief reference by one of the classical writers suggests that the village of Gebelein, south of Luxor, was his home.[9] A monument giving the names of his parents dates from between 495 and 491 B.C. It is an inscription in the Wadi el Hammamat, where an architect named

---

[6] See P. Barguet, *La Stèle de la Famine à Sehel* (Cairo, 1953).

[7] See B. Gunn, in *Annales du Service*, XXVI (1926), 177–96.

[8] There are other titles from later periods; for these, see Kurt Sethe, "Imhotep," in *Untersuchungen*, Vol. II, Part IV.

[9] It is Mercur who mentions that Askelepios was buried in Crocodilopolis (Gebelein) not far from Kena.

---

10. *A bronze statuette of Imhotep, Late Period. (Cairo Museum.)*

Khnum-ib-Re, who was quarrying stone there, ordered an inscription set up listing his distinguished ancestors, many of whom were architects. The oldest name is that of Ka-nefer, who was Director of Works of Upper and Lower Egypt. The second name was that of his son, Imhotep. In any case, we see from Imhotep's titles that he was directly connected with the artistic activities of the period, enjoyed great authority in the royal house, and, as High Priest of Heliopolis, held the highest religious position in the land. The king bestowed a singular favor on him by allowing his name to appear on the base of a royal statue.

As time went on, Imhotep became a legendary, godlike figure. Manetho, the Egyptian historian, mentioned Zoser and added: "Under him lived Imuthes (Imhotep), whom the Greeks consider as Askelepios because of his skill as a physician; this man also discovered the art of building with hewn stones, and occupied himself with enthusiasm in writing." According to a papyrus which dates from the second century A.D., King Menkure established temples and endowments for Imhotep and two others, but no early document has been found to support this. The earliest definite reference to Imhotep's reputation dates back to the Middle Kingdom. It is contained in the "Song of the Harper," which was composed in the Eleventh Dynasty (2100 B.C.) and was still popular during the New Kingdom. The song speaks of the wisdom of Imhotep, although no works attributed to him have appeared among the several papyri recording the wise sayings of the ancient sages. The memory of Imhotep was held in respect during the Middle Kingdom, and New Kingdom scribes regarded him as their patron. Before writing on their papyrus rolls, they poured out a few drops of water from their water pots as a libation to him.

It is much later, in the sixth century B.C., that we first notice a real deification of Imhotep. This occurred during the Persian period, or perhaps a little earlier, when temples were built in his honor and he was called the "Son of Ptah." Worship of Imhotep may have been introduced as a reaction of the Egyptians to the rising power of Assyria, Greece, and Persia. At any rate, by the time of the "Famine Stela," Imhotep was worshiped and temples were built for him. People sought his advice through oracles and held his decisions in respect. The Egyptians worshiped him as a magician, skilled in charms, and as the inventor of stone masonry.. They also saw in him the wise physician whose prescriptions contained all the secrets of medicine. The temples of Imhotep were the mecca of the sick, and pilgrims flocked to them to be cured.[10] The center of the worship of Imhotep was at Memphis, but his temples were found everywhere in the Delta and in Upper Egypt. He was worshiped even in Nubia and in the distant oases of the western desert. Archeologists hope to discover Imhotep's tomb so that we may learn more about this remarkable man. He is probably buried at Saqqara, not far from Zoser's pyramid, but this is not definite.

Imhotep did not design all of Zoser's monuments. He was not responsible for the design of Zoser's tomb at Beit Khallaf, built early in his reign. This tomb, south of Abydos, was in the traditional form of a large rectangular mastaba built of mud brick. It measures about 95 meters long, 50 meters wide, and over 10 meters high. A passage more than 17 meters long descends steeply from the top of the mastaba to a wide, horizontal passage with twelve chambers. (In these chambers were found many stone vases, but none with Zoser's name. It did occur, however, on the clay stoppers, together with the names of several vineyards and those of various officials.) Zoser also built temples at Heliopolis and at Horbeit in the Delta, of which fragments have been found. The sculptor's models of faces and hieroglyphs in the Metropolitan Museum of Art in New York City are attributed to this early period.[11] However, Imhotep supervised the building of the Step Pyramid and all the royal buildings thereafter. It is the Step Pyramid that most interests Egyptologists. No other monument in Egypt, with the exception of the Temple of Karnak at Luxor, has so fascinated archeologists as this pyramid and its complex. It exhibits the genius of a great architect and the flowering of Egyptian architecture.

The buildings in the Step Pyramid complex are beautiful and im-

---

[10] The story of Nechatis, who was a priest in the temple of Imhotep, tells how his mother and he were miraculously cured in the temple. In grateful recognition, Nechatis translated an Egyptian papyrus, attributed to Imhotep, into Greek. See Grenfell and Hunt, *Oxyrhynchus Papyri*, Vol. XI (1915), and J. B. Hurry, *Imhotep, the Vizier and Physician of King Zoser* (Oxford, 1926). They also might be from the Saite period and an imitation of the old art style.

[11] See W. C. Hayes, *The Scepter of Egypt* (New York, 1953), pp. 60–61.

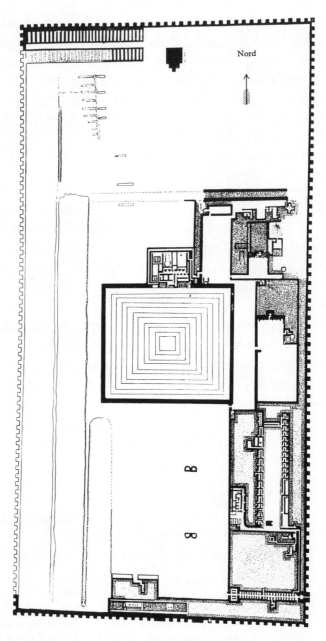

Nord

11. *General plan of the Step Pyramid complex, Saqqara.*

12. *A model reconstruction of the Step Pyramid complex. (By Lauer.)*

pressive and have two distinguishing features. First, the monuments are
built of fine limestone as simulacra of buildings which stood in the royal
residence in Memphis. The architect faced many difficulties in representing in stone elements which were originally constructed in mud brick,
wood, reeds, and tree trunks, but his genius found a solution for every
problem. Second, most of the architectural elements appear here for the
first and last time. Even the various types of columns, with their graceful
fluting, were not repeated in later periods, and similar architectural details have not been found near the pyramids.

A great wall of fine white limestone encloses the pyramid and subsidiary structures. The wall originally stood 20 Egyptian cubits (10.4
meters) high, and measured 545 meters from north to south and 277
meters from east to west. It had fourteen bastion gates, of which thirteen
are simulated; there is only one real gateway. This wall may have had
the same dimensions as the palace of Zoser in Memphis. Imhotep used

13. *A decorated gallery in the so-called Southern Tomb.*

very small blocks of stone in order to copy in shape and size the large bricks used at that time, and he indicated in the walls the places where minor gates pierced the palace inclosure.

The entrance must have remained open, because no pivot-holes have been found to indicate the presence of doors. But pivots were represented in the masonry on the inner side of the thick gateway, indicating that the original building had wooden doors opening inward. The gateway leads to a long, impressive gallery. Twenty piers, each 6.6 meters high, project from each side. At the end of each stood an engaged column, or wall-tongue, probably stone representations of similar brick supports in the palace. The bricks were probably covered with wood or the stems of reeds. Most of the drums of the columns were found in the debris, and have been restored to their places. The stone ceiling imitates palm logs. Near the end of the gallery, on the western side, stands a small rectangular hall. The eight piers supporting its roof are unique in Egyptian architecture. At the end of the gallery is a narrow passage with a curious simulated door, constructed as though it were standing half open. After passing through this door, the visitor finds himself inside the great inclosure. To the right is the pyramid, in front the so-called Southern Tomb.

The name "Southern Tomb" was applied when this building was discovered in 1928, but we have no proof that it was ever intended to be a tomb, or was used as such. It stands beside the pyramid inclosure wall, with an entrance in the southern side. As in the original mastaba built for Zoser, there is a pit 7 meters square and 28 meters deep. At the bottom is a room built of granite blocks, which measures 1.6 meters square. There are also galleries decorated with blue faience tiles. On one of the walls are three false doors carved with the figure, name, and titles of King Zoser. Over the subterranean passages rose a large rectangular superstructure with a concave roof. It measured 84 meters long and 12 meters wide, and contained a chapel. At the corner of this monument stands a part of the original limestone wall, decorated with a frieze of cobras.

Most Egyptologists describe the Southern Tomb as a symbolic burial for Zoser as King of Upper Egypt (the South) or as a burial place for the canopic jars containing his viscera. In my opinion, it is an earlier

14. *The names of Zoser from a gallery in the so-called Southern Tomb.*

form of the subsidiary pyramid which was built beginning with Sneferu (and perhaps earlier) at the southern side of each pyramid. We do not know what function these subsidiary pyramids served. The excavators of the tomb found the pit, the trench leading to the tomb, and the steps completely blocked with masonry, but thieves had penetrated into the interior by cutting a hole in the southern side of the pit and then working their way through the rubble which filled it. Archeologists found nothing inside.

In the large open court, the visitor then passes one of two B-shaped stone buildings which were probably connected with the ceremonies of Heb-Sed. To the east are three fluted piers standing among the ruins of a small, rectangular temple. From the remains, excavators determined that its red painted stone ceiling was also made to imitate palm logs. Interesting details include the half-opened dummy door at the eastern side and the torus molding at the corners. The latter originated in the bundles of bound reeds which stood in the corners of huts to strengthen the walls.

To the east of the small temple are the remains of a large, oblong court called the Jubilee, or Heb-Sed, Court. Although it is in ruinous condition, the parts that remain are enough to indicate its arrangement. Remains of chapels lie along both its eastern and western walls. Those against the western wall have a small entrance leading to a room containing a niche. The façades of those against the eastern wall are plain, but those on the west are decorated. Each chapel on the western wall has three engaged columns, with the center one higher than the other two. Above these rests a curved projecting cornice, and the roof is also curved. The capitals of the columns are unique in Egyptian architecture. A hole extends through the column, above which the surface of the stone is smoothed. At each side are stone petals. A short distance below is another hole, and below that two bosses. The only reasonable explanation for these holes is that they were used for inserting a bracket to support standards of the gods. (These are represented in scenes of the Sed Feasts.) Some archeologists have suggested that the holes were emplacements for imitation rhinoceros horns, but this seems improbable. Stone imitations of low wooden fences appear on the walls separating the chapels. At the southern end of the court there is a large stone platform, on which probably stood two thrones side by side, one for the king as ruler of Upper Egypt and the other for him as ruler of Lower Egypt. At the northern end stood a shrine containing four statues, of which nothing now remains but the feet.

North of the Jubilee Court, in its own court, are the ruins of a structure known as the "Building of the South." Its beautiful façade is ornamented with four engaged, fluted columns and other architectural ornaments. The existing parts of these columns measure a little over 3.5 meters high, but their original height, according to Lauer's studies, must have been 12 meters; their capitals were like those of the Jubilee Court. East of the façade there is a recess and the remains of columns which probably had capitals with two large pendent leaves. To the northeast, in another court, are the remains of the "Building of the North," arranged more or less like its neighbor. On the east are columns with papyrus capitals (the papyrus was the heraldic plant of the north). They are in a better state of preservation than those of the Building of the South, and have been restored.

Both the Jubilee Court and the two neighboring buildings, as well as

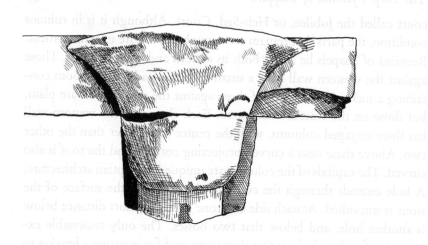

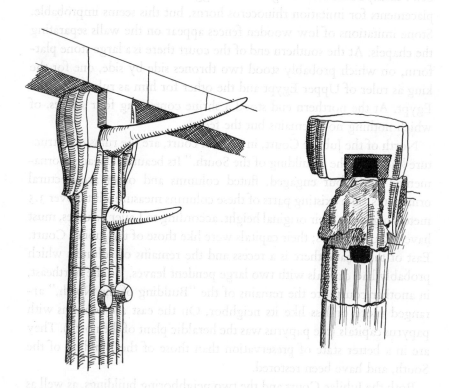

*15. Architectural elements from the Step
Pyramid complex.*

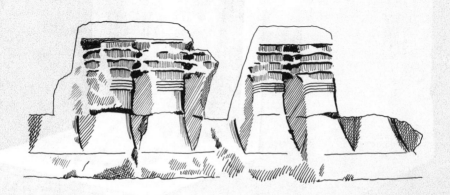

the B-shaped structures in the court, were connected with the Heb-Sed, or Sed Festival. During this series of ceremonies, which date back to the First Dynasty, the king, wearing a special costume, performed certain dances and ran a prescribed number of times around the walls of his palace. He had to perform every ceremony twice, once as King of Upper Egypt and once as King of Lower Egypt. The rites originated in an old custom which survives among a few tribes in central Africa, especially those of the Nilotic group. According to custom, a ruler is allowed a maximum reign of thirty years, after which he is put to death because the welfare of the crops and herds is directly connected with his health and activity. Among some tribes today, a ruler can renew his youth by means of special ceremonies or sacrifices, and thus extend his reign. At the dawn of history, the Egyptians undoubtedly practiced this custom, but the ritual murder of rulers had ceased before the First Dynasty. The kings celebrated the Sed Feast as a means of renewing their youthful vigor and thus extending their reigns. The Heb-Sed practice continued until the end of ancient Egyptian history. There are many representations of its ceremonies on the walls of temples and tombs. Unfortunately, although we know these reliefs and can read the hieroglyphic inscriptions which accompany them, we are still far from being able to understand the whole ceremony.

Most kings did not wait thirty years before celebrating the feast; it was reckoned that, after celebrating it once, a new period of thirty years began. Zoser celebrated one of these feasts, although he reigned only nineteen years. There must have been several buildings of brick and reeds constructed for the performance of the various ceremonies. Imhotep erected copies of these buildings in stone around the eternal dwelling of the body and soul of his master.

At the northern side of the pyramid are the remains of a temple and, built against its east side, a small room called a "serdab." In the latter, which provided a place for a statue to look out on the temple, archeologists found the statue of Zoser which is now in the Cairo Museum. (A replica has replaced it in the serdab.) The temple differs in plan from the pyramid temples of later periods. It is difficult to define its functions exactly or to decide if it is a Mortuary Temple. (Such temples exist on the eastern side of pyramids, but their plans differ from this one.) From

16. *The statue of Zoser found in the serdab of the Step Pyramid.*

the remaining walls we can see that it consisted of two symmetrical parts and included two bathrooms with stone basins in the floor. It has been suggested that this building represents in stone a part of the royal palace in which important feasts took place.

The monuments in the Step Pyramid complex were admired in ancient times; many graffiti were written on the walls of the Building of the North. The writer of one of them, a certain Thay, lived in the days of King Tutankhamen (Eighteenth Dynasty, about 1370 B.C.). Another scribe who lived during the same time—Ahmes, son of Iptah—says that he came to see the temple of Zoser and found it as though heaven were inside and Ra rising within it.[12] The modern visitor also admires the sober simplicity, elegance, and proportions of the buildings as fitting adjuncts of the pyramid itself.

The building of the Step Pyramid underwent several phases. Before workmen constructed the first mastaba—the bottom layer of the pyramid—they sank a shaft in the rock, 28 meters deep and 7 meters square. At the bottom of the shaft they built an oblong burial chamber of granite blocks and also cut a tunnel, extending northward a little over 20 meters. This tunnel would have had its entrance outside the original mastaba. But the burial chamber was to be reached only through a round hole in its ceiling from a limestone room (now destroyed) above it; the granite plug for closing this hole weighs over three tons and measures 2 meters in height.

Four underground galleries and connecting passages were cut around the burial chamber to contain the funerary equipment and the many vases buried with the king. Some of these galleries were never finished; others were covered with panels of blue, glazed tiles, which resemble the mats which hung upon the walls of the king's palace.

Zoser's family was buried near his tomb. Eleven shafts over 32 meters deep were cut at the eastern side. Each ended in a corridor 30 meters long directed westward under the original mastaba. (Grave-robbers entered all eleven burial chambers in ancient times, but archeologists found in one of them two alabaster coffins, one of which contained the remains of a mummy of a child.) Zoser wanted to in-

---

[12] For a translation of these graffiti, see C. M. Firth and J. E. Quibell, *The Step Pyramid*, I, 77–85.

corporate the burials of his family within his own tomb, so the mastaba was extended eastward (the third extension). The entrances to the eleven shafts were now inaccessible, so a stairway was cut leading to the northern ones.

When it was decided to build additional mastabas above the original one, the builders had to add to the ground area for the superstructure at the northern side. Consequently the original entrance to the trench and stairway leading to the burial chamber had to be blocked. The builders cut a new entrance farther to the north (inside the area of the temple), beginning with steps and then a tunnel. Instead of connecting the new tunnel with the old one, they carried it around the galleries and passages until it met the original tunnel near its end, not far from the burial chamber. No one can tell whether all the passages and galleries under the Step Pyramid were made by the ancient builders; some may have been tunneled by thieves. Moreover, there are galleries which have not yet been fully examined because of the weak shale in which they are cut.

The original stone mastaba of the Step Pyramid was the first royal tomb with a square plan. Each side measured about 63 meters long and about 8 meters high. (The core consisted of the local limestone of

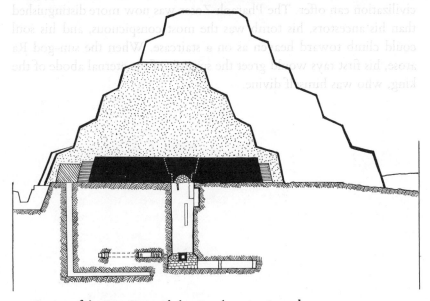

17. *Section of the Step Pyramid showing the successive enlargements.*

Saqqara, but the pyramid was cased with beautiful, fine white lime-stone brought from the opposite side of the Nile.) In later years, Im-hotep added to the original mastaba, the first alteration being an extension of 3 meters on all sides. The second addition—about 9 meters on the eastern side—made the tomb rectangular. Before the builders had finished casing this new mastaba, they extended each side about 3 meters. This altered mastaba now became the lowest stage of a stepped pyramid consisting of four mastabas erected one above the other. The architect intended this stage to be final and began the temple on its northern side. Before this temple or the pyramid casing was complete, however, he planned another alteration. The pyramid was to be extended toward the north and west, and the number of superimposed mastabas increased to six. Before this was done, a final alteration added slightly to each side. In its final dimensions, the Step Pyramid measured about 140 meters from east to west and about 118 meters from north to south and stood 60 meters high.

There is no doubt that Zoser was buried in the pyramid and not in his brick mastaba at Beit Khallaf. The latter must have been a cenotaph; this is the only explanation which our present knowledge of Egyptian civilization can offer. The Pharaoh Zoser was now more distinguished than his ancestors, his tomb was the most conspicuous, and his soul could climb toward heaven as on a staircase. When the sun-god Ra arose, his first rays would greet the summit of the eternal abode of the king, who was himself divine.

4

The Successors

of Zoser

It might be expected that Zoser's successors would have surpassed the technical and artistic achievements of his reign, but we search in vain for any advance. Perhaps later excavations will yield an explanation of this curious situation.

The Third Dynasty is an obscure period in Egyptian history. Even the number of kings and the order of their succession is a matter of controversy. Manetho records eight names, the list of Abydos mentions six, and the Turin papyrus preserves only five. The dynasty began with Zoser, who was followed by Sekhem-khet, Kha-ba, Neb-ka, and others; it ends with Hu (or Huni), who was the predecessor of Sneferu, the founder of the Fourth Dynasty.[1]

The monuments of Zoser, which stand at the edge of the western plateau overlooking the capital, probably inspired the kings who succeeded him on the throne. One of these built his pyramid at Saqqara, not far from that of Zoser. Two preferred a neighborhood a little to the north, at Zawiet el Aryan. There are other pyramids whose construc-

[1] For the list of Manetho, see W. G. Waddell, *Manetho* (Cambridge, Mass.: The Loeb Classical Library, 1940). See also Petrie, *A History of Egypt* (London, 1923), I, 39 and 274. For the succession of these kings, see William Stevenson Smith, *Ancient Egypt* (Boston, 1952), p. 172, and W. C. Hayes, *The Scepter of Egypt*, p. 58.

tion suggests a Third Dynasty date, but their identity cannot be established without excavation. One of these is the pyramid of Seila in the Faiyum; another is at Zawiet el Amwat, opposite Minya in Middle Egypt; and a third is at El Kola, north of Idfu in Aswan Province. Although the pyramid at Meydum was finished by Sneferu, the founder of the Fourth Dynasty, it was in all probability begun during the reign of Huni, and so is included in this chapter.

SEKHEM-KHET'S PYRAMID AT SAQQARA

From time to time the press announces the discovery of a pyramid. On such an occasion the American or European reader is perplexed, and asks himself how such a high and massive building could be overlooked. A small object, such as a statue or a vase, might easily be lost, but a pyramid is a different matter! The reader is right. It would be impossible to hide a great pyramid; but several of those in question are small ones, the upper parts of which have been quarried away and the lower parts covered by the drifting sands of the surrounding desert. In many cases, only the lower courses of the masonry and the substructure remain; in other cases, the pyramids were never finished. There are several mounds in the Memphite necropolis which still preserve such monuments under masses of debris and sand. Some day they will be explored, and excavations will reveal their identity. Archeologists will then speak of the discovery of "new" pyramids, which in reality are only the remains of those long buried.

In May, 1954, the press of the world announced the long-awaited results of excavations made in the entrance of a newly "discovered" step pyramid at Saqqara. Speculation had been rife as to what the monument would contain, and there was great disappointment when the sarcophagus was found to be empty. But, in spite of the unfulfilled expectations, the discovery was one of the most important in the history of archeology, especially for the study of the pyramids.

For many years archeologists had known of the existence of a vast, rectangular inclosure buried under the sand west of the Step Pyramid at Saqqara. It was marked on several maps and was clear in air photographs of the district. The latter showed a huge rectangle, divided into two sections, which together were larger than the inclosure of Zoser's monument.

The Antiquities Department decided in 1951 to investigate the site, and intrusted the work to the Curator of Saqqara, Mohammed Zakaria Ghoneim. He cleared part of the high inclosure wall, which was more or less a copy of that surrounding the Step Pyramid complex. Unfinished, it measured 550 by 200 meters (Fig. 18). The name of the king who built it was unknown, but some archeologists interested in the excavations at Saqqara have held that he must have been one of Zoser's successors because his tomb is so close to Zoser's. Several Ptolemaic mummies were found in the sand, as well as objects dating from the Twenty-sixth Dynasty onward. Work advanced in 1954, and revealed a building

18. *The unfinished temenos wall of the newly discovered pyramid of Sekhem-khet.*

19. *The newly discovered Step Pyramid at Saqqara.*

which is undoubtedly an unfinished step pyramid. It consists of the lowest stage of such a monument and part of the second stage (Fig. 19). Its total height is about 7 meters, but its square base measures about 120 meters on each side, indicating that its builders planned it to be almost as large as the Step Pyramid itself.[2]

An interesting feature of this pyramid is the construction ramps, which were found *in situ*, almost covering the monument. These ramps were of rubble, but at intervals had a layer of flat, rough-hewn stones, which seem to have formed a kind of crude pavement. The ramps were enlarged and lengthened, the main ramp for the supply of material being to the west.

[2] This information is based on personal visits to the monuments and conversations with my colleague the excavator, Mr. Mohammed Zakaria Ghoneim. See M. Zakaria Ghoneim, "La nouvelle pyramide à degrés de Saqqara," in *Les Grandes Découvertes Archéologiques de 1954, Le Revue du Caire* (1955), pp. 18–31. His account of the excavation has recently appeared: *The Buried Pyramid* (London, 1956) and *Horus Sekhem-khet* (Cairo, 1957).

20. *The exterior of the entrance to the Unfinished Pyramid at Saqqara.*

21. *The entrance passage showing the masonry wall blocking it, Unfinished Pyramid at Saqqara.*

The entrance to the pyramid lay 24 meters from the northern face, at the end of a passage (Fig. 20). As workmen uncovered the latter, the excavator had the impression that the pyramid had not been tampered with in modern times, because the masonry blocking the entrance was intact. But he also noticed that, while half of this blocking had been carefully built and seemed to be original, the other half was rather carelessly constructed, as though it might have been opened at some time in

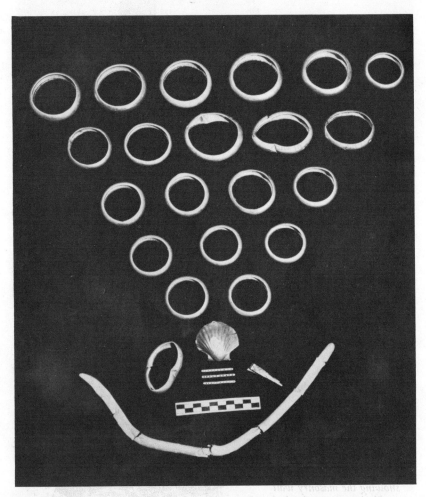

22. *Gold objects found in the passage underneath the pyramid of Sekhem-khet.*

23. *The burial chamber, Unfinished Pyramid of Sekhem-khet.*

24. *The alabaster sarcophagus (notice the foliage on top) in the Unfinished Pyramid of Sekhem-khet.*

the past and then closed again (Fig. 21). Within the pyramid itself, excavation revealed a shaft cut in the superstructure. Although much of it was blocked by sand and debris, its contents indicated that it had never been used for a human burial but contained the remains of oxen, as well as those of birds and other animals. The most important discovery, sixty-two fragments of a papyrus written in demotic, was found in the lowest layer of filling.

When excavators reached the interior of the pyramid, they found subterranean galleries, one of which had 120 storerooms. These contained stone vases in all stages of completion, resembling in form, material, and technique those found under the pyramid of Zoser. The most important find was the name of the builder of the pyramid, King Sekhem-khet, which occurred seven times on jar-stoppers. Among the thrilling finds made in May, 1954, were twenty-one gold bracelets, some very small and others of normal size. There were also a gold necklace and a pair of electrum tweezers. The finest of these gold objects was a small box with a lid in the form of a cockle shell (Fig. 22). All these objects were reported to have been placed in a wooden box which had decayed. They were found in a crevice in the floor of one of the galleries.

The burial chamber lies at a distance of 72 meters from the entrance. It is rectangular, measuring 8.20 by 5.22 meters, and is 5 meters high (Fig. 23). In the middle stands an alabaster sarcophagus which measures 2.37 meters long, 1.4 meters wide, and 1.8 meters high. A vertically sliding door at one end was shut and sealed with plaster, and remains of foliage still rested on top of the sarcophagus (Fig. 24). Hopes were now raised to a high pitch, but when the sarcophagus was opened, it was found to be empty and unused. Had any king ever been buried here? The excavator believes so, because of the vases and gold jewelry, and intends to look for the burial in another part of the pyramid. Other archeologists are not convinced and suggest that the pyramid may have been a cenotaph, or that, being unfinished, it was never used for burial. The interior of this pyramid has not yet, at the time of writing, been completely excavated, and the other parts of the inclosure remain to be investigated.

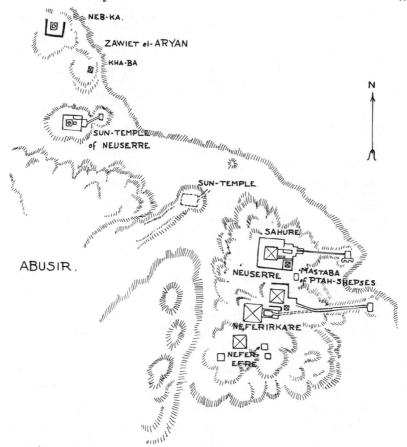

25. *Pyramid fields of Zawiet el Aryan and Abusir.*

THE PYRAMIDS OF ZAWIET EL ARYAN

There are two pyramids at Zawiet el Aryan, a site between the pyramids of Giza and those of Abusir (Fig. 25). Both of the buildings belong to an early period of Egyptian architecture and are generally known today as the "Layer Pyramid" and the "Unfinished Pyramid." The latter was built for King Nefer-ka-(Re) Neb-ka. The identity of the other still remains a problem.

The visitor to the site of the "Layer Pyramid" can see only the lower courses of the monument, which is built of small blocks of local limestone; the interior is inaccessible. The site presents a scene of wild confusion, and appears as though it had never been scientifically investigated. In reality, the contrary is the case. Lepsius noted the pyramid as early as 1840,[3] and in 1885 Maspero tried unsuccessfully to enter it. In 1896 De Morgan discovered a staircase at the northeastern angle but did not continue his investigation.[4] In March, 1900, Maspero instructed Alexander Barsanti to search for the entrance, and he at last succeeded in finding it. The results were disappointing because the builder of the pyramid had never been buried in it. Not even his name was found. After another ten years, the Harvard University–Museum of Fine Arts Expedition excavated the pyramid, as well as the cemeteries surrounding it, and published the findings in the Boston Museum Bulletin.[5] They were subsequently discussed by Reisner in his monograph on tomb development published in 1936.[6]

According to the investigations and studies of Reisner and Fisher, the pyramid consists of a square nucleus, about 11 meters on each side, covered with fourteen layers of stone masonry, each about 2.6 meters thick. The base of the pyramid thus measures 83.8 meters on each side. The angle is 68° (Fig. 26).

The burial chamber is reached by a stairway about 10 meters long, which begins near the northeast corner of the pyramid and continues as an inclined passage to a shaft. There it makes a right-angle turn to the south, and then leads down to a chamber in the rock, 54 meters from the turning point. The room is 3.63 meters long by 2.65 meters wide and is 3 meters high; it is situated under the center of the pyramid. Another passage at the bottom of the shaft leads to three galleries into which open thirty-two small chambers, twenty on the north, six on the east, and six on the west.

In constructing the pyramid, the builders used stones of an inferior quality limestone from a quarry south of the monument. They did not

[3] Lepsius, Denkmäler (Text), I, 128–29.

[4] Mentioned by Barsanti in his report in Annales du Service, II (1901), 92–94.

[5] G. A. Reisner and C. S. Fisher, "The Work of the Harvard University–Museum of Fine Arts Egyptian Expedition," Bulletin of the Museum of Fine Arts, IX, 54–59.

[6] G. A. Reisner, The Development of the Egyptian Tomb down to the Accession of Cheops (Cambridge, Mass., 1936), pp. 133–36.

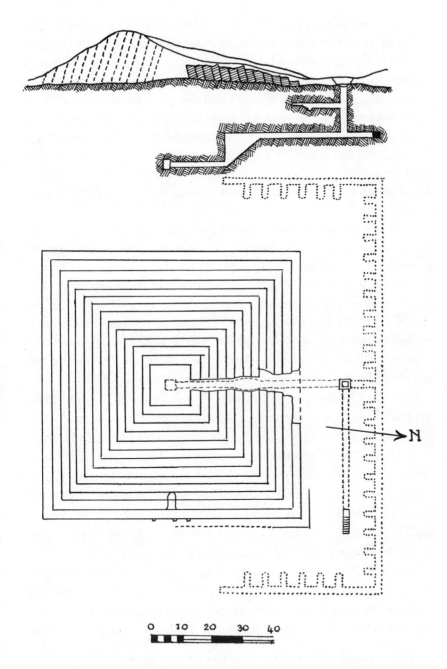

26. *Plan and section of the Layer Pyramid.*

lay the stones horizontally, but sloped them toward the interior at an angle of 22°. (This method, used in older pyramids, was discarded in Sneferu's northern pyramid; from that time on, builders laid the stones horizontally.) No remains of a stone casing were observed, but Reisner noticed crude bricks, and thought that the pyramid might have been cased with them. Many Old Kingdom tombs were cased with white-washed mud bricks, although such a casing has not yet been found on a pyramid. Reisner agrees with Barsanti that this pyramid had never been used for burial. No remains of a chapel at the eastern side were found, but if such a building had been made of mud brick, it might well have disappeared.

Reisner generally attributes the "Layer Pyramid" to the Third Dynasty but also points out similarities between its entrance and those of several tombs of the Second Dynasty. His excavations in the area proved the existence of tombs of the First, Second, and Third Dynasties. The last-mentioned contained bowls bearing the name of King Kha-ba, the third king of the Third Dynasty, but Reisner did not feel that the presence of this king's name gave any clue to the builder of the pyramid. He maintained that "the identification of the builder remains obscure and the site of his final burial-place is probably yet undiscovered."

In spite of Reisner's arguments, the "Layer Pyramid" can be attributed with some certainty to the Third Dynasty. It was built of small stone blocks, and was probably intended to be a step pyramid. The suggested resemblance between the arrangement of its entrance to those of Second Dynasty tombs may be due to architectural traditions. The architect introduced the technique of adding layers of masonry to the core of the superstructure. Edwards prefers to date the pyramid from the Third Dynasty,[7] as does Lauer, the principal authority on step pyramids.[8] As for the identity of the builder, the connection of the name of Kha-ba with the cemetery around it makes his name the most probable one, at least for the time being. To the south of the monument, less than 2 kilometers away, I have come across a cemetery of mud-brick mastabas, which have not yet been excavated. Probably the objects and in-

---

[7] I. E. S. Edwards, *The Pyramids of Egypt* (London, 1947), p. 69.

[8] J.-P. Lauer, *La pyramide à degrés*, I, 8–9.

scriptions to be found here will throw some light on the problem and help us to ascertain the true date of the pyramid.

Although the "Layer Pyramid" is poorly constructed and its architect did not follow in Imhotep's footsteps, less than $1\frac{1}{2}$ kilometers from it lies another monument which was planned to be no less magnificent than the famous Step Pyramid of Saqqara. This is the "Unfinished Pyramid" begun by King Nefer-ka-(Re) Neb-ka, Kha-ba's successor. Work on this pyramid did not proceed beyond the preparatory stages. The site today consists only of a huge pit cut in the rock and a long trench that slopes down through the rock to its northern side. Granite and limestone blocks lie scattered round about; sand covers the floor of the trench and pit.

Before May 15, 1900, no one suspected the existence of this structure, which lies less than 4 miles from the pyramids of Giza. On that day, Alexander Barsanti, the architect of the Antiquities Department of the Egyptian government, was riding back from his work. He was then excavating the "Layer Pyramid" 1 mile south, and traveled every day to the pyramids of Giza, taking the regular road at the edge of the cultivation. On that particular day, he decided to take a short cut and ride across the desert. His foreman, who accompanied him, drew his attention to the fact that the surface of the area was covered with small chips of granite. This suggested the presence of a monument built with granite. Barsanti climbed at once to the top of one of the hills and perceived the outline of a large rectangle. Extremely excited at the idea of discovering a new monument, he started work there on May 16 but had to stop shortly afterward. The site was later given as a concession to the University of California, under the direction of George Reisner. It was not until 1904 that Barsanti resumed his work there,[9] and from then until 1911 he continued intermittently. When he died, he was not yet convinced that his work was finished.[10]

Barsanti's excavations revealed the substructure of a pyramid (Fig. 27), as well as the remains of a razed superstructure. The measurements

[9] G. A. Reisner, *The Development of the Egyptian Tomb*, p. 152.

[10] The reports of Barsanti are published in *Annales du Service*, VII (1906), 260–86; VIII (1907), 201–10, and XII (1911), 57–63. Barsanti's photographs and drawings are our main source of information. His were the only excavations made at the site.

of the latter—180 by 200 meters—correspond more or less to those of the base of the Step Pyramid. The open trench begins with an incline and a horizontal platform; after this comes a staircase cut in the rock, but divided into two parts by a smooth ramp in the center, a little higher than the steps. At the end of the staircase is another horizontal section on the same level as the floor of the pit (Fig. 28).

The pit was filled to a depth of 4.5 meters with stone masonry; the lowest courses were of granite and limestone blocks. On top of the masonry, serving as a floor of the burial chamber, were granite blocks weighing nine tons each, surrounding a single block of forty-three tons. An oval granite sarcophagus was sunk in the floor on the western side, with its long axis north-south. Nothing was found in the oval cist, although its well-polished lid was cemented over (Fig. 29).

Reisner believed that the dimensions of the superstructure and the arrangement of the trench and pit show unmistakable points of similarity between this unfinished pyramid and that of Zoser, and that "probably both were intended to be step pyramids."[11]

The large limestone blocks used as filling were raised to the surface and can now be seen near the pit. Each one weighs between three and four tons, and they total about 4,200 cubic meters. Many had quarry

[11] G. A. Reisner, *The Development of the Egyptian Tomb*, p. 153.

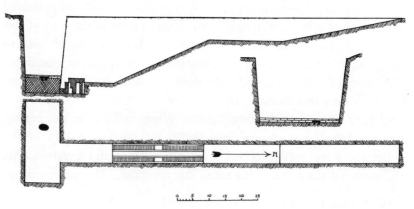

27. *Plan and section of the passage in the substructure of the Unfinished Pyramid at Zawiet el Aryan. (After Barsanti.)*

28. *The rock-cut substructure of the Unfinished Pyramid at Zawiet el Aryan.*

29. *The floor of the pit showing the sarcophagus sunk in the floor and its cover.*

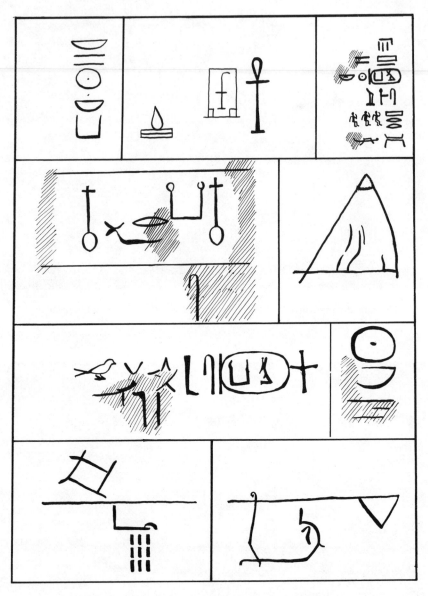

30. *Some of the quarry marks on the stones of the Unfinished Pyramid at Zawiet el Aryan.*

marks in red pigment traced by the gangs of masons and stonecutters (Fig. 30). The name of the owner of the monument appears many times, sometimes written inside a cartouche, and there is little doubt that he was Nefer-ka-(Re) Neb-ka, one of Zoser's successors. The cutting of the rock walls and steps and the handling, cutting, and polishing of the heavy granite blocks (brought from the Aswan quarries) prove that the ancient masons and craftsmen of Neb-ka had mastered their professions.

At the time of Barsanti's first report in 1906, Maspero—at that time Director-General of the Antiquities Department—doubted that anything more could be found, or that the cist in the floor was a sarcophagus.[12] Barsanti was firmly convinced, however, that the real burial chamber and the true sarcophagus were still to be discovered. He continued to remove stones from the floor and to tunnel in the limestone blocks. In his last report, written just before his death, he mentioned that the money at his disposal had run out when he was "two fingers" from his goal, and he expressed the wish to resume his research. We cannot tell what made him so certain and persistent, but it seems that one incident, mentioned in his first report, was mainly responsible. On March 31, 1905, there was a great rainstorm, and the pit was flooded with water to a depth of 3 meters. Suddenly, about midnight, the waters sank to a depth of 1 meter and stopped; the rest had to be emptied away. Barsanti believed that there was a subterranean gallery into which the 380 cubic meters of water had escaped.[13] Until his death he searched for that mysterious gallery, which might have contained a royal burial. It is possible, however, that the water suddenly found its way into a fissure in the rock under the masonry. No archeologist of our generation shares Barsanti's theory of another burial chamber, and he has been severely criticized. Petrie, however, has stated that the site ought to be examined again,[14] and every archeologist will agree that the "Unfinished Pyramid" of Neb-ka ought to be re-explored, not in the hope of finding any new galleries, but in order to explain and study the trench and the floor in the light of our present knowledge.

[12] G. Maspero, *Annales du Service*, VII (1906), 257–59.

[13] G. A. Reisner, *The Development of the Egyptian Tomb*, p. 153.

[14] W. M. F. Petrie, *A History of Egypt* (1923), I, 41.

During the winter months of 1953–54, the site was chosen as the scene of part of a film on ancient Egypt, and the pyramid was partly freed from sand. By the time work on the film had ended, however, the desert had already begun to encroach, and by August, 1954, there was nothing but sand to be seen on the floor of the pit. Whether or not the sarcophagus and the stairway can be seen, the visitor to the site gains a clear idea of the colossal amount of work needed to prepare the substructure of a pyramid.

THE PYRAMIDS OF SEILA, ZAWIET EL AMWAT, AND EL KOLA

These three pyramids, as yet incompletely explored, are thought to belong to the Third Dynasty, according to the observations of the archeologists who have visited them. They are not in the Memphis area; indeed, they are far from it. One is in the Faiyum Province, one in Minya Province, and one in the extreme south in Aswan Province.

The small pyramid of Seila, which has never been explored, stands on one of the spurs of the strip of desert separating the Faiyum from the Nile Valley. It commands a beautiful view over the green fields of the Faiyum on one side, and over the pyramid of Meydum on the other (Fig. 31). From its top one can see the Middle Kingdom pyramids of Hawara and El Lahun—black, conical hills on the edge of the horizon. In 1898 Borchardt visited the site, and wrote the first description of it.[15] Since then archeologists have rarely visited it, because it is rather difficult to reach.[16] It was not until 1937 that A. Pochan published five new photographs of it.[17] From the archeologist's point of view, these added nothing new to Borchardt's observations.

The pyramid of Seila looks like a mastaba built of large limestone blocks. It measures 22.5 meters on the western face, but the length of the other sides cannot be ascertained without cleaning the site, so we cannot say whether or not it is square in plan. There is sufficient evidence, how-

[15] L. Borchardt, "Die Pyramide von Silah," in *Annales du Service*, I (1900), 211–14.

[16] It is situated at 28°23′ latitude N. and 31°3′ longitude E., at a distance of three miles to the west of the canal Wahbi, near Ezbet Zananiri.

[17] A. Pochan, "Pyramide de Seila (au Fayoum)," *Bulletin de l'Institut français d'Archéologie orientale*, XXXVII (1937), 161.

ever, to indicate that it was built as a step pyramid. The substructure is unexplored. As for its date, it is generally accepted as a Third Dynasty structure; but this opinion is based on Borchardt's report, written more than sixty years ago. No remains of a chapel can be seen on the eastern side, and there is no room for a Valley Temple, since the pyramid stands almost at the edge of the plateau, with a steep slope on the east. No tombs are reported near it, and nothing but a few fragments of pottery

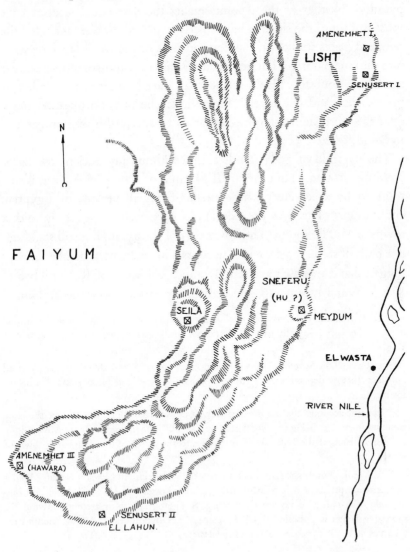

31. *Pyramid field from Lisht to Faiyum.*

and chips of limestone can be seen around it. Borchardt reports picking up a piece of basalt, which would indicate the existence of statuary or a temple.

I have visited this site on several occasions, most recently in October, 1954, and on every visit I have tried to understand the basis for the Third Dynasty dating. There is no evidence except the nearby pyramid of Meydum, and the fact that its construction suggests that of a step pyramid. Neither of these points makes the date conclusive, and we must wait until the site can be properly explored. Reisner included the pyramid in his studies on the development of the royal layer mastaba into the true pyramid, but he concludes that its reconstruction as a layer mastaba is doubtful.[18] He describes it as "faced rubble with rubble filling; nucleus and one layer." In the index he places a question mark after the word, indicating his hesitation to accept this monument as a pyramid.[19]

The pyramid of Seila stands alone, without any ancient tombs or buildings around it; but the small pyramid of Zawiet el Amwat is surrounded by a cemetery with remains from all periods of Egyptian civilization.[20] This was the necropolis of Hebenu, one of the oldest towns in Middle Egypt. The lower part of the pyramid is still standing; it is built of stone blocks with the courses inclined inward. The remains suggest that it was built as a step pyramid. The work of R. Weill before World War I is our only source of information about the building.[21]

[18] G. A. Reisner, *The Development of the Egyptian Tomb*, p. 339, dates it in the Second or Third Dynasty. He states that it is impossible to be certain that it was the tomb of a king.

[19] L. Grinsell, in *Egyptian Pyramids* (Gloucester, 1947), p. 176, describes this pyramid but notes that he depends entirely upon Borchardt's paper and photographs for his information.

[20] In some accounts the site is called Zawiet el Maieteen. Both words have the same meaning in Arabic, being the plural of *maiet*, "dead." The site of Zawiet el Amwat is on the eastern back of the Nile, about five miles to the north of the flourishing town of Minya.

[21] R. Weill, "Fouilles à Tounah et à Zaouiêt-el-Maietin," in *Comptes Rendus* (Académie des inscriptions et belles-lettres, 1912), p. 488. Porter and Moss, *Topographical Bibliography*, IV, 134, give no other reference. A photograph with arrows showing the successive layers is published by J.-P. Lauer, "Les pyramides à degrés, monuments typiques de la IIIe dynastie," *Revue Archéologique*, XLVII (1956), 6 (Fig. 3).

He cleaned its sides, but found nothing which furnished a clue to its date. He even failed to find the entrance. He cut a tunnel through the masonry from north to south in the hope of finding the burial chamber, but without success. No chapels seem to be connected with it. Reisner mentioned this pyramid in his study, and compared it with the "Layer Pyramid" of Zawiet el Aryan.[22] Lauer, Grinsell, and Edwards do not discuss it at all.

The pyramid of El Kola lies on the west bank of the Nile near the small village of El Bissalieh, opposite the famous ancient site of El Kab in Aswan Province. The guidebooks mention it, but we know nothing definite about its date or purpose.[23] Reisner hesitates to call it a pyramid. The expedition of the Fondation Égyptologique Reine Elizabeth, under Capart, excavated the site in 1946 in the hope of finding the entrance. A few years later, Jean Stiénon, the architect of the expedition, made a study of the superstructure of this monument,[24] and from his description we can come to several conclusions:

It was built as a layer pyramid, consisting of one nucleus and three layers (Fig. 32). It has three levels. The lowest is composed of twelve courses of masonry and is 4.3 meters high; the second has ten courses; the third is now almost totally destroyed.[25] The small stones of which this monument is built were quarried locally and were inclined inward. The mortar is dry mud mixed with chopped straw and a little crushed lime. The base is 18.6 meters long on the northwestern side. Stiénon does not give the length of the other sides, but in his plan the pyramid is

[22] G. A. Reisner, *The Development of the Egyptian Tomb*, p. 339. In his index he puts a question mark after the word "pyramid."

[23] For the bibliography of this monument, see again Porter and Moss, *Topographical Bibliography*, V, 167. See also G. Steindorff in Baedecker's *Guide to Egypt and the Sudan* (English, eighth edition, 1929), p. 364. Maspero, more than sixty years ago, tried to enter it, but the tunnel which he cut in one of its sides did not obtain any results (see *Histoire ancienne des peuples de l'Orient*, II, 58). This monument is a favorite place of "treasure hunters" who have tried several times to gain access to the supposed treasure still hidden inside it!

[24] Jean Stiénon, "El Kôlah," *Chronique d'Égypte*, XLIX (January, 1950), 42–45.

[25] There is a reference to the pyramid in Vyse, *Operations Carried On at the Pyramids of Gizeh*, III, 85, where it is mentioned that it had twenty-seven courses, built in three stages, and that in 1839 it was 38 feet, 6 inches high.

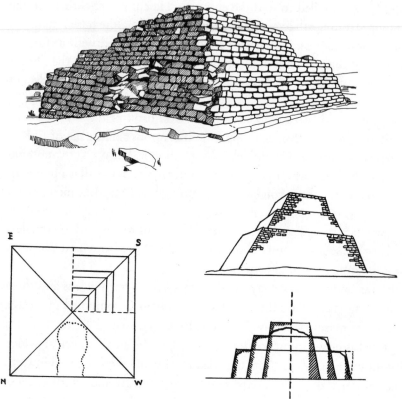

32. *The pyramid of El Kola.* (*After Stiénon.*)

square. Its height was originally 9.4 meters.[26] An unusual feature is that
the corners, rather than the sides, face the four cardinal points. (The
diagonal orientation is probably due to the direction of the Nile in this
region.) No traces of a casing were found.[27]

As for the date of the pyramid, it is believed to be of the Third Dy-

[26] The dimensions given by Borchardt to Reisner and published in *The Development
of the Egyptian Tomb* (p. 339) were taken before the clearance of the angles in 1946:
Borchardt measured the monument as 13.5 by 12 meters.

[27] There is a possibility that we might add to these pyramids another monument, that
at Nubt, near Naqada, in Qena Province. This was examined by Petrie in 1892 (*Naqada
and Ballas*, pp. 65–70); it is also of the layer-mastaba type with inclined courses and has
a nucleus and three layers. There are no remains of any other stages to indicate that it
might have been a step pyramid.

nasty, although Stiénon says cautiously that it must belong to a very early period. I should like to point out that this pyramid lies a short distance from Kom el Ahmar, the site of the ancient Hierakonopolis (the first capital of the south). Many important monuments were found there, especially from the earliest dynasties.

To summarize the facts about these three structures: All of them are small and have no chapels. Two do not seem to be connected with cemeteries. One of them, that of Seila, has not been examined, but the other two have defied all efforts to find the substructure or any burial chamber. Were these structures built for royal burials, or for burials at all? Do they really belong to the Third Dynasty and not to an earlier or later period of the Old Kingdom? These two important questions cannot be answered now. It is generally accepted that there were no important stone buildings before Zoser's time, when Imhotep built the Step Pyramid. But these three pyramids are built of comparatively small stones, quarried locally, and in their technique do not surpass the First and Second Dynasty monuments built of stone; and layer and stepped mastabas in brick were known before the Third Dynasty. There is another problem, not less irritating. If these buildings were indeed step pyramids and were intended to be burials, why were they constructed so far from the cemeteries of the period? Should we consider them as cenotaphs? Once more we find ourselves at a loss to explain.

THE PYRAMID OF MEYDUM

For many miles the pyramid of Meydum dominates the area in which it stands. Its present shape makes it look like a colossal tower standing on a hill at the edge of the desert (Fig. 33). Books on archeology and history published prior to 1945 attribute the pyramid to King Sneferu. As a result of recent excavations at Dahshur, however, archeologists now identify the so-called southern pyramid of Sneferu—once thought to refer to that at Meydum—with the Bent Pyramid of Dahshur. Thus the ownership of the Meydum pyramid becomes unclear. However, we may note that it is the final development of the step pyramid type, and was almost certainly the immediate predecessor of Sneferu's pyramids.

The pyramid of Meydum has drawn and held the attention of many investigators from the earliest years of Egyptology. Drawings were

33. *The pyramid of Meydum.*

made of it before and during the eighteenth century, and it was among
the pyramids investigated by Perring and Vyse in 1839.[28] The site attracted the attention of Mariette, who found several important tombs
there, notably that which contained the statues of Prince Rehotep (Fig.
34) and his beautiful wife Nefert. They are among the most famous in
the Cairo Museum. Petrie excavated the site as early as 1890, and resumed work on it with G. Wainwright. Petrie published two works
which for many years provided our chief source of information on the
pyramid, its temple, and the surrounding cemeteries.[29] Borchardt investigated the pyramid in 1927 and wrote a famous paper, containing the
most accurate plans to date.[30] A few years later, an expedition of the

[28] Vyse, *Operations Carried On at the Pryamids of Gizeh*, III, 78–80.

[29] W. M. F. Petrie and others, *Meydum and Memphis* (London, 1910), Vol. III; W. M.
F. Petrie, *Medum* (London, 1882).

[30] Borchardt, *Die Entstehung der Pyramide, an der Baugeschichte der Pyramide bei Mejdum
nachgewiesen* (Berlin, 1928).

34. *Statue of Prince Rehotep, who was buried at Meydum near the pyramid.*

museum of the University of Pennsylvania continued excavating the site. However, this expedition concentrated on the temple and the cemeteries around it, rather than the pyramid itself. The final publication has not yet appeared, although Alan Rowe published a preliminary report in 1931.[31] The site has been deserted since the work of this expedition ended in 1934. It still has much to reveal, and may be one of our most valuable sources for the study of Old Kingdom civilization.[32]

The pyramid of Meydum is surrounded by the earliest complete pyramid complex so far discovered (Fig. 35). The pyramid stands at the edge

[31] University of Pennsylvania, *Museum Journal*, XXII (1931), 5–46.

[32] Porter and Moss, *Topographical Bibliography*, IV, 88–96.

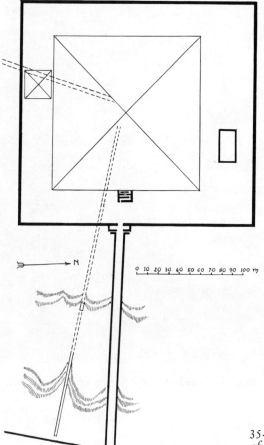

0 10 20 30 40 50 60 70 80 90 100 m

35. *The pyramid complex of Meydum.*

of the plateau, surrounded by an inclosure wall in ruinous condition. From an entrance in the eastern side, a walled, roofless causeway led down to the edge of the cultivation. It was paved with stone, and its walls were topped by a rounded coping. The Valley Temple at the end of the causeway is now under water because of a rise in the level of the subsoil water; but it is not beyond the possibility of excavation.

On the southern side of the pyramid itself are the remains of a small pyramid. On the east is a small Mortuary Temple with its own inclosure wall (Fig. 36). This temple was almost intact when found by Petrie, and its ceiling is still in excellent condition. In a small, open courtyard, built against the casing stones of the pyramid, stood an offering-table flanked by two tall, rounded stelae. To the east lay two small, roofed chambers. The whole building was inclosed within the temenos wall of the pyramid (Fig. 37). On the inside walls of the chambers are graffiti written by visitors to this site, some of which refer to King Sneferu. One of these graffiti may date from the end of the Old Kingdom, but most are from the Eighteenth Dynasty. One, dated in the year 41 of Thotmes III, was

36. *The Mortuary Temple of the Meydum pyramid.*

written by the scribe Aakheperkare-seneb, who mentions that he came
here to see the beautiful temple of Sneferu. At the end of his inscription,
he prays for the *Ka* of King Sneferu and of Queen Meresankh, who was
probably the king's mother. This text and the other graffiti oblige us to
consider carefully who the owner of the pyramid might have been. The
ancient scribes were not ignorant, and we have every reason to believe
that some had read the name of Sneferu on nearby monuments, or had
obtained their information from priests in the vicinity. We know from
ancient sources that King Sneferu had two pyramids, which have been
identified at Dahshur. It would be unusual for a king to have three such
monuments. Sneferu's predecessor, King Hu, reigned for at least
twenty-four years. In my opinion Hu built his monument at Meydum,
but it was either left unfinished at the time of his death or considered too
simple. During Sneferu's reign, this unfinished (or too modest) building
was enlarged and completed. Consequently, we can consider the completion of the pyramid of Meydum and its complex to date from the
reign of Sneferu.

The pyramid originally stood 92 meters high, and was 144 meters
square at the base. It has an angle of 51°53′. According to Petrie's investigations, it stands on a prepared platform or pavement which runs
under the casing stones. The superstructure consists of a core comprising

0   1   2   3   4   5m

→ N

37. *The plan of the Mortuary Temple
of the Meydum pyramid.*

a nucleus mastaba with eight added layers of masonry, which converted it into an eight-stepped mastaba of the layer type (Fig. 38). As the additions were made, the structure was increased in height, and each succeeding stage carefully cased and dressed smooth. Finally, when the builders had constructed a smooth, eight-stepped pyramidal monument, they filled in the steps, cased the whole structure once again, and achieved a true pyramid for the first time.

The entrance lies in the center of the northern face of the pyramid, almost 30 meters from the ground. It gives access to a passage, 57 meters long, which descends into the rock below the superstructure. Apparently the passage was closed at its lower end by a wooden door, the emplacement of which may still be seen. At the end of the passage are two antechambers in the form of a corridor, and finally there is a vertical shaft directed upward, with the burial chamber at the top. It measures 5.9 by 2.65 meters. The floor of the burial chamber is level with the base of the superstructure. The room itself is lined with limestone and has a fine corbelled roof composed of seven steps. It was here that Petrie discovered in 1891 the remains of a wooden coffin, which he believed to

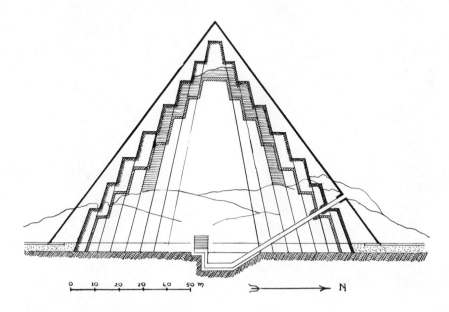

38. *Section of the pyramid of Meydum showing the different stages of construction.*

have belonged to King Sneferu. In the roof are socket holes for cross-
beams, in one of which still remains the stump of a wooden beam. (This
resembles the cedar beams found inside the Bent Pyramid of Sneferu at
Dahshur and is probably contemporary with that structure.)

The outer casing of the pyramid was destroyed in ancient times, perhaps during the New Kingdom, and it is the debris of this destruction
which, covering the lower part of the building, gives it the appearance
of standing upon a conical hill. Removing this huge mound of debris
will probably reveal other interesting facts and may even tell us whose
pyramid it was.

5

The Pyramids of Sneferu

at Dahshur

Six miles south of Saqqara, on top of a spur of the Libyan Plateau over-looking the ancient site of Memphis, the two stone pyramids of Dahshur rise proudly on the horizon (Figs. 39 and 40). There King Sneferu, the founder of the Fourth Dynasty, built his gigantic royal tombs. In later periods, several kings of the Twelfth Dynasty built their brick pyramids near the edge of the cultivation. The earlier stone pyramids have always presented something of a problem. Explorations and excavations during the past few years have shown that Dahshur is an especially important site for the study of pyramid archeology (Fig. 41).

King Sneferu was the founder of a new royal dynasty. His right to the throne was insured by his marriage to the royal heiress, the famous Queen Hetepheres. (An intact cache of her funerary furniture was found in the Giza necropolis in 1926 by the Boston Museum expedition; the marvelous objects now occupy an entire room in the Cairo Museum.) Sneferu's predecessor is considered to be King Hu, but all that is known with certainty is that he followed Hu on the throne, and may have been related to the previous royal house. Although Sneferu undertook build-ing operations at Meydum, he chose a place nearer the capital as the site of his tomb. The records on the Palermo Stone—one of the valuable sources for the history of ancient Egypt, particularly the kings of the

39. *The two stone pyramids of Sneferu at Dahshur.*

first five dynasties—tell us about his activities and the temples he built throughout the land. This stone also records that he sent a fleet of forty large ships to the coast of Lebanon to bring back cedar. (Many beams of this wood, in remarkably sound condition, are still preserved inside the southern pyramid.) Sneferu was also famous for an expedition which he sent south to restore order in the countries on Egypt's southern frontiers. This expedition brought back 7,000 captives and 200,000 oxen and sheep. Sneferu's name was recorded in the mines of Sinai, a situation which indicates that he promoted mining in this region. His memory lasted for many centuries among the Egyptians, who long after his death referred to him as a beneficent, kind, and beloved king.[1] Several kings of the Twelfth Dynasty chose to be buried near him seven hundred years after his death, and we know that at that time he had been deified and was worshiped side by side with Re, Osiris, Soker, and other gods.

The site of Dahshur shares the same fate as the rest of the Memphite necropolis. Its temples and pyramids were demolished in ancient times,

[1] B. Gunn, "Concerning King Snefru," *Journal of Egyptian Archaeology*, XII (1926), 250–51.

and its tombs robbed. Indeed, it was the work of modern grave robbers which first drew attention to the archeological importance of the site. The two stone pyramids, as well as the others built of brick, aroused the interest of archeologists at the beginning of the nineteenth century. The most famous names connected with them are those of the British archeologists Perring and Vyse, who cleared the interior of the pyramids in 1839.[2] The first expedition to carry out any serious work of excavation was that of De Morgan, who, in 1894 and 1895, excavated the pyramids of Amenemhet II, Senusert III, and others near the edge of the cultivation.[3] His work revealed many tombs dating from the Old and New Kingdoms; the name of Sneferu appeared frequently, especially in the necropolis near the northern stone pyramid. (It was in the tombs of several princesses of the Middle Kingdom that De Morgan found a world-famous collection of jewelry which now fills many cases in the Cairo Museum.) Since De Morgan's time, it has been well established that the northern stone pyramid belonged to Sneferu. According to texts found in tombs and on other monuments, it was known that Sneferu had two pyramids, a northern and a southern one. This is why we find the northern stone pyramid of Dahshur and the pyramid of Meydum (to the south) usually attributed to Sneferu. The Bent Pyramid at Dahshur, one mile south of the northern pyramid, remained a problem. Those who ventured to guess attributed it to King Hu.

No one excavated at Dahshur for about thirty years after De Morgan's time because of the great difficulties involved. In 1924, Gustave Jéquier tried to investigate around the Bent Pyramid, but transferred his work to the more northerly site around the Mastabet Fara'un and the pyramid complex of Pepi II after only a month's digging. Complete silence then reigned over Dahshur for twenty years. In 1945 the Egyptian government created a new section in the Antiquities Department for pyramid studies, and intrusted it to the late Abdel Salam Hussein. He undertook successful work around the Bent Pyramid and found the name of Sneferu among the quarry marks on some of the blocks. It occurred several times, especially on blocks built under the corners of

[2] Vyse, *Operations Carried On at the Pyramids of Gizeh*, III, 65 ff.

[3] J. de Morgan, *Fouilles à Dahchour, mars-juin 1894* (Vienna, 1895); *Fouilles à Dahchour en 1894-95* (Vienna, 1903).

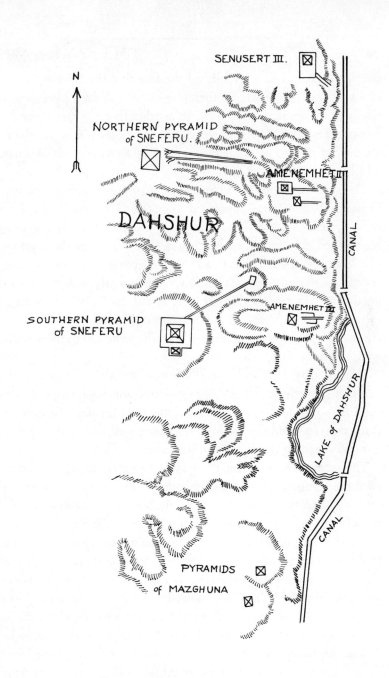

N

SENUSERT III.

NORTHERN PYRAMID
of SNEFERU.

AMENEMHET II

DAHSHUR

SOUTHERN PYRAMID
of SNEFERU

AMENEMHET III

CANAL

LAKE of DAHSHUR

CANAL

PYRAMIDS
of MAZGHUNA

41. *Pyramid field of Dahshur.*

40. *The Bent Pyramid of Sneferu as seen from cultivation.*

the pyramid, and thus established the fact that the Bent Pyramid had also been built by Sneferu; therefore the king's two pyramids, mentioned in the ancient texts, were none other than the two stone monuments of Dahshur. This discovery of course raised a new problem—the identity of the builder of the pyramid of Meydum—the solution of which still awaits research.

The premature death of Hussein in 1949 put an end to the work at Dahshur. When I was appointed in 1951 as Director of the Pyramid Research Project, I realized that there was no pyramid site in Egypt which needed investigation more than Dahshur. From the beginning of my work there, I felt that it was more important to examine the area around the pyramid than its interior. Consequently, in addition to clearing the interior, I decided to excavate east of the Bent Pyramid, in hope of finding the Mortuary Temple. Jéquier had made soundings in the area in 1924, but none of them had been deep enough to show that there were monuments.[4]

Work started in March, 1951. We explored the interior of the pyramid in a short time, cleared all its galleries, and discovered the western entrance. Outside the pyramid, we found the Mortuary Temple, as well as the parts of buildings inside the inclosure wall, and cleaned part of the causeway leading down toward the valley.

The second season, which began in October, 1951, and continued until the summer of 1952, brought many discoveries. The line of the causeway was clearly discernible on the surface of the desert, and there was a large area covered with limestone chips in the gorge leading down to the cultivation. It looked as though the causeway ended somewhere in this vicinity and that we might find here the remains of the Valley Temple. The temples of the area had been used as quarries as early as pharaonic times. Medieval Cairo needed stone for building its fortresses, city walls, and mosques, and even in the days of Mehemet Ali, as recently as 1815, one of his relatives took stone from the site to build a palace. All the stones of the temenos wall and those of the Mortuary Temple, as well as much of the pyramid's casing, had been removed.

[4] For the reference to previous work done at the site, as well as the preliminary reports on my excavations there, see Ahmed Fakhry, *The Bent Pyramid of Dahshur* (Cairo, 1954); see also Ahmed Fakhry, *The Monuments of Sneferu at Dahshur*, Vol. I: *The Bent Pyramid* (Cairo, 1959), pp. 1–13.

42. *A part of the Valley Temple during the excavations, South Pyramid,*
Dahshur.

One might logically conclude that workmen had done this only after
having exhausted all the available stone near the cultivation. My only
hope was to find enough remaining of the Valley Temple to enable us
to make a plan of it; I had not the slightest expectation of finding anything more. The sand was very deep, and I told my assistants on the first
day of work to expect nothing of importance. I did not think we would
find any trace of the temple for at least two weeks.

We generally begin our work at 7 A.M., with a half hour's break at
9 A.M. for breakfast. On October 16, 1951, the first day of the work, I
divided the workmen into two gangs. After exactly one hour and
twenty minutes, one of the gangs came across the top of a high-standing

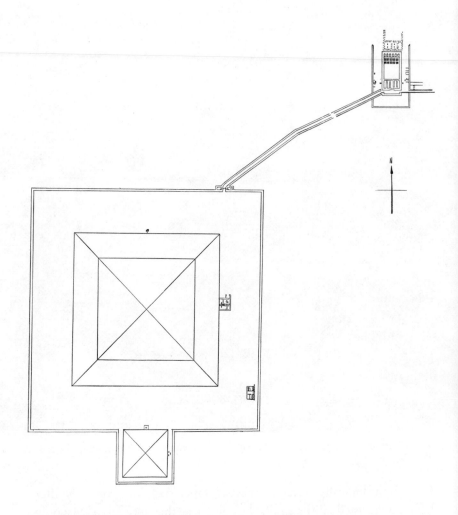

43. *General plan of the Bent Pyramid complex, Dahshur.*

wall of limestone masonry. A few minutes later, part of a statue and some fragments of reliefs appeared. At 9 A.M. I sat near that newly discovered wall, looking at these fragments, and could hardly believe my eyes. What were these inscriptions, and how had that huge wall survived the depredations of the ancient quarrymen? Was there a possibility that a part of the Valley Temple had escaped destruction? It had long been a common belief among Egyptologists that the walls of the temples were

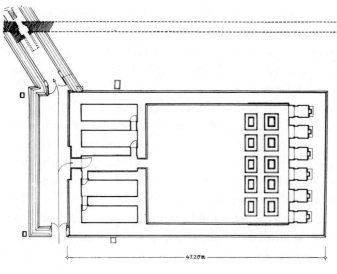

44. *Plan and isometric drawing of the Valley Temple of Sneferu at Dahshur.*
(After Ricke.)

not decorated with reliefs before the end of the Fourth Dynasty. If this were essentially true, where had these reliefs come from? The days that followed brought new finds, and the realization that the reliefs and wall did indeed belong to the Valley Temple. It was completely excavated that season, and some 1,400 fragments of relief came to light. The walls of the building were still standing to a good height, so that we could see the plan clearly (Fig. 42). We found statues, stelae, and many other objects, but all were dwarfed by the magnificent reliefs of Sneferu, which depicted him performing ancient ceremonies. Further work carried out around the small pyramid south of the Bent Pyramid resulted in the discovery of a large stela bearing the names of Sneferu. The work around the Bent Pyramid is still far from complete; the short description that follows summarizes the finds and what we have learned about the pyramid and temples of this great king.

THE SOUTHERN, OR BENT, PYRAMID

The approach to the southern pyramid complex of King Sneferu at Dahshur is through a Valley Temple situated near the edge of the cultivation (Fig. 43). At the time of writing, this is the earliest Valley Temple discovered. As we have already seen, there was no temple of this type for the Step Pyramid of Zoser, nor any remains of a causeway which would suggest that such a building had ever existed. Nor were Valley Temples or causeways found in connection with any of the other pyramids of the Third Dynasty. The pyramid of Meydum, which has both a causeway and a Valley Temple (yet to be excavated) is now supposed to have belonged to King Hu, and was in all probability completed, if not entirely built, by Sneferu. We cannot say as yet whether the Valley Temple was introduced by Sneferu or whether it was a traditional feature of the pyramid complex, the earlier evidence for which has escaped us.

The Valley Temple of Sneferu is a simple, rectangular building measuring about 47.16 by 26.20 meters (90 by 50 ancient Egyptian cubits), its long axis directed north-south (Fig. 44). It was surrounded by a thick temenos wall of mud brick, which was pierced by a large gateway near its center on the east (the side near the cultivation). A ramp, bordered on each side by brick walls, led to the entrance. At a later date this

45. *A part of the nome list of Upper Egypt, Valley Temple of Sneferu, Dahshur.*

causeway was blocked and a smaller entrance made near the southeast corner of the inclosure. The ramp of the original entrance perhaps led to a quay, but this area has not yet been excavated. On the outer side of the southern inclosure wall stood two huge limestone stelae adorned with the names and figure of the king. The doorway of the temple proper is in the center of the southern wall, and opens into a long, narrow hall, with sculptured friezes on the western and eastern walls. The frieze on the west depicts the royal estates in Upper Egypt; they are personified as women, and identified with the names of the districts, or *nomes*,[5] in which they were situated (Fig. 45). On the eastern wall, a similar frieze,

[5] The nomes were the administrative districts. The word is from the Greek and is usually translated as "province."

46. *Sneferu embraced by a lion goddess.*

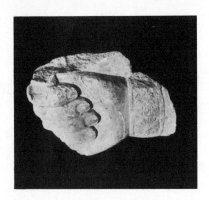

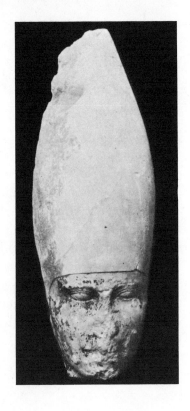

47. *A head of one of the large limestone statues of Sneferu and the hand of another statue showing an ornamental bracelet.*

much destroyed, had figures representing the king's estates in Lower Egypt. Most of the walls above the friezes have disappeared, but enough remains to show that they were sculptured in relief and painted with scenes representing the king in the presence of the gods.

Two storerooms lay on each side of this Hall of Nomes. That on the east had a small crypt in the floor; a golden bead and fragments of gold foil indicate that it served as a storage place for valuables. A doorway at the northern end of the hall opens into a rectangular, open courtyard, with plain walls. At the northern side of this court were six shrines, protected by a portico upheld by ten rectangular pillars in two rows.

The walls under the portico were adorned with reliefs and a continuation of the frieze showing the royal estates. The pillars had sculptures on at least two sides. Unfortunately, the temple was used as a quarry, and not one of the pillars was found standing in its place. All of them had been smashed to fragments in the open court, which served as a workshop. However, we found many parts of these pillars, and have been able to fit some of the fragments together. The scenes show King Sneferu performing various ceremonies, such as the Sed Festival, the ceremonial visit to the shrines of Buto, and the foundation of the temple. Others depict him standing in the presence of the gods or being embraced by them (Fig. 46).

None of the sculptured walls of the six chapels have been preserved intact, but we have recovered enough to enable us to reconstruct their appearance. The inner part of each shrine was a monolithic naos of fine limestone; a large statue of the king contained in each was actually carved from the same piece of stone. These statues, of which we have recovered fragments of three, were life-size or larger and seem to have differed in pose and costume (Fig. 47). One well-preserved statue shows the king wearing the crown of Upper Egypt and a kilt of finely pleated linen, held up by a belt. The buckle bears his name. His arms hang at his sides, and on his wrists are wide bracelets decorated with a design of rosettes and the emblem of the god Min. The chapel façades had figures in high relief, modeled with astonishing realism. Above the opening to each naos were carved the names of the king, flanked by emblems and topped by a band of five-pointed stars representing the sky. On each side stood a large figure of Sneferu. (One of these shows him in exactly

the same costume described above on a naos figure, even to the design
on the bracelets.)

As we have mentioned before, the cult of Sneferu flourished for centuries after his death, and here in his Valley Temple we found much evidence of the great esteem in which he was held. Under the portico in
front of the shrines we found statues of private persons, as well as stelae
and altars. They date from both the Old and Middle Kingdoms. The
temple was apparently destroyed during the Eighteenth Dynasty, for
pottery from that period was found in the open court and in the later
mud-brick dwellings that existed inside and outside the temple.

In all the later Valley Temples, the causeway leads upward from the
western door of the temple itself. Here it begins outside the building, at
the southwest end of the stone inclosure. Its limestone walls have been
entirely quarried away, except for small portions at the beginning. They
had a batter and were surrounded by a curved coping. The causeway
was unroofed. A curious feature is that it was paved with mud brick,
laid over a limestone pavement. After a distance of over 700 meters, it

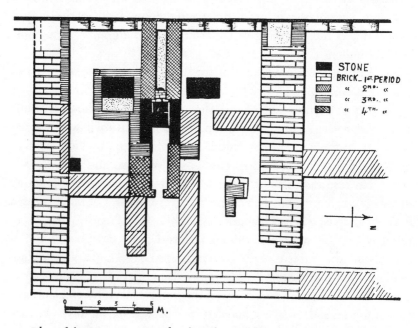

48. *Plan of the Mortuary Temple of Sneferu, Dahshur.*

curves to join the temenos wall of the pyramid and leads into the pyramid courtyard.

Straight ahead, on the eastern side of the pyramid, lies the Mortuary Temple of King Sneferu. This temple underwent several structural alterations (Fig. 48). It was planned on a modest scale. Simpler than that of Meydum, it consisted merely of a small shrine, or shelter, open to the east and west, under which was placed a great limestone slab surmounted by an alabaster offering table. The shrine was flanked by two huge stelae, similar to those found outside the Valley Temple, but on a larger scale. A mud-brick wall surrounded the stelae and the shelter. As it was originally planned, the temple opened to the north, and apparently contained no other structural features. Later, perhaps near the end of the Old Kingdom, the temple was enlarged. Brick walls were built in front of its entrance, and the simple court surrounding the offering table and the two stelae was divided into several rooms, which seem to have been roofed. During another alteration, possibly during the Middle Kingdom, builders walled in the southern stela and added, just inside the main entrance, a mud-brick altar reached by a short flight of steps. At a very late date, possibly in Ptolemaic times, a long, narrow room with a vaulted roof was constructed between the original limestone shelter and the face of the pyramid. At the same time, brick walls, extended eastward from the eastern face of the stone shelter, formed an antechamber to it. This last alteration gives the impression that it was the effort of a small group of priests determined to revive the cult of the good King Sneferu. There is something touching in the way that they sought out three of the ancient incense altars and set them up on the alabaster offering table. We found them there, still standing upright and unharmed. On one was a bowl of charcoal, waiting in vain for the attendant priest to come and sprinkle incense upon the embers. The incense altars, which have so astonishingly withstood the destruction of the rest of the monuments, seem to date from the Middle Kingdom. Two are of limestone, and one is of red pottery. The former, which are inscribed, were made for King Sneferu by a family of priests, all of whom were named after him.

In the southeast corner of the pyramid courtyard a low, rectangular mound proved, upon investigation, to be a collection of brick buildings, including granaries.

South of the parent building lies a small pyramid. From the time of the pyramids of Meydum and Dahshur, builders always added one or more small pyramids south of the parent building. Comparing them with the so-called "Southern Tomb" of Zoser at the Step Pyramid of Saqqara, some Egyptologists have interpreted these small pyramids as burial places for the jars which contained the king's viscera. Others consider them as burials for the Ka of the king—hence the name "*Ka*-pyramid," often used to describe them. Nothing proves either of these theories, and a great deal of negative evidence tends to disprove them. Actually we are completely ignorant of their use. All we know is that the Egyptians considered them a very important and necessary feature of every pyramid complex.

The Subsidiary Pyramid of Sneferu is located about 55 meters south of the center of the Great Pyramid. Its interior was cleared in 1946–47 by Abdel-Salam Hussein, and found to be empty. A quarry mark on one of the stones was incorrectly read as part of the name of Queen Hetepheres, Sneferu's wife, and some attributed this building to her. But the reading

50. *The Bent Pyramid. The circle shows the location of the unsuspected western entrance. To the right is the small subsidiary pyramid.*

49. *Sneferu as depicted on a newly discovered stela in front of his subsidiary pyramid at Dahshur.*

was a mistake, and the chamber inside is so small that it could never have contained a burial, much less the elaborate funerary equipment which was later removed from her original (and still undiscovered) tomb and re-buried near the great pyramid of her son Khufu at Giza. This small pyramid yielded only fragments of broken pottery, and no trace of a burial of any kind.

Hussein had cleared the northern face of the Subsidiary Pyramid; I decided to finish clearing the others. In so doing I discovered the remains of a chapel in front of the entrance, on the north, and two huge limestone stelae near the eastern face, within the girdle wall. One of them, the upper part of which has been destroyed, was still standing upright. The other had fallen down and was broken into three large pieces. It was easily repaired, to reveal sculpture in almost perfect preservation (Fig. 49). It is almost the same as the other stelae found near the Valley Temple and Mortuary Temple, and its presence here settles forever the question of the ownership of the small pyramid. No matter for what purpose it was designed, there is now no doubt that it belonged to King Sneferu himself, and the missing original tomb of Queen Hetepheres still remains one of the many incentives for future excavations at Dahshur.

The Bent Pyramid is constructed of local limestone and cased with fine white limestone (Fig. 50). This casing is laid in sloping courses; that is, the casing blocks are tilted down from the outside to the inside, similar to those on Third Dynasty pyramids. The pyramid has retained much of its casing, because it is very difficult to dislodge stones laid in this manner.

The building measures 188.6 meters square, and is 101.15 meters high. The angle of the slope is 54°31'13" to a height of 49.07 meters, and then changes to 43°21' (Fig. 51). This change in the angle gives the pyramid its characteristic appearance, from which originated its various names— the "Bent Pyramid," "Blunted Pyramid," and "Rhomboidal Pyramid." Scholars have offered several explanations to account for the change of angle. Some feel that, if the builders had retained the original angle, the great weight of the masonry would have crushed the ceiling of the interior rooms and corridors; it is true that these show cracks, which were repaired with plaster in ancient times. Others suggest that the builders

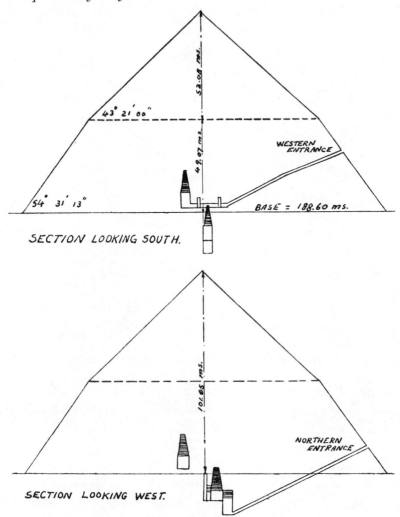

51. *Diagram showing the dimensions and angles of the Bent Pyramid at Dahshur.* (*Hassan Mustapha.*)

changed the angle in order to finish the pyramid quickly, or because they feared that the casing would slide down from a steeper angle. This last theory is quite untenable; the very fact that the casing was laid in a sloping position would make such an occurrence impossible.

The entrance is in the northern face of the pyramid, at a height of

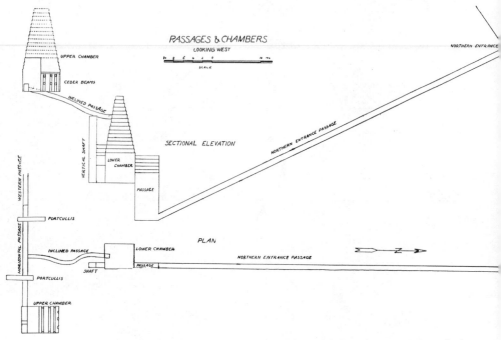

52. Passages and chambers in the Bent Pyramid at Dahshur. (Hassan Mustapha.)

11.8 meters. On each side of it, near the top, are sockets for a flap door.
A descending passage, 79.53 meters long and only 1.1 meters high, ends
in a horizontal corridor, which has a fine corbelled roof 12.6 meters
high. In order to proceed further, the visitor has to scale the southern
wall of this passage to a height of 6.25 meters, to find himself on the
floor of the lower chamber of the pyramid (Fig. 52). Beginning at 12.3
meters from the floor, the walls are corbelled from every side; each
course of masonry projects inward 0.15 meters until the ceiling measures
only 0.3 by 1.16 meters (Fig. 53). The southern wall of this room has
openings into two passages. One leads to a shaft which rises vertically,
but does not seem to connect with any of the known passages or chambers. Much higher in the wall—about 12.6 meters from the floor—
hidden near the ceiling, is another passage which slopes slightly upward.
This crooked, irregularly cut corridor terminates in a horizontal passage, running east-west. To the east, beyond a portcullis, is a second
room.

53. *The corbelled ceiling of the lower chamber of the South Pyramid of Sneferu at Dahshur.*

54. *The cedar beams inside the upper chamber of the South Pyramid of Sneferu at Dahshur.*

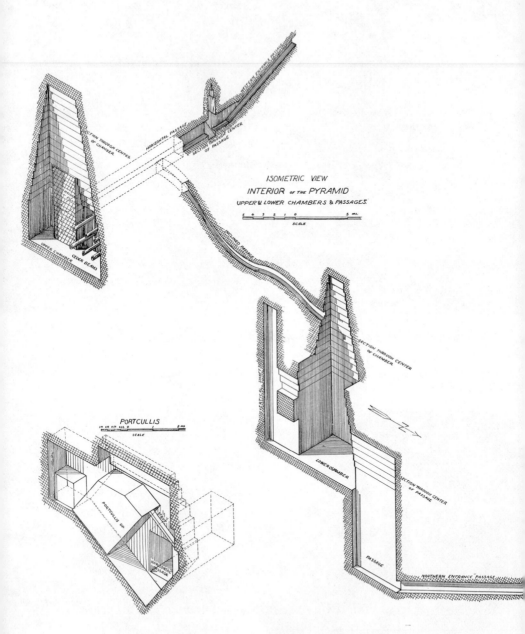

ISOMETRIC VIEW
INTERIOR of the PYRAMID
UPPER & LOWER CHAMBERS & PASSAGES.

SCALE

PORTCULLIS

SCALE

55. *Isometric view of the upper and lower chambers and passages of the South Pyramid of Sneferu at Dahshur.*

The walls and ceiling of this upper chamber are built like those of the lower chamber, but here the roofing blocks are damaged. A curious feature is several large cedar beams laid along the walls (Fig. 54). At first glance, these appear to be a scaffolding, but closer inspection shows that this cannot have been their purpose. When Perring and Vyse investigated the pyramid, they found both the lower and upper rooms filled with small blocks of white limestone, with the cedar beams lying among them. Both beams and blocks are a puzzle, but it may be that the sarcophagus was built of stone masonry (this is known to have occurred elsewhere), and the beams may represent a kind of funerary canopy over the burial. In any case, we may assume that the beams, which are in an excellent state of preservation, represent part of the cargo of cedarwood which Sneferu imported from Lebanon.

Retracing our steps to the horizontal passage and passing under another portcullis, we make our way westward through a passage measuring 64.63 meters long and only 1.1 meters high (Fig. 55). This passage slopes upward at first at an angle of 24°17' and then at an angle of 30°9'. It ends abruptly in the western face of the pyramid, at a height of 33.32 meters from its base, and 13.7 meters south of the dead center of the face. So far, this is the only pyramid known to have a second entrance on the west side. Moreover, it was evidently considered to lead to something very important, as the passage was filled with huge limestone blocks, which were exceedingly difficult to remove. The Bent Pyramid has proved to be a hard task for all who have tried to work in it, and it may not yet have revealed all its secrets.

In the account of their operations, Perring and Vyse relate an incident which suggests a tantalizing train of speculation. They mention that while their men were working on the clearance of one of the passages, they suffered greatly from the heat and lack of air. On October 15, 1839, conditions were such that they could hardly continue the work. By that time the men had forced an entrance into one of the chambers. Suddenly a strong, cold wind began to blow from the interior of the pyramid outward. This current of cool air was so strong that it was only with difficulty that the men could keep their lamps lit. The wind blew strong for two days and then stopped as mysteriously as it had started;

56. *The Northern Pyramid of Sneferu at Dahshur.*

no one could explain from whence it came. Perring expressed the opinion that the chambers of the pyramid must have had some other connection with the outside.[6] This could not have been the western entrance, because it was opened for the first time in 1951.

While working inside this pyramid in recent years, I have noticed that, on some windy days, a noise can be heard, especially in the horizontal corridor between the two portcullises at the end of the ramp leading to the western entrance. This noise sometimes continues for almost ten seconds and has occurred many times. The only explanation for it is that there is still an undiscovered part of the interior which leads to the outside. The problem must be settled in future investigations.

From the above account, it will be appreciated that the interior of the Bent Pyramid is quite unlike those of other pyramids. It is most impressive to behold, and its clean, white walls and corbelled ceilings leave the visitor with an unforgettable memory.

[6] Vyse, *Operations Carried On at the Pyramids of Gizeh*, III, 67.

THE NORTHERN PYRAMID

The various ridges of the desert near the southern pyramid of Sneferu are surmounted by tombs and mastabas which date from the Old Kingdom and later. These have been partly destroyed by thieves but have never been scientifically excavated. Sneferu's northern pyramid also awaits investigation. We tried to examine the ground in front of the eastern face in 1953, but had to abandon the work temporarily because of the large stone blocks which had fallen from the pyramid and covered the spot. It is to be hoped that the Valley Temple and causeway of this pyramid will be found, so that we can learn more about the funerary cult of King Sneferu.

This pyramid may have been started before its southern neighbor was almost completed. It is similarly constructed of local limestone with a casing of fine white limestone, nearly all of which has been stripped off. In size this pyramid is a close rival to the Great Pyramid of Khufu at Giza. It measures about 220 meters square, only 10 meters less than the Great Pyramid. It is 99 meters high and has an angle of 43°40′; this slope

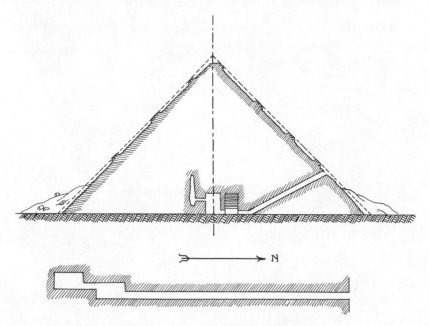

57. *Plan and section of the North Stone Pyramid at Dahshur.*

is considerably less than that of most other pyramids, and creates a characteristically flattened appearance (Fig. 56).

The entrance, about 4 meters east of dead center in the northern face, is situated 28 meters above ground level, and is walled and roofed with slabs of white limestone. It opens on a passage about 60 meters long which descends at an angle of 27′56° and joins a horizontal passage 7 meters long and 1.2 meters high (Fig. 57).

The horizontal passage leads to three chambers, all of which have the same type of corbelled roof as those in the Bent Pyramid. The first and second are almost identical in size and appearance, each measuring about 9.3 by 3.6 meters, and are situated on the same level. The third is reached through an opening about 7.5 meters from the floor in the southern wall of the second room. It is the largest of the three, measuring about 9.3 by 4.05 meters by 15 meters high (Fig. 58). When it was investigated by Perring and Vyse, and also when cleaned in 1947, the pyramid did not reveal any trace of a royal burial. But it is certain that the last word has not yet been said, and investigation of this pyramid with modern scientific methods will probably reveal surprises, as was the case with the Bent Pyramid.

Before ending this chapter on the pyramids of Sneferu, a few more sentences are necessary. There are three pyramids in the Memphite necropolis which are associated with the name of Sneferu—that at Meydum and the two at Dahshur. The reader is no doubt curious about where Sneferu was buried. I am convinced that this king was buried in the Bent Pyramid of Dahshur, in the upper burial chamber at the end of the western gallery. There may exist some of his funerary monuments near the Northern Pyramid, but the principal ones are those discovered near the Bent Pyramid between 1951 and 1955; it is this pyramid that was the eternal house of his body.

58. *Corbelled ceiling in the*
Northern Pyramid of Sneferu at Dahshur.

59. The Great Pyramid of Giza.

6

The Great Pyramid

of Giza

The Great Pyramid of Giza represents the culminative effort of the pyramid builders. Not only is it the largest monument of its kind ever constructed, but for excellence of workmanship, accuracy of planning, and beauty of proportion, it remains the chief of the Seven Wonders of the World (Figs. 59 and 60).

This pyramid has attracted great interest since earliest times. It was probably entered and robbed at the fall of the Old Kingdom, during the time of weakness and unrest called the First Intermediate Period. This may have led to a story related by Diodorus, who wrote that the Egyptians so hated the builders of the pyramids that they threatened to enter these great tombs and destroy the mummies of the kings.

We know hardly anything about the Great Pyramid during the Middle Kingdom, and it is not clear whether the building remained open or whether a pious king cared to close it. We do know that the Egyptians of that time paid little respect to the temples of the pyramids. They used those of Giza as quarries for the northern pyramid of Lisht, which dates from the early years of the Twelfth Dynasty. Excavations by the Metropolitan Museum of New York revealed many decorated and inscribed blocks, and probably many more still lie embedded in its walls. Some of the blocks had belonged to the walls of Old Kingdom

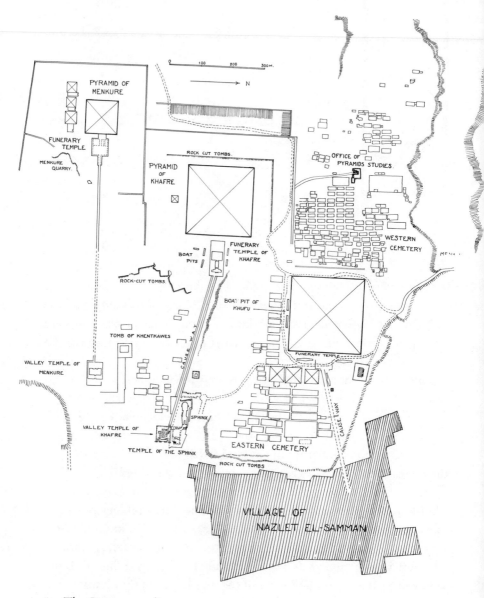

60. *The Giza necropolis.*

tombs, but a great many undoubtedly came from the temples and causeways of the pyramids of Giza.

The same silence concerning the Great Pyramid continued during the New Kingdom, although reference is made to "the sanctuaries of Khufu and Khafre" in the neighborhood. Prince Khaemwese, the eldest son of Ramses II, took a keen interest in the Memphis necropolis, so it is very likely that he made restorations on the Great Pyramid, as he had done to several of the monuments of Abusir and Saqqara. The record of such work, if it ever existed, would have been on the casing stones of the pyramid, which have since been quarried away.

The Twenty-sixth Dynasty witnessed the revival of old traditions, and people paid special reverence to the monuments of the Old and Middle Kingdoms. We do not know what the kings of this period did for the Great Pyramid and its temples, but it is generally believed that the cult of Khufu continued and that priests attended to his temples and worship.

It is certain that during the Roman period the interior of the pyramid stood open and parts were accessible to visitors. Some of the galleries and chambers were partly filled with debris and used for later burials. The entrance was subsequently closed by the accumulation of blown sand and ever falling debris, and thus escaped the notice of all who searched for it. The pyramid was opened in the ninth century during the reign of El Mamun, the son of Caliph Harun al-Rashid. El Mamun's men did not succeed in finding the real entrance, but forced a passage through the masonry so they could reach the interior. The writers of the time related fantastic stories about the work of El Mamun; analysis of these tales indicates that the original burial had been robbed, and that the mummies and coffins found there belonged to late, intrusive burials.

Herodotus and others referred to the inscriptions which were said to cover the outside of the pyramid. Even in the days of the Arab period, Abd el Latif (b. A.D. 1179) mentioned that the inscriptions, if copied, would fill 10,000 pages. The graffiti and other inscriptions left by visitors through the ages were unfortunately lost when the casing stones were quarried away during and after the thirteenth century. Since then the Great Pyramid has looked more or less as it does today, although the interior has now been completely cleared and examined, and its base freed from the mounds of sand, rubble, and stone blocks which had accumulated around it.

Early travelers recorded several descriptions and sets of dimensions, and a few plans, of the Great Pyramid. But not until the early nineteenth century did scientific exploration begin. An Italian, T. B. Caviglia, examined the interior of the pyramid in 1811.[1] A courageous but uneducated naval officer, he carried on archeological research for several Europeans in Egypt, who paid him to look for antiquities to add to their collections. Shortly afterward, in 1837–39, Perring and Vyse made a thorough examination of the Great Pyramid and took careful and accurate measurements. Their observations were superseded by those which Petrie made in 1881–82.[2] The Antiquities Department cleaned the interior in the late nineteenth century. Its steep galleries have been fitted with handrails, and electric lights installed; it is now open to the public, except for the subterranean chamber.

It is astonishing that we know so little about King Khufu, the man who ordered the erection of the Great Pyramid as the eternal home of his mortal body. He was the son and successor of King Sneferu by Queen Hetepheres, the daughter and heiress of King Hu. She was probably buried near one of the two pyramids of Sneferu at Dahshur. Evidently thieves entered her tomb during her son's reign, so it was decided to bring her funerary furniture, including her alabaster sarcophagus, for reburial at the bottom of a deep shaft east of the Great Pyramid. The mummy of the queen and the jewelry adorning it have not been recovered.

According to ancient records, Khufu reigned for twenty-three years; he married more than one wife and had many sons and daughters. He sponsored several building projects, and monuments bearing his name occur all over Egypt. Khufu also exploited regions of Sinai, Nubia, and the Arabian Desert for their mineral wealth. Archeologists have found many tombs belonging to Khufu's family, priests, and officials. Although their inscriptions do not afford any details of events during his reign or indications of his personality, they bear eloquent testimony to

[1] For an account of Caviglia's work, see Vyse, *Operations Carried On at the Pyramids of Gizeh,* II, 152 ff.

[2] W. M. F. Petrie, *The Pyramids and Temples of Giza.*

the great artistic progress made in his time. This testimony is confirmed by the excellence of the workmanship and architectural skill displayed in the building of the Great Pyramid.

In later times, Khufu's name was considered a powerful charm. It was engraved on scarabs to be used as amulets, and connected with many legends. The most famous of these are related in the Westcar Papyrus. This document, a copy of a papyrus dating from the Hyksos period, contains several stories originally written no later than the Twelfth Dynasty. They relate the wonders performed by great magicians who lived in ancient times and by wise men who could foretell the future, as told to King Khufu by his sons. The first one was supposed to have taken place during the reign of King Zoser; the second, related by Prince Khafre, told of events which happened during the reign of King Nebka; the third, told by Prince Bauefre, concerned King Sneferu; the fourth and last story was told by Prince Hordedef, and took place during the reign of Khufu himself. It prophesied the end of Khufu's dynasty, and will be discussed in a later chapter.

Some of the classical authors wrote that Khufu was a great tyrant and was hated by his subjects because he enslaved the whole nation to build his great tomb; unfortunately, such ideas are still repeated. But ancient Egyptian history provides no evidence at all to support these stories. Khufu was apparently an able and energetic ruler, during whose reign the land flourished and art reached perfection. The student of history should not forget that it is a great mistake to judge from our modern viewpoint, moral standards, and principles. Khufu was divine, and his subjects were certainly willing to take part in erecting his eternal monuments. His reign fostered Egyptian architecture and art. Had he really been an oppressive tyrant, he could never have left the land in such a stable economic position as to enable his son, Khafre, to build the Second Pyramid, a monument almost as colossal as that of his father. If the stories of the later authors had an element of truth, it would have been impossible to preserve the cult of Khufu for so many centuries after his death. Monuments referring to Khufu's priests date from several periods of Egyptian history down to Ptolemaic times, more than two thousand years after his death.

The pyramid complex was evolved during Sneferu's reign. But there are vital differences between his temples and those of Khafre—changes which denote a modification in the mortuary cult of the king. Khufu's pyramid complex should supply the connecting link in these changes, but unfortunately the evidence is meager. Part of Khufu's complex has never been excavated, while another part has been almost entirely destroyed.

The Valley Temple of the Great Pyramid has never been excavated. It probably lies at the end of the causeway under the modern village of Nazlet el Samman or a little farther east of it. Khufu's monuments were used as a quarry by a king of the Middle Kingdom, so there is no hope of finding the Valley Temple intact. But it should be excavated so that archeologists could examine its plan, which ought to provide the transitional link between Sneferu's temple at Dahshur and Khafre's at Giza.

When Lepsius visited Egypt a little over a hundred years ago, he found the causeway almost intact, except for its white limestone pavement and passage underneath it that enabled people to reach the other side without walking around the pyramid complex. Herodotus greatly admired it, stating that it was a work almost equaling the pyramid itself; he also mentioned that it was adorned with sculptures. Today many blocks of the causeway road remain *in situ*, a testimony to the vastness and solidity of the structure. Excavations made by Selim Hassan in front of the Great Pyramid in 1938 brought to light a few blocks, adorned with reliefs, from the upper end of the passage. At the time of this discovery, the prevailing theory held that the walls of Old Kingdom temples were not decorated before the end of the Fourth Dynasty. The statement of Herodotus was interpreted to refer only to graffiti left by visitors, and many scholars regarded the 1938 discoveries as Twenty-sixth Dynasty restorations. Only in 1951, when the inscribed walls of Sneferu's Valley Temple came to light, did Egyptologists realize that temples were decorated before the reign of Khufu; consequently the blocks from the causeway passage are certainly contemporary with the rest of the pyramid complex.

Khufu's Mortuary Temple stood east of the Great Pyramid. Nothing remains of it except the rock-cut foundations and part of the basalt pavement of the court. But, incomplete as these remains are, they do furnish enough information to enable Egyptologists to trace the plan of the eastern part of the temple (Fig. 61). This is entirely different from the Mortuary Temples which preceded and followed it. The entrance opened into a large, colonnaded court, with its long axis directed north-south. The roof of the portico was upheld by granite pillars, of which only fragments remain. The westernmost section of the temple has been completely destroyed, but it cannot have been very complex, because the space it occupied is small and narrow. In his reconstruction of the temple, Ricke suggests that there were five statue niches.[3] There is no evidence, however, to prove their existence, and we should remember that in the pyramid complex of Sneferu at Dahshur these niches totaled six, and were situated in the Valley Temple. The few fragments found indicate that the walls were of limestone. These, combined with the basalt pavement and the red granite pillars, must have been very effective in appearance. This polychrome technique may have inspired the builders of the Abusir pyramids.

The Great Pyramid was surrounded by a temenos wall, of which only the foundations remain. Its northern and western sides were 23.6 meters from the pyramid base; the southern side, 18.5 meters.

In May, 1954, the press announced to an excited public that an intact

[3] H. Ricke, *Bemerkungen*, I, 37, Fig. 10.

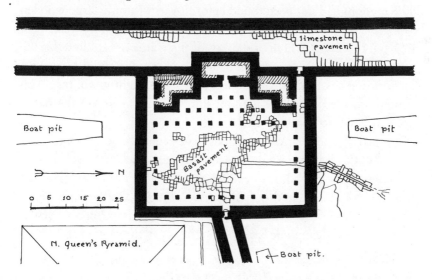

61. *Plan of the Mortuary Temple of the Great Pyramid. (After Lauer.)*

cedar boat had been discovered by the Egyptian architect Kamal El-Mallakh while cleaning the south side of the Great Pyramid. Accounts described it as lying in a rock-cut pit over 30 meters long; another boat was reported lying in line with it immediately to the west. Unfortunately, this news was mixed from the beginning with wild speculation as well as unscholarly rivalry, but there is no doubt that this was one of the outstanding discoveries of recent years.

We must bear in mind, however, that archeologists were long aware of the presence of such vessels beside the tombs of kings or private individuals. Plastered mud-brick pits in the form of boats have been found near many of the First and Second Dynasty tombs at Helwan.[4] They also occur near First Dynasty tombs at Saqqara.[5] Boats were also known to have been buried near the Great Pyramid of Khufu; three of the pits which contained them can be visited. Five boat pits can be seen near the Second Pyramid, a stone's throw from the newly discovered wooden boats. These were the subject of a detailed study by S. Hassan in 1946, when he published the results of his sixth season's excavations at Giza, between 1943 and 1945.[6] Reisner cleared the boat pits near the Great Pyramid in the 1920's, and found in one of them fragments of gilded wood and pieces of rope. However, large wooden boats dating from the Old Kingdom had not been found before 1954. The only large wooden boats previously known, found at Dahshur more than fifty years ago, date from the Twelfth Dynasty. (Two of them are now exhibited in the Cairo Museum; a third is in the Chicago Natural History Museum.) The importance of this great discovery lies in the light it will throw on the methods used by Old Kingdom shipwrights. These are the oldest large ships ever to be discovered.

The boats found near the pyramids have generally been called "solar boats," but this is by no means an accurate term. Various kinds of boats were intended to provide the dead king with material substitutes for the vessels he would need in the afterlife. According to the Pyramid Texts, at least eight different boats were to be used by the king in his celestial voyages; two of them were for crossing the sky in the retinue of the sun-

[4] Zaki Saad, *Royal Excavations at Saqqara and Helwan* (Cairo, 1947).

[5] W. B. Emery, *The Tomb of Ḥor-Aḥa* (Cairo, 1939).

[6] Selim Hassan, *Excavations at Giza,* Vol. VI, Part I.

god—one by day and the other by night. Thus, only two of the vessels could accurately be called solar boats. With the limited knowledge we now possess, it would be preferable to call the vessels ritual, or funerary, boats; they were certainly connected with religious ideas about resurrection. We do not know where in the pyramid complex the two boats for the solar journey were located, or even if they had any special form to distinguish them from the others. Khufu is now known to have had five boats, two to the south of the pyramid, two to the east, and one lying parallel with the causeway. Two sides of the pyramid have not been examined in this connection, and it would not be surprising if other boats were to be found beside the causeway.

The newly discovered boat pits undoubtedly belonged to Khufu, but it is clear that they were closed after his death and that his successor finished the work. In accordance with ancient Egyptian usage, almost every stone roofing the pit bore quarry marks and graffiti (Fig. 62); the only royal name occurring in these is that of Rededef, Khufu's successor.

62. *Quarry marks on one of the stones roofing the boat pit at Giza.*

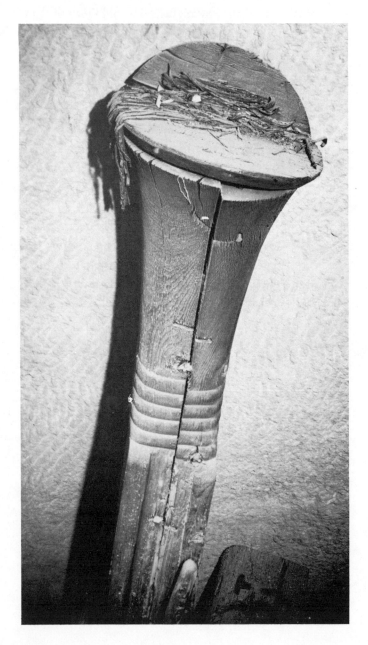

63. *The prow post.*

On his shoulders fell the duty of burying Khufu and finishing his incomplete monuments.

The newly excavated boat lies in a pit 17.85 meters from the base of the pyramid. It measured 31.2 meters long, 2.6 meters wide, and 3.5 meters deep and was covered by forty-one large blocks of limestone and one smaller block. The large stones measure 4.8 meters long, .85 meters wide, and 1.6 meters high; they weigh an average of sixteen tons. The stones were cemented together with plaster, and their ends rested on rock-cut ledges on each side of the pit. Six months after the discovery, when workmen began removing the blocks, it became clear that the boat had been dismantled before being placed in the pit, but its timbers had been placed as nearly as possible in their original position to give the appearance of a complete boat. Some of the parts, including the bowsprit (Fig. 63), were carelessly placed in the pit, while the poles of the canopy, the large steering oars, and the smaller rowing oars were scattered over the deck. There must have been at least one cabin, because doors were lying on the deck. There were also coils of rope and many mats (Fig. 64). The timbers had been fastened together by tenons, wooden pegs, and copper hooks and staples.

The great task now confronting the Antiquities Department is the preservation of the boat, which is made of cedar with small amounts of sycamore and other Egyptian and foreign woods. It is planned to consolidate every fragment of the ship, then remove it from its place, assemble it, and house it in a special building between the boat pit and the southern side of the Great Pyramid. Not until this has been accomplished will the second boat pit be examined.

As of January, 1968, the various parts of the boat were still lying near the pit, having been treated chemically for preservation. The authorities know the position of every fragment, and the boat is ready to be placed in the museum when it is completed, probably by 1970. The boat was assembled temporarily to learn its dimensions, which are as follows: from prow to stern, almost 43.5 meters; height at prow, 5 meters; height at stern, 7 meters. It is composed of 651 pieces of timber, mostly cedar from Lebanon, as well as several hundred small pieces of rope, nails, mats, and other items. There is a large cabin on the deck, with three wooden palmiform columns to support the ceiling.

64. *Parts of the dismantled wooden boat of Khufu.*

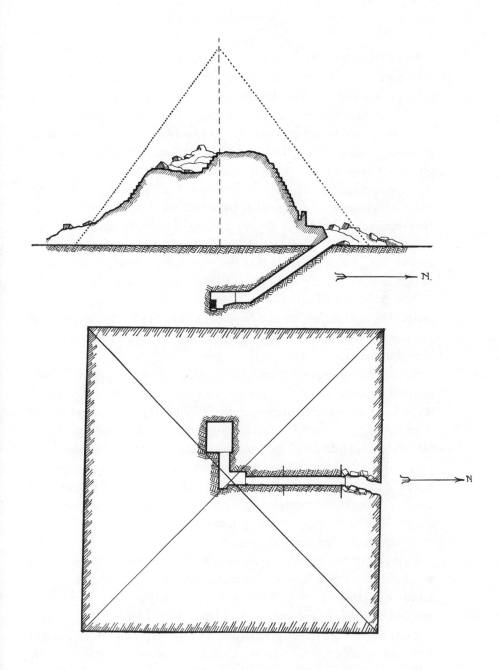

65. *Plan and section of the northern small pyramid.*

East of the Great Pyramid lie three small ones. These were probably built for three of King Khufu's wives, although an ancient tradition attributes two of them to his daughters. Herodotus quotes a story current in his time that the central one was built by a daughter whom Khufu was said to have prostituted in order to gain funds with which to complete his pyramid. The lady is said to have asked each of her lovers to give her a stone so that she could build her own pyramid. Needless to say, it is unnecessary to look for historical confirmation of this story. The southernmost of these small pyramids was built for the Princess Ḥenutsen, according to a stela found in the adjacent Temple of Isis. Although the stela is a "forgery," purporting to be a restoration of a more ancient one, it is quite likely that this attribution is correct. The name *Ḥenutsen* was common during the Old Kingdom, and means "Their Lady." She may well have been a daughter of Sneferu, and was probably married to her brother (or half-brother) Khufu. It is quite unlikely that she was his daughter; all the king's children, even the eldest son, were buried in mastaba tombs.

Apparently the northernmost of the three small pyramids was planned to stand some meters east of its present location; the rock was leveled and the substructure begun there. Evidently this plan interfered with the shaft cut for the reburial of the funerary furniture of Queen Hetepheres, so the small pyramid was moved west. This limestone pyramid is 45 meters square; at present it is about 6 meters high and has an angle of about 51° (Fig. 65). The entrance opens above ground level in the center of the northern face and is roofed with a huge slab of limestone. A steep passage 16.5 meters long leads to an antechamber, from which another corridor descends to the burial chamber. On the eastern side of this pyramid are remains of a Mortuary Chapel, and at its southern side is a large rock-cut boat pit. At a later period, the interior of this pit was divided into a series of compartments by walls of rubble and mud. Apparently it served as a storeroom.

The central small pyramid has a core of local limestone, but was cased with fine white limestone, of which a few courses still remain on the eastern side. It is possible to see three inner facings, showing that it was built on the accretion, or layer, plan. The pyramid stood upon a platform of limestone slabs and, like its northern neighbor, is 45 meters

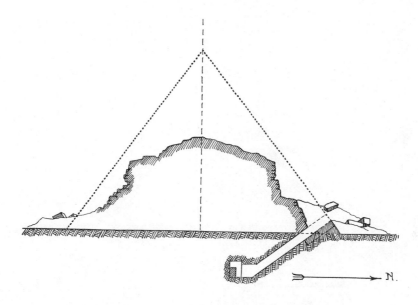

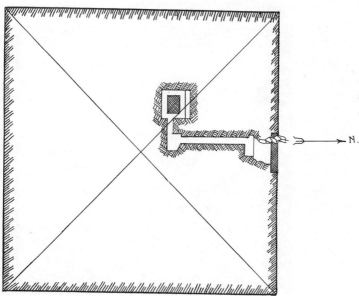

66. *The central small pyramid.*

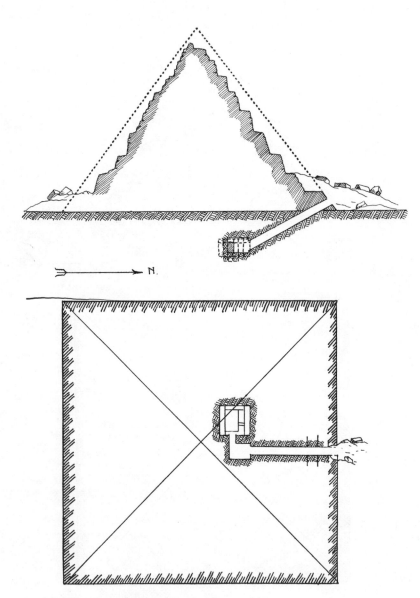

N.

67. *Plan and section of the southern small pyramid.*

square. At present it is about 9 meters high; it slopes at about 52° (Fig. 66). The entrance, in the northern face, is about 1 meter square, and opens into a substructure resembling that of the northern pyramid. To the east are the remains of a small chapel, in which can be seen the emplacement for a false door. There is also a boat pit south of this pyramid. It was excavated in 1952 but immediately filled in because it projected into the roadway.

The southern small pyramid is much better preserved than its neighbors. It is built of coarse local limestone and had a casing of white limestone, several courses of which remain on the eastern and southern sides. Three inner accretion facings are visible. It measures 45 meters square, and is now 11 meters high. The angle is about 51° (Fig. 67). The entrance and substructure resemble those of the other two small pyramids. On the left, or eastern, wall of the descending passage is an inscription reading "Re-opened 1837," apparently referring to the work of Perring and Vyse. East of this pyramid are remains of its Mortuary Chapel with parts of a "palace-façade" decoration on the walls. This decoration on the stone depicted the façade of a palace, because the pyramid was considered the eternal house of that queen. Theoretically her soul could communicate with the outer world by going and coming through the false façade. This small chapel formed the nucleus of the later Temple of Isis, mentioned earlier. The southern side of the pyramid has not yet been cleared, so that we cannot say with certainty whether a boat pit existed there.

The Great Pyramid itself now stands 137 meters high; its original height of 146 meters is indicated by an iron post erected on the summit. Each side originally measured 230 meters (440 cubits), and the angle was 51°50'. (At present each side measures 227 meters, due to the loss of the casing stones.)

The pyramid was surrounded by and built partly upon a pavement or platform of limestone blocks, portions of which can be seen at the northern and eastern sides. A few blocks of the fine limestone casing remaining at the base of the northern side show how accurately the stones were dressed and fitted together.

The core masonry consists of large blocks of local limestone taken from the nearby quarries and built around and over a rocky knoll. The

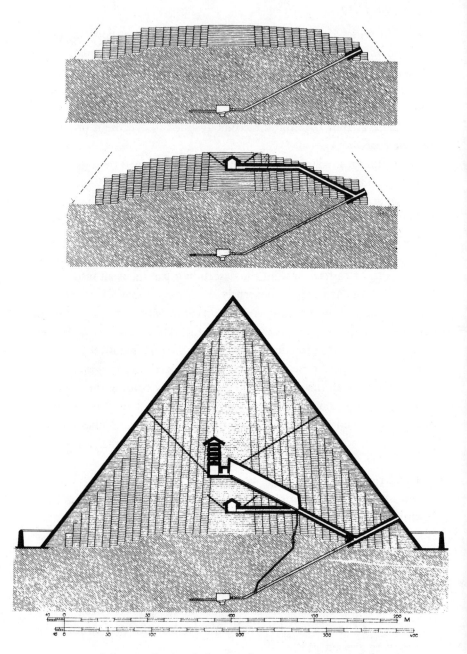

68. *Section of the Great Pyramid, showing the successive changes of plan.*

size of this knoll cannot be determined, since it is completely covered by the pyramid. It is estimated that when the casing was complete, the pyramid must have contained about 2,300,000 blocks of stone, averaging about two and a half tons each, although some weighed as much as 15 tons.

Many persons feel that no mere description can do the Great Pyramid justice or even convey an idea of its enormous size. Statisticians have worked out several painstaking calculations in order to compare its height and bulk with other well-known monuments. According to their estimates, the area of the base of the Great Pyramid could contain the Houses of Parliament and St. Paul's Cathedral and still leave a large space unoccupied. Other calculations reveal that the area of the base would contain the cathedrals of Florence and Milan, St. Peter's in Rome, and St. Paul's Cathedral and Westminster Abbey in London. If all the stone in the pyramid were sawed into blocks 1 foot square and these blocks laid end to end, they would stretch two-thirds of the way around the earth at the equator. During his campaign in Egypt, Napoleon calculated that the Great Pyramid and its neighbors contained enough stone to build a wall 3 meters high and 1 meter thick which would entirely surround France. A mathematician among the savants accompanying the expedition confirmed Napoleon's calculations.

The entrance to the pyramid is in the center of the northern face (Fig. 68). It is located in the thirteenth course of masonry from the base, about 20 meters from the ground. This entrance, now accessible, has a pointed roof formed of massive slabs of local limestone, and opens into a long, steeply descending passage.[7] Visitors now enter the pyramid through a passage known as "Mamun's Hole," which was forced by the Caliph Mamun in the ninth century. It was cut in the sixth course of masonry, below and a little west of the original entrance. After traversing about 36 meters, this passage reaches the junction of the original descending and ascending passages (Fig. 68, middle). The former continues downward at an angle of 28° to an unfinished chamber cut in the rock (Fig. 68, top). This is the original burial chamber.

[7] To the north of the entrance is a neatly cut inscription in hieroglyphs. This is not ancient but was made by Lepsius commemorating a visit of his expedition to the Great Pyramid on the occasion of the birthday of the King of Prussia.

Egyptologists generally believe that the Great Pyramid underwent alterations. It was originally planned on a much smaller scale, but the builders decided to enlarge it before finishing the first burial chamber. Accordingly they constructed an ascending passage, 36 meters long and a little over 1 meter high. It leads to a horizontal passage 35 meters long and 1.75 meters high, which terminates in what is incorrectly called the "Queen's Chamber" (Fig. 68, middle). In reality, this was the burial chamber of the pyramid in accordance with the enlarged plan. At the juncture of the ascending and horizontal passages is an opening of a shaft which descends, partly vertically and partly at a very steep angle, to a depth of 60 meters. It opens into the lower part of the descending passage, and is believed to have been an escape shaft for the workmen who filled the ascending passage with huge stones after the king's funeral.[8] Once the plugs had been slid into place, they would have made the ascending corridor impassable, and the workmen would have been trapped inside.

The so-called Queen's Chamber is built entirely of limestone. It measures 5.2 by 5.7 meters, and the maximum height of its pointed roof is about 15 meters. The north and south walls each have a small hole a few centimeters square about 1 meter from the floor. These lead into narrow channels that originally opened on the exterior of the pyramid; their outer ends are now embedded in the superstructure masonry because of the enlargement of the pyramid. They are usually referred to as "air channels," but most Egyptologists believe that they had a religious significance related to the soul of the king. In the eastern wall of this room is a large niche with a corbelled roof; from its back wall a short passage leads to a shaft which ascends to the antechamber in front of the upper burial chamber. This passage and shaft were made by treasure-hunters.

After constructing the second burial chamber, the builders of the Great Pyramid changed their plans once again. They enlarged the structure and built a third, higher burial room. The visitor retraces his steps to the beginning of the horizontal passage and comes upon the Grand Gallery, which leads upward to the final resting place of King Khufu. This majestic passage is the most wonderful and impressive feature in

[8] This shaft was discovered by Davison in 1763.

69. *The grand gallery.*

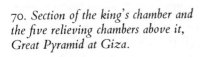

70. *Section of the king's chamber and the five relieving chambers above it, Great Pyramid at Giza.*

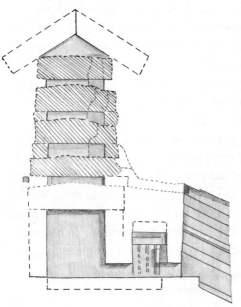

the interior of any pyramid (Fig. 69). It is 47 meters long and 8.5 meters high, and has a corbelled roof. In the center of the floor is a sunken ramp about 60 centimeters deep. On the raised parts of the floor are rectangular holes, perhaps for holding beams to retain the plug stones destined to block the gallery.

At the top of the southern wall, or upper end, of the Grand Gallery is a small opening that leads to the lowest of five "relieving" chambers. These were designed to take the enormous weight of the pyramid's upper portions off the roof of the burial chamber (Fig. 70). Each of these chambers is built of limestone and roofed with granite, and is about 1 meter high. Quarry marks on some of the stones in these chambers record the seventeenth year of Khufu's reign, showing that the building had reached this stage at that time. These are the only places where Khufu's name occurs inside the pyramid.

The Grand Gallery ends in a horizontal granite passage which serves as an antechamber. It measures 8.4 meters long and 3.1 meters high, and has slots for three portcullises; part of one may still be seen. In the southern wall is a series of vertical grooves, which some believe were used in raising or lowering the portcullis slabs. [9]

Beyond the antechamber is the so-called "King's Chamber," which is lined, roofed, and paved with finely dressed and polished red granite. It measures 5.2 meters by 10.8 meters and is 5.8 meters high. Its flat roof is formed of nine monolithic slabs of granite, estimated to weigh 50 tons each. In the western part of this room is a lidless granite sarcophagus, finely polished but uninscribed. The northern and southern walls each have an "air channel," one of which still functions and serves to keep the air of the chamber wonderfully fresh.

None of the chambers, corridors, or passages of the Great Pyramid can be called a storeroom. However, some of them undoubtedly contained the funerary furniture and the vases of food. All these things were stolen thousands of years ago, and archeologists found nothing inside.

Most visitors to the Great Pyramid wonder how it was built. Even equipped with modern tools and instruments, and profiting from nearly five thousand years of experience, architects and engineers today

[9] For a study of the mechanism of these portcullises, see Borchardt, *Einiges zur dritten Bauperiode der grossen Pyramide bei Gise* (Cairo, 1932), pp. 7 ff., Plates 3–5, 10.

might well quail if called upon to erect a duplicate. Theories concerning the building's construction are many and varied.

The earliest account is that of Herodotus, who seems to have inquired of the priests, and reports in detail:

Up to the death of Rhampsinitus, the priests said, Egypt was excellently governed, and flourished greatly; but after him Cheops [Khufu] succeeded to the throne, and plunged into all manner of wickedness. He closed the temples, and forbade the Egyptians to offer sacrifices, compelling them instead to labor, one and all, in his service. Some were required to drag blocks of stone down to the Nile from the quarries in the Arabian range of hills; others received the blocks after they had been conveyed in boats across the river, and drew them to the range of hills called the Libyan. One hundred thousand men labored constantly, and were relieved every three months by a fresh lot. It took ten years' oppression of the people to make the causeway for the conveyance of the stones, a work not much inferior, in my judgment, to the pyramid itself. This causeway is half a mile in length, 60 feet wide, and in height, at the highest part, 48 feet. It is built of polished stone and is covered with carvings of animals. To make it took ten years, as I said—or rather to make the causeway, the works on the mound where the pyramid stands, and the underground chambers, which Cheops intended as vaults for his own use; these last were built on a sort of island, surrounded by water introduced from the Nile by a canal. The pyramid itself was twenty years in building. It is a square, 800 feet each way, and the height the same, built entirely of polished stone, fitted together with the utmost care. The stones of which it is composed are none of them less than 30 feet in length.

The pyramid was built in steps, battlement-wise, as it is called, or, according to others, altar-wise. After laying the stones for the base, they raised the remaining stones to their places by means of machines formed of short wooden planks. The first machine raised them from the ground to the top of the first step. On this there was another machine, which received the stone upon its arrival, and conveyed it to the second step, whence a third machine advanced it still higher. Either they had as many machines as there were steps in the pyramid, or possibly they had but a single machine, which, being easily moved, was transferred from tier to tier as the stone rose—both accounts are given, and therefore I mention both. The upper portion of the pyramid was finished first, then the middle, and finally the part that is lowest and nearest to the ground. There is an inscription in Egyptian characters on the pyramid which records the quantity of radishes, onions, and garlic consumed by the laborers who constructed it; and I perfectly well remember that the inter-preter who read the writing to me said that the money expended in this way was 1,600 talents of silver.[10] If this then is a true record, what a vast sum must have been spent on the iron tools used in the work, and on the feeding and clothing of the laborers, considering the length of time the work lasted, which has already been stated, and the additional time—no small space, I imagine—which must have been occupied by the quarrying of the stones, their con-veyance, and the formation of the underground apartments.[11]

According to this statement, the time taken to build the Great Pyra-mid and its causeway amounted to thirty years, ten for the causeway and twenty for the pyramid. Yet the ancient records credit Khufu with a reign of only twenty-three years. Herodotus seems to have been de-ceived by an ignorant guide on some points, such as the translation of the inscription on the pyramid. From his account one would imagine that all the stones were quarried on the eastern bank of the Nile and ferried over, but we know that the core is of local stone, and that the only stone brought from the eastern quarries was the white limestone for the casing. The story of the subterranean vaults being surrounded by water introduced from the Nile is also entirely untrue. Even today, with the subsoil water at a higher level, the substructure of the pyramid is never damp. The original height of the monument never equaled the length of its base, although the latter dimension is fairly accurate.

In view of these inaccuracies, how much trust can be put in the theory of the wooden "machines"? Supposing that they existed, work-ing with a single machine moved from tier to tier would have taken far longer even than the twenty years allotted by Herodotus; if there were machines for every tier (and every stone) it would have taken an impossible quantity of wood. Yet modern scholars have taken this ex-planation seriously, and have tried to explain the type of machine which could have been used.

According to Diodorus, the pyramid was constructed by means of "mounds," that is, ramps. This is the most reasonable view, and is favored by Somers Clarke, an architect, and R. Engelbach, engineer.

[10] Like his descendants of the present day, this "interpreter" was inventing a transla-tion for an inscription which he certainly could not read!

[11] George Rawlinson, *The History of Herodotus*, I, 177–79.

In *Ancient Egyptian Masonry*, they discuss the problem of pyramid-building and admit the possibility of the use of ramps, both the long, wide "supply ramps," with a comparatively easy gradient, and the shorter, steeper ramps for the use of laborers and for bringing lighter materials.[12] They warn that their notes on the subject are not to be regarded as a complete and final exposition of the many problems hitherto unexplained, but rather as preliminary deductions which may have to be considerably modified in the future.

As it happens, the recent discovery of the unfinished pyramid of King Sekhem-khet at Saqqara proves that this pyramid was certainly built with the aid of ramps, which can still be seen there. As we have already mentioned, the whole structure of this early pyramid is buried in these rubble heaps. It is worth mentioning that the roadway at Giza by which the modern visitor ascends to the pyramid plateau from the north is nothing but an embankment of ancient builder's waste, such as composes the eastern edge of the plateau, north of the Great Pyramid causeway. It is tempting to see in this modern road the remains of an ancient supply ramp. Remains of a similar ramp, composed of rubble mixed with mud, still exist a short distance from the southern side of the causeway, and the houses of the western side of the modern village are built upon it.

The Great Pyramid of Giza has always inspired thoughtful persons. It has also given rise to many mystical and occult theories. Star-worshipers in the Middle Ages held their meetings inside it and considered it a source of wisdom. Since the end of the last century, when Piazzi Smyth wrote *Our Inheritance in the Great Pyramid*, books on mystic beliefs, astrology, and spiritualism in connection with the Great Pyramid have greatly increased.

It is Khufu's monument alone that holds the attention of the "pyramidologists." They find in the dimensions of its passages and chambers the basis for many theories which explain or predict historical events. Some of them have found all the great occurrences of the Old and New Testaments recorded inside the Great Pyramid; one even calculated that the date of the birth of Jesus Christ was recorded there. Other en-

[12] S. Clarke and R. Engelbach, *Ancient Egyptian Masonry: The Building Craft*, pp. 117–29.

thusiasts believe that the pyramid was built, not to embody prophecies, but, through secrets now lost to us, to heal certain diseases by radiation or by the atmospheric conditions of parts of its passages.[13]

One thing most of these theorists agree on is that the Great Pyramid was not built as a tomb for Khufu. They offer every kind of explanation for its purpose except the one accepted by archeology. More than one Egyptologist has vehemently refuted all these mystical doctrines, but many persons still believe in them. Archeological research has proved beyond doubt that the Great Pyramid is nothing more or less than a tomb for King Khufu. Its features represent simply a development of earlier Egyptian architecture; the dimensions of its stones cannot bear any relation to future events. No one will deny that we have not yet solved many of the problems concerning the pyramid and its construction. But our lack of knowledge should not allow us to disregard archeological evidence based on concrete, tangible records.

The facts alone are impressive enough. The Great Pyramid is the largest tomb ever built for a single individual, and the most famous monument of antiquity. Never before and never again did any king have so sublime a resting-place. Although it failed in one of its purposes —that of protecting Khufu's body—it succeeded in preserving his name. Generations of men yet unborn will stand before the Great Pyramid in amazement and admiration. As long as it stands on the edge of the Libyan plateau, the name of Khufu will endure.

[13] Those interested in knowing more about these beliefs can find a résumé and bibliography in Kingsland's *The Great Pyramid in Fact and Theory*. There is also an excellent résumé in J.-P. Lauer's *Le Problème des Pyramides d'Égypt*, pp. 113–60.

7

The Descendants
of Khufu

During and after Khufu's reign, dissension troubled the royal family. Khufu had several wives, some of them no doubt princesses of the royal blood, and he had sons and daughters by all of them. More than one queen wanted to see her own son on the throne. Consequently some kind of conflict arose between two principal lines of Khufu's children, Rededef and Khafre, and may even have extended to the priests and people.

One of Khufu's wives was believed to have been a Libyan woman, who became the mother of Rededef, Khufu's immediate successor, and several other children. The theory concerning her Libyan origin was based on the appearance of Queen Hetepheres II, the wife of Khufu, in the Giza tomb of her daughter, Queen Meresankh III. This representation shows her with blond hair and blue eyes. Another curious feature is the unusual costume worn by the ladies of the family, whose dresses have a kind of starched, triangular projection over the shoulder. In the light of our present knowledge, we cannot say whether this style of dress or the blond hair and blue eyes can prove beyond doubt the Libyan origin of the family. (For one thing, the blond hair may have been a wig.)

The line of succession among Khufu's descendants is not always clear. Rededef was his father's immediate successor and was followed by

Khafre, another of Khufu's sons. After Khafre's death, the dispute between the two branches of Khufu's family flared up again. We know from the Turin Papyrus and other sources that the period between Khafre and Menkure was relatively short. Two kings ruled in a space of five years; they probably came from the branch of the family to which Rededef belonged. They undoubtedly had no opportunity during their short, troublesome reigns to build pyramids. It is possible that they continued to live after their defeat or abdication and were buried in ordinary mastabas in the Giza necropolis. (Reisner tried to identify these kings and to recognize the Egyptian form of their names from the Greek forms.[1])

An inscription discovered on the rocks of Wadi el Hammamat in 1950 gives us important, if somewhat puzzling, information on this subject. It provides a list of royal names written in cartouches. They are arranged as follows: Khufu, Rededef, Khafre, Hordedef, and Bauefre.[2] Although the inscription does not predate the Twelfth Dynasty, it must be based on reliable information because it agrees with our knowledge gained from the Turin Papyrus, Manetho, and other sources. Hordedef was a son of Khufu and was buried in a large mastaba east of the Great Pyramid.[3] As for Bauefre, no monuments of his are preserved. However, we know of two sons of Khufu called Khnumbaef and Horbaef.[4] One of them may have assumed the name "Bauefre" upon his accession to the throne. In the Westcar Papyrus, as we have seen, the story told by Prince Bauefre follows that of Khafre and precedes Prince Hordedef's. It is difficult to say whether these men really occupied the throne, each of them as sole ruler of the land. There was unrest in the country, and

[1] G. A. Reisner, *Mycerinus: The Temples of the Third Pyramid at Giza* (Cambridge, Mass., 1931), p. 246; see also E. Meyer, *Chronologie*, p. 142, and Walter Federn, "Zur Familiengeschichte der IV. Dynastie Ägyptens," *Wiener Zeitschrift für die Kunde des Morgenlandes*, XLII, 165–92.

[2] F. Debono, "Expedition archéologique royale du desert orientale," *Annales du Service*, LI (1951), 89.

[3] The tomb of Hordedef is No. 7210. See G. A. Reisner, "Hetepheres, Mother of Cheops," *Boston Museum Bulletin* (Supplement to Vol. XXX [May, 1927]), p. 4. See also Reisner, *ibid.* (October, 1927), p. 74.

[4] There was a son of Khufu called Khnumbaef (tomb No. 7310 at Giza), and another named Horbaef, whose sarcophagus is in the Cairo Museum (Mariette, *Notices . . . Musée Boulac*, 1874, p. 93, nos. 6, 7).

they may have ruled only during the latter years of Khafre or the early years of Menkure. They were, however, recognized as legitimate kings by the compiler of the Turin Papyrus and by the writer of the Wadi el Hammamat inscription, and their names also occur in Manetho's work.

We do know that Menkure was followed on the throne by his son Shepseskaf, whose unusual tomb departed radically from the pyramid form. It served as a model for the tomb of one of Menkure's daughters, Queen Khent-kawes, whom we may regard as the link between the Fourth and Fifth Dynasties.

THE PYRAMID OF REDEDEF AT ABU RAWWASH

Rededef, Khufu's immediate successor, built his pyramid at Abu Rawwash, about 5 miles north of his father's pyramid at Giza. We do not know why he chose this distant, lonely site, high on a lofty spur of the plateau. Reisner and many other scholars see in this action a result of the split in the royal family. Some even suspect Rededef of the murder of the legitimate heir to the throne, Prince Ka-wab, whose mastaba lies east of the Great Pyramid at Giza. However, there is no evidence for this accusation. The commanding site Rededef chose for his pyramid had already been used as a necropolis from the time of the First Dynasty. It was thus more or less a part of the vast Memphis necropolis, and, because of its commanding position, was a logical place to build a pyramid. Whether or not there was any foreign blood in Rededef's branch of the family, we find no sign of exotic influence in his monuments at Abu Rawwash, nor any innovation which would lead us to think that there had been a break in the religious or architectural traditions inherited from the time of Sneferu and Khufu.

Abu Rawwash was visited by interested travelers during the early nineteenth century.[5] No investigations of any scientific value, however, were made there before 1839, when Perring and Vyse included the area in their operations.[6] Perring's description and plates indicate that more of the pyramid's lower superstructure remained standing then than can be seen today. Petrie records that in his time the pyramid complex was

[5] Porter and Moss, *Topographical Bibliography*, III, 1.

[6] Vyse, *Operations Carried On at the Pyramids of Gizeh*, III, 8.

being used as a quarry; he was told that as many as 300 camel-loads of stone were removed from the site daily.[7]

A few scattered blocks of limestone slightly west of the modern village of Abu Rawwash probably indicate the still unexcavated site of the Valley Temple. From this area begins what was probably the most splendid of all the pyramid causeways (Fig. 71). This wonderful structure, over 1.5 kilometers long, extends in a southwesterly direction, and rises to a height of about 12 meters above the desert where it joins the rock of the plateau. We do not know whether it was walled or roofed, because it has not been properly examined. As in the case of the Bent Pyramid at Dahshur, the causeway seems to have terminated near the northeastern corner of the pyramid inclosure; only the northwestern corner of the temenos wall remains.

At the eastern side of the pyramid are the remains of the Mortuary Temple, excavated by the Frenchman E. S. Chassinat in 1901. It is unfortunate that the results of his excavation were never published in detail. South of the pyramid, and apparently within its temenos wall, there was a small pyramid, now almost totally demolished.

[7] W. M. F. Petrie, *The Pyramids and Temples of Giza*, p. 140.

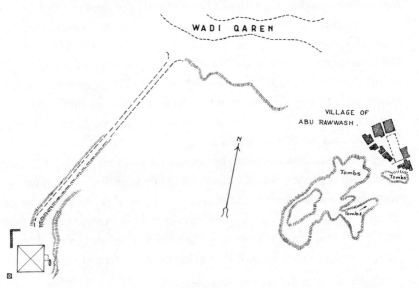

71. *Map of the monuments of Abu Rawwash.*

72. *Plan and section of the pyramid of Abu Rawwash.*

South of the Mortuary Temple on the east side is a large rock-cut boat pit. With its long axis pointing north-south, it measures 35 meters long, 3.75 meters wide at its widest part, and 9.3 meters deep. At the bottom of the debris filling this boat pit, Chassinat found three beautiful heads from statues of Rededef. They had been wantonly knocked off the bodies and flung there during the upheavals that followed the Old Kingdom. (Two of the heads are now in the Louvre, and one is in the Cairo Museum.)

The pyramid of Rededef measures about 100 meters square and is at present about 12 meters high. The superstructure that remains consists of between eight and ten courses of limestone masonry covering a core of natural rock. It is frequently suggested that the pyramid was never completed, because Rededef reigned only eight years. However, several blocks of red granite are still *in situ* on the eastern face, which would suggest that the monument was cased with granite for at least three courses. The work must have been well advanced to have reached this stage. The extremely dilapidated condition of the pyramid is probably due to its well-documented use as a quarry, and not to the inability of the king to finish it. Vast areas around the monument, especially on the northern side, are literally covered with granite chips, showing that granite was used there extensively.

In the center of the northern side of the pyramid is an entrance to a descending passage which measures about 48 meters long and is now between 8 and 9 meters wide (Fig. 72). This rock-cut passage, descending at an angle of between 22° and 35°, was originally lined with either limestone or granite. It ends in a large burial chamber, now measuring 9 meters wide, 21 meters long, and 9 meters deep. The chamber and the sloping passage leading to it are now open to the sky, except for a slight section of masonry projecting over the chamber. Originally the walls were lined to a thickness of about 2 meters with limestone or granite, which would have reduced the measurements of the room to a length of 17 meters and a width of 5 meters. According to Petrie, the lining was removed during the reign of Mehemet Ali.[8] Perring believed that relieving chambers, similar to those found in the Great Pyramid, had been constructed over the roof.[9]

According to Lepsius, there was another pyramid at Abu Rawwash.[10]

[8] *Ibid.*

[9] Vyse, *Operations Carried On at the Pyramids of Gizeh*, III, 8–9.

[10] R. Lepsius, *Denkmäler*, Vol. I, Plates 11 and 12.

73. *The Second Pyramid of Giza.*

74. *The famous diorite statue of Khafre from his Valley Temple at Giza.*

This lay north of the village, immediately east of a group of mastabas. No trace of it can now be seen, but Lepsius records that it was built of mud brick and stood 17 meters high. The 1929 edition of Baedeker's *Egypt* mentions that the brick superstructure of this pyramid had been entirely removed, but that the rock-cut core, the passage, and the burial chamber still remained. A more thorough examination of the tombs in the vicinity might identify the pyramid's owner.

The site of Abu Rawwash is in need of further excavation. Rededef's Valley Temple has never been examined, although its position is known, and the Mortuary Temple itself needs more work. The presence of one boat pit suggests that there are others. It should be remembered that Rededef completed one of Khufu's boat pits, as the Giza discoveries of 1954 have shown.

THE SECOND PYRAMID AT GIZA (THE PYRAMID OF KHAFRE)

The Second Pyramid at Giza (Fig. 73), built by Khafre, another son of Khufu, has the most completely preserved pyramid complex of the Giza group. The Valley Temple lies at the edge of a sandy plain near the modern village of Nazlet el Samman; in the older accounts it is referred to as the "Temple of the Sphinx" because of its position immediately south of that monument. This temple, once buried in the sand, was first excavated by Mariette in 1853, although he cleared only part of the interior. It was not then considered a free-standing building. It was Mariette who discovered the magnificent diorite statue of Khafre which is now one of the glories of the Cairo Museum (Fig. 74). Uvo Hölscher realized the true significance of the Valley Temple, and excavated it completely at the beginning of the present century.[11]

The Valley Temple faces east. Beside the entrance is a quay, fronting on a canal that runs north and south. The southern end of the canal runs under a tunnel built of massive limestone blocks, and apparently passes under a later temple, which seems to be that of Osiris, Lord of Rostaw. This temple is mentioned on the stela and graffiti in the Temple of Isis near the Great Pyramid. The canal has never been excavated, and its northern end disappears under a mound of sand northeast of the actual Temple of the Sphinx.

---

[11] U. Hölscher, *Das Grabdenkmal des Königs Chephren* (Leipzig, 1912).

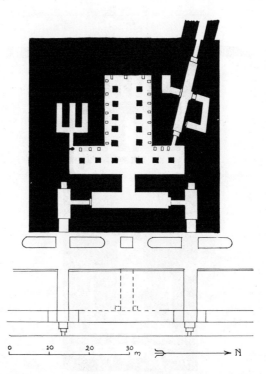

75. *Plan of the Valley Temple of the Second Pyramid, Giza.*

The Valley Temple is built around a core of massive blocks of local limestone, covered with finely dressed and polished red granite. Almost all the corner blocks were cut in an L-shape. This device obviated vertical joints in the interior corners of the building and thus made for greater durability. Most of the granite casing on the outside of the building has been quarried away, but that on the inside is almost perfect. Alabaster was used for the floor of the building, as well as the walls of some of the smaller rooms.

The temple is entered through two doorways in its eastern façade, one at the north and one at the south (Fig. 75). Hölscher believed that the oblong indentations in the pavement flanking these doors held the bases of sphinxes, placed in pairs before each entrance. Both open into a long, narrow vestibule. It was in a well in this entryway (now filled in) that Mariette found the diorite statues of Khafre. A doorway in the center of the western wall opens into a T-shaped hall, the roof of which was originally supported by sixteen square red granite pillars.

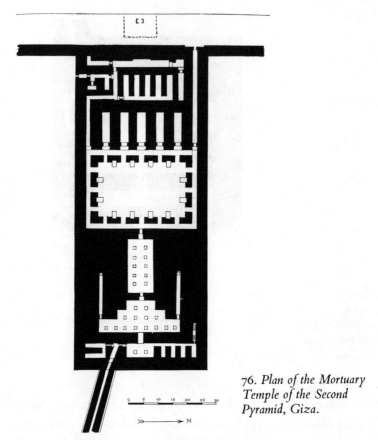

76. *Plan of the Mortuary Temple of the Second Pyramid, Giza.*

Around this hall stood twenty-three statues of the king, the emplacements of which are visible on the floor. This hall, now open to the sky, was originally lighted by small clerestory windows, so arranged that each cast a ray of light upon one of the statues. From the southwest corner of the hall, a short passage leads to six storerooms with low ceilings. These are arranged in two stories; the three lower ones are made of highly polished slabs of red granite, and the upper three are of alabaster.

From the northwest corner of the hall a narrow passage leads upward to the temple exit, where the causeway begins. Nearly halfway up this passage, a ramp on the right (north) leads up to the flat roof of the temple. Opposite it, in the southern wall of the passage, is a small chamber lined and paved with alabaster.

As noted earlier, the washing of the dead body of the king, as well as its mummification and the "Opening of the Mouth" ritual, all probably took place in this temple. Remains of basins and holes for tent poles are found in front of the temple and on the roof.

The causeway of Khafre's pyramid is hewn almost entirely out of living rock. Part of the walls are visible at the easternmost end, near the Valley Temple, but we do not know whether it was roofed or whether the walls were originally sculptured with bas-reliefs. It ascends the plateau obliquely to the northwest, and meets the Mortuary Temple near the southern end of its eastern façade.

The Mortuary Temple of Khafre, a large and imposing monument, was excavated by the Von Sieglin expedition in the early years of the present century. Although ruined, it still has an air of imposing grandeur, and its plan is easily discernible (Fig. 76). The building bears little resemblance to its predecessor, the Mortuary Temple of Khufu, and still less to the small chapels of Sneferu and Hu. Some unknown development in the royal mortuary cult must have led to radical changes in the plan of the pyramid temples.

Like the Valley Temple, this building seems to have been constructed with a core of local limestone and a casing of some other material, perhaps granite. Its floor was of alabaster. The entrance gives access to a narrow passage, connecting on the south with two chambers and on the north with a vestibule, the roof of which was supported by two pillars. The passage continues farther north to four storerooms and a staircase, cut in the thickness of the northern wall, that leads to the roof. From the center of the rear wall of the vestibule, a passage leads to an elongated hall, the western part of which recedes into two large bays. Its roof was supported by fourteen square pillars; this feature is reminiscent of the pillared hall west of the colonnaded court in Khufu's Mortuary Temple. At the northern and southern ends of this hall are two long, narrow statue chambers. Beyond this room is yet another hall, its roof originally held up by ten pillars. Proceeding westward, the visitor finally emerges into the great court of the temple, which was surrounded by a colonnade supported on massive, rectangular pillars, each of which formed the backing for a large statue of the king.

On the western side of this court we now encounter for the first time (as far as we know) the five niches which were to become an invariable feature of all later kings' Mortuary Temples. (In queens' temples they numbered only three.) The reader will recall that, in Sneferu's pyramid complex, there were six of these niches, located in the Valley Temple. We do not know why they were decreased in number and placed in the higher temple. In spite of the many theories on the subject, we still do not have a clear idea about their real function in the royal mortuary cult.

South of the row of niches, a corridor leads to five smaller niches or storerooms lying behind the first row. To the south are two small rooms and a doorway leading to the outside of the building. At the extreme western end of the temple is a long, narrow sanctuary, in the center of which stood a great granite stela, parts of which may be seen lying in the ruins. From the northwestern corner of the great colonnaded court, a passage runs westward to the pyramid courtyard.

Flanking the Mortuary Temple are five rock-cut boat pits; a narrow cutting in the rock northeast of the temple suggests that six were intended. Two pairs lie parallel with the northern and southern walls of the temple; their axes are directed east-west, and they are arranged prow to prow. In each pair, the westernmost pit has retained its original roofing slabs, and the interior of the hall is carved to represent the internal structure of a wooden boat. When excavated, they contained fragments of pottery and statuary, but no trace of wooden ships. South of the temple is a pit directed north-south; the unfinished cutting to the northeast has the same direction.

At the center of the pyramid's southern side once stood a small pyramid. Nearly all the superstructure has been quarried away, but the entrance and the descending passage may be seen. Although this pyramid originally measured about 20.1 meters square, the entrance and passage are so narrow that an average adult would find it difficult, if not impossible, to enter. This indicates once more that these small subsidiary pyramids were never intended for burial, or for any purpose which required anyone to enter them.

The Second Pyramid was surrounded on the north, south, and west by a temenos wall, parts of which are still visible. West of the wall are ruined parallel walls built of rough stones. They are divided by partitions into 110 small rooms, which Petrie believed were barracks for the workmen who built the pyramids. He estimated that they could have housed between 3,500 and 4,000 workmen.

Khafre's pyramid was one of the last to lose its casing. It retains some at the summit, and, although the once-white limestone has weathered to shades of brown and mauve, the stones still retain some of their high polish. At night they reflect the white light of the moon.

The area chosen for the site sloped sharply from west to east, so that considerable labor was required to prepare it for building. The rock was scarped on the north and west, and huge blocks of stone removed in the process were used at the southern and eastern sides to build up the hollows in the plateau.

Originally the pyramid was 143.5 meters high and 215.5 meters square, with a slope of 53°10′. The entrance was hidden for a long time, and early travelers looked for it in vain. Some even thought that the pyramid had no interior passages or chambers. It was not until 1818 that Giovanni Belzoni, the Italian archeologist, succeeded in finding the

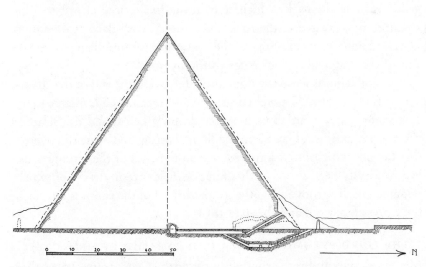

77. *Section of the Second Pyramid at Giza.*

entrance and reaching the burial room. Actually the pyramid has two entrances on the northern face (Fig. 77). The one discovered by Belzoni stands about 11 meters from the ground. The other is cut in the rock at ground level a few meters from the pyramid. The existence of two entrances has generally been thought to be the result of a change of plan during its construction. Such an explanation is not convincing. In my opinion, the two entrances in this and other pyramids are related to the burial of the king. One, and the galleries to which it led, was carefully built with masonry and fortified with great, heavy portcullises; the other served to let workmen in and out, and was later blocked.

The interior arrangement is very simple. Belzoni's entrance, with his name and the date of his discovery inscribed over it, leads to a passage which is walled and roofed with red granite. It descends at an angle of 26° to a horizontal passage which is closed by a vertically operated granite portcullis. The lower entrance also leads to a descending passage, with a slope of 22°. This seems to have been the original entrance, as the sloping passage ends at a portcullis; then follows a horizontal corridor and another sloping passage, which leads to an empty, rock-cut burial chamber. The horizontal passage continues beyond this, and, after another portcullis, slopes upward again. It joins the passage leading from the upper entrance, and both merge into a long, horizontal gallery, cut in the rock, which ends in the final burial chamber. The chamber is excavated in the rock but is roofed with slabs of limestone placed obliquely; it is not under the center but is more than one meter east of the diagonal of the center of the pyramid.

A sarcophagus is set in the floor at the far (western) end of the chamber; it is of beautifully polished granite and measures 2.6 meters long, 1.05 meters wide, and about 1 meter deep. When found by Belzoni, it was open and its lid lay upon the floor. Perring and Vyse discovered that the lid, which fitted into grooves on the ends of the sarcophagus, had originally been sealed with a kind of melted resin, traces of which remained in the grooves. On the southern wall of the room is inscribed the name of Belzoni and the date 1818.

THE THIRD PYRAMID AT GIZA (THE PYRAMID OF MENKURE)

Menkure's pyramid is the southernmost of the Giza group. Its smaller size was offset by the splendid appearance of the granite casing which covered at least the lowest sixteen courses. The Mortuary Temple was designed on a large and magnificent scale, but Menkure died before the casing of the pyramid was completed, so his successor, Shepseskaf, had to finish the monuments. He skimped on his father's pyramid complex, building it of mud brick, and did not try to build a large pyramid for himself.

The Third Pyramid attracted the attention of early travelers. Herodotus related a story, current in his day, that it was built by the courtesan Rhodopis; he had the good historical sense to discredit it on the grounds of the antiquity of the monument and the fact that such a woman would not have had the means to build a pyramid. In modern times the Third Pyramid was included in Burton's description,[12] and the plan and elevation were published in the *Description de l'Égypte*. The first scientific excavation was undertaken by Perring and Vyse in 1837; they seem to have been the first people in modern times to penetrate its interior.[13] Reisner made extensive excavations near this pyramid, chiefly in the Mortuary and Valley Temples,[14] but the areas north and south of the monument have not yet been properly examined, and it is possible that there are still other monuments, including perhaps boat pits, awaiting discovery.

Menkure's Valley Temple lies near the Moslem cemetery of the village of Nazlet el Samman, and the pyramid city, which merges with that of Queen Khent-kawes, runs under the modern graves.

The temple is built of mud brick, with the column bases and parts of the pavements and thresholds in limestone. Its eastern entrance opened into a small vestibule, the roof of which was borne by four columns (Fig. 78). On either side are four storerooms opening into a corridor which runs the width of the building and meets another long corridor on the south. A doorway in the middle of the rear wall of the vestibule leads into the great court. This has a mud-brick pavement and walls of mud brick decorated with niches. Running across the center from east to west is a narrow gangway of limestone slabs. South of this is a limestone basin, from which a covered limestone drain leads obliquely back under the gangway. The western end of the gangway

[12] See Porter and Moss, *Topographical Bibliography*, III, 7.

[13] Vyse, *Operations Carried On at the Pyramids of Gizeh*, II, 71 ff.

[14] G A. Reisner, *Mycerinus*.

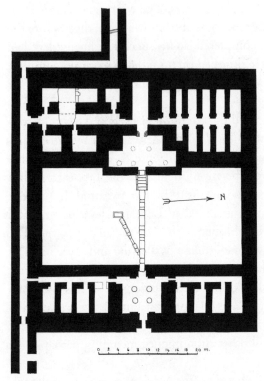

78. *Plan of the Valley Temple of the Third Pyramid at Giza. (After Reisner.)*

terminates at the entrance to a pillared hall, recessed on the west, whose roof is supported by six columns. Beyond are the sanctuary and several smaller chambers, including six reminiscent of those in Sneferu's Valley Temple. It was in the room to the south that Reisner found the beautiful schist triads of Menkure, as well as fragments of other statues. (Each of the triads represents Menkure flanked by a goddess or a god and a *nome* deity.)

There seems to have been no access between the main part of the temple and the causeway; instead, a corridor ran along the southern side of the building, turned north, and then ran west again to join the causeway—another feature reminiscent of Sneferu's Valley Temple. The causeway was built of massive blocks of local limestone, paved and walled with mud brick, and roofed with palm logs. It joined the temenos wall which surrounded the complex.

Menkure's Mortuary Temple is fairly well preserved, and its basic plan is not difficult to comprehend (Fig. 79). The core masonry of the

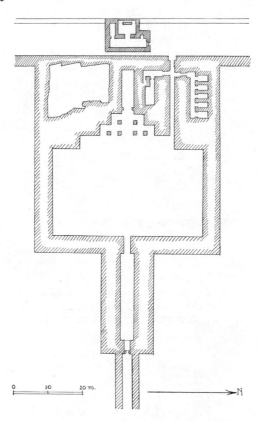

79. *Plan of the Mortuary Temple of the Third Pyramid. (After Reisner.)*

walls is of huge blocks of local limestone, which were originally to be lined on the inside with granite. A long entrance corridor, built of mud brick, leads to a large central court. Here the walls were cased with mud brick and a final layer of limestone. In the center of the court were a basin and a drainage system. At the western side of the court is a recessed hall, which originally had six red granite pillars. Behind this is a long, narrow chamber, resembling the sanctuaries in the temples of the Fifth Dynasty and later. South of this is a large area which was never completed. From the northern end of the pillared hall a passage leads to five small rooms.

The western end of the temple consists of a sanctuary or offering shrine built against the face of the pyramid. It was paved with red granite, and a large, rectangular depression in its floor probably marks the place of a false door and an offering table. Immediately east is a cor-

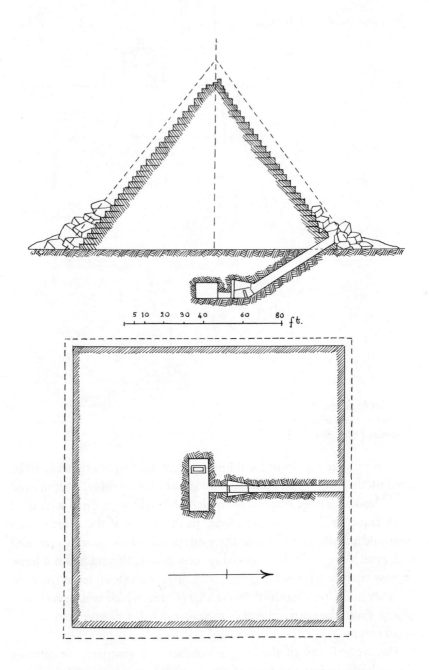

The plan and section of the easternmost of the three small pyramids to the south of the pyramid of Menkure.

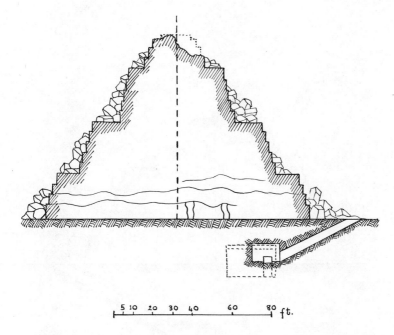

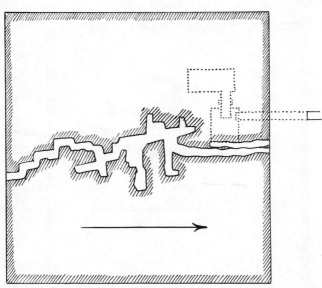

81. *Plan and section of the central small pyramid to the south of the pyramid of Menkure. (After Reisner.)*

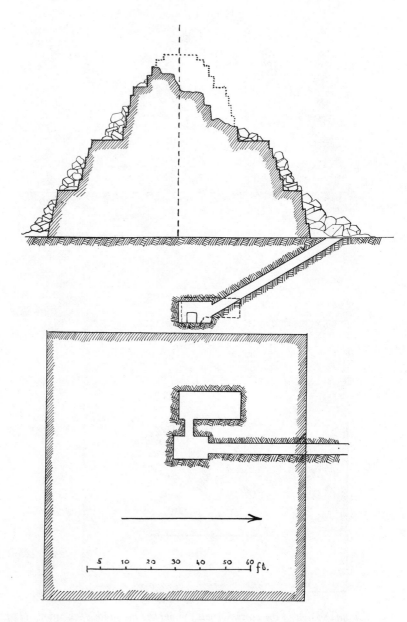

82. *Plan and section of the westernmost of the small pyramids south of the pyramid of Menkure.* (*After Reisner.*)

ridor with limestone pillars. The latter, as well as several limestone rooms on the north (also built against the pyramid), are later constructions, probably dating from the Sixth Dynasty. North of these structures are several mud-brick chambers.

The only real evidence of the splendid scale on which this building was designed is furnished by the granite portions of the construction, especially the black granite walls of the northern corridor.

South of the Third Pyramid are three small pyramids, one of which is possibly the usual subsidiary pyramid. These were also investigated by Perring and Vyse. The easternmost of the three (Fig. 80) measures about 10 meters high and is 36 meters square. It is built of large blocks of local limestone, apparently without accretion faces, and was at least partly cased with red granite. The entrance in the northern face, now inaccessible, led to a descending passage terminating in a burial chamber. In the western end of the room, sunk in the floor, is a red granite sarcophagus. East of this pyramid is a small mud-brick chapel. Some Egyptologists have suggested that the pyramid belonged to Queen Khamerernebty, the sister-wife of Menkure and the lady represented with him in a famous group now in the Boston Museum of Fine Arts.

The central pyramid stands about 9 meters high and is 36 meters square (Fig. 81). It was built of local limestone in four accretions, and there is no evidence that it was ever cased. The entrance, still accessible, is in the northern face, but the lower end of the descending passage is nearly choked up at present. It leads to a burial chamber, in which Perring and Vyse found a small granite sarcophagus containing the skeleton of a young woman. One of the stones in the room has a quarry mark giving Menkure's name. A small mud-brick chapel was found east of the pyramid.

The westernmost of the small pyramids, also 9 meters high and 36 meters square (Fig. 82), was built in accretions of large blocks of local limestone; again there are no traces of casing stones. Its entrance, blocked at present, leads to a descending corridor, an antechamber, and a burial room. Apparently no traces of a burial were found here, and it is possible that this is the subsidiary pyramid of Menkure's complex. Like the other two, it has a small mud-brick chapel on the eastern side.

83. *The pyramid of Menkure* (*Third Pyramid*), *Giza.*

Menkure's pyramid was built on a slope of the plateau, and the site was leveled with limestone masonry (Fig. 83). Much of its original granite casing remains in place, but, except for the area forming the rear of the Mortuary Temple sanctuary and a few blocks around the entrance, all these blocks were left in the rough—a feature which would indicate that the casing blocks were sent from the quarry rough-hewn and dressed only after being set in place.

According to Herodotus, this casing of "Ethiopian stone" extended for half the height of the pyramid. As is the case with the other Giza pyramids, the Third Pyramid has lost most of its white limestone surface, and the structure itself has suffered damage, especially on the northern side. It is said that in A.D. 1196 one of the Moslem rulers of Egypt deliberately tried to destroy this pyramid but had to stop because of the great expense.

The building measures about 108.5 meters square, and originally stood 66.5 meters high; the angle is 51°. The entrance is, as usual, in the northern face, about 4 meters above the base in the fifth course of masonry (Fig. 84). The descending passage, with a slope of 26°2′, measures about 31 meters long and is walled and roofed with granite from the entrance to the point where it enters bedrock. A vestibule at the bottom, its walls paneled with stone, leads into a horizontal passage

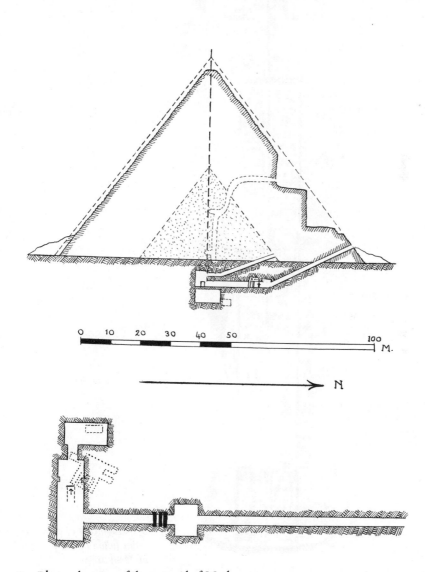

84. *Plan and section of the pyramid of Menkure.*

85. *Fragments of a wooden coffin found in the pyramid of Menkure.*

86. *The burial chamber of the Third Pyramid showing the vaulted roof and the basalt sarcophagus.*

with three portcullises. Beyond is the burial chamber, where Perring and Vyse found a wooden coffin thought at the time to have been Menkure's (Fig. 85). Its inscription reads: "Osiris, the King of Upper and Lower Egypt, Menkure, living forever. Born of the sky, conceived by Nut, heir of Geb, his beloved. Thy mother Nut spreads herself over thee in her name of 'Mystery of Heaven.' She caused thee to be a god, in thy name of 'God,' O King of Upper and Lower Egypt, Menkure, living forever." This inscription is a version of a well-known passage in the Pyramid Texts. The coffin contained the remains of the mummified body of a man, possibly Menkure. Both the mummy and the coffin fragments are now in the British Museum.

Apparently this pyramid was originally designed on a much smaller scale, because there is another descending passage. It opens from the upper part of the northern wall of the burial room and extends upward to what was once the original entrance, but is now a cul-de-sac. From the western end of the burial chamber floor, a granite-lined passage leads westward to a staircase, then down to a chamber containing six niches. (This arrangement resembles the substructures of the tombs of King Shepseskaf and Queen Khent-kawes, both children of Menkure.) Still farther west lies another splendid burial chamber with red granite walls and roof (Fig. 86). The vaulted ceiling was made by first erecting a pointed roof and then hollowing out the slabs to make them concave. It was here that Perring and Vyse discovered the king's beautiful basalt sarcophagus (Fig. 87). It had the typical Old Kingdom "palace-façade"

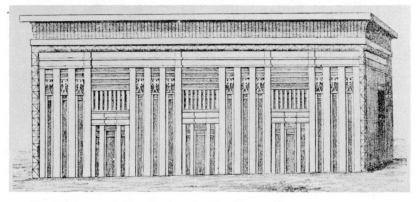

87. *The basalt sarcophagus found in the Third Pyramid.*

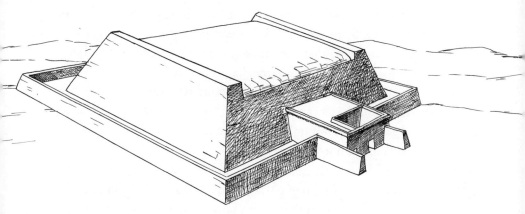

88. *A reconstruction of the Mastabet Fara'un. (After Jéquier.)*

paneling, and was no doubt contemporary with the pyramid. The sarcophagus was shipped to England, but was lost en route when the ship carrying it was wrecked off the Spanish coast.

THE MASTABET FARA'UN

The gigantic pyramids and temples built by Sneferu's descendants needed a large number of priests and great endowments to perpetuate the cults of their builders. Consequently the influence of the priests of Heliopolis increased. We find the name of Ra, the sun-god, as an element of royal names from the Second Dynasty onward. Beginning with the Fifth Dynasty, the kings added a new name to the already-existing four—"Sa-Ra," meaning "the son of Ra."

Although Menkure's son Shepseskaf began his reign by completing his father's monuments, it would seem that he felt the pressure of the priests and took certain steps to limit their power. Unfortunately we have no document to tell us the story of the clash between the palace and the hierarchy, but we can see one of its results. From the days of Zoser, kings had been buried in pyramids, which were symbolic of sun worship. Three generations built their royal monuments on the Giza plateau. But Shepseskaf decided to build a different type of royal tomb and chose a new area midway between Zoser's Step Pyramid and the pyramids of Sneferu, a site now known as Saqqara South.

On a site commanding an excellent view of the fields around the great and flourishing city, Shepseskaf built his royal tomb, the Mastabet Fara'un, in a form which differed completely from those used by his ancestors. It was neither a pyramid nor a true mastaba, but had the form of a gigantic rectangular sarcophagus and somewhat resembled the tombs of the kings of the First and Second Dynasties (Fig. 88). It measures 100 by 72 meters and is 18 meters high. A temenos wall surrounds it, and a chapel stands on the eastern side. A causeway leads down to a Valley Temple, not yet excavated.

The entrance to the substructure, in the middle of the northern side, leads to a long descending passage and a horizontal corridor, at the end of which is an antechamber with a burial room on the right and several storerooms on the left (Fig. 90). The plan is clear, and its execution, as well as the dressing of the stone, is excellent (Fig. 89). Apparently the interior was never finished, and, according to its last excavator, it was never used for a burial.

Lepsius examined the Mastabet Fara'un in 1843, and it was subsequently entered by Mariette in 1858. Jéquier excavated it carefully in 1924 and revealed that it had been built for Shepseskaf.[15] The chapel suffered such great destruction that the name of the owner was never found complete. However, the lower part of the name was found inscribed on a pedestal, and Jéquier decided that it must be that of Shepseskaf, because his name and cult were mentioned in nearby private tombs. (It is curious that in writing the name of this royal tomb, the determinative was usually shown as a pyramid, as in all the other pyramid names. In only a few is the determinative written in its correct form of a sarcophagus, the true shape of the monument.[16])

Shepseskaf's reign lasted only four years. Another king, named Djedef-Ptah (Thampthis), apparently ruled for two years after him. We cannot tell if he belonged to the same family. The great dynasty founded by Sneferu had passed the zenith of its power and artistic achievement, and the struggle between the two branches of the family

---

[15] G. Jéquier, *Le Mastabet Faraoun* (Cairo, 1928).

[16] For a good example, see Ahmed Fakhry, *Sept Tombeaux à l'est de la grande pyramide de Guizeh* (Cairo, 1935), pp. 5–6.

had brought destruction. Before proceeding to the pyramids of the
Fifth Dynasty, however, we may discuss briefly the last of the Fourth
Dynasty queens.

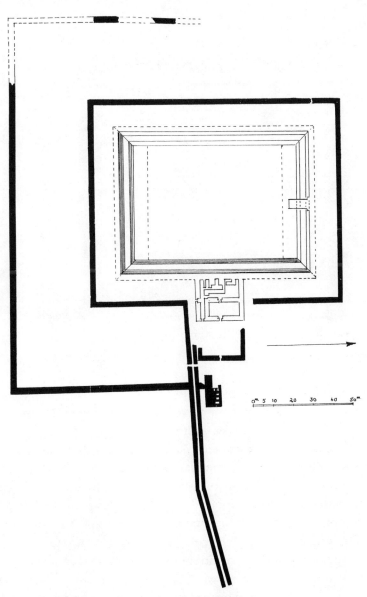

89. *The plan of the Mastabet Fara'un. (After Jéquier.)*

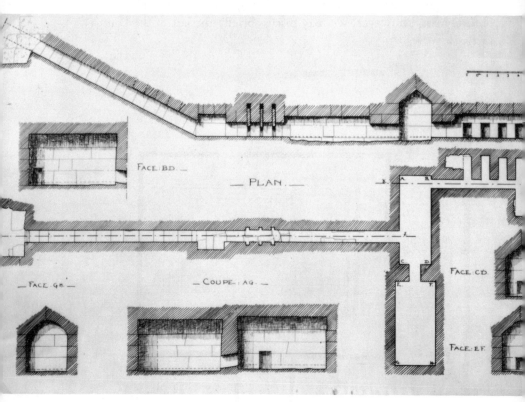

90. *Plan and section of the substructure of the Mastabet Fara'un.* (*After Jéquier.*)

THE TOMB OF QUEEN KHENT-KAWES

The royal tomb of Shepseskaf served as the prototype for another tomb, which was built at Giza south of the Second Pyramid. It was unidentified for many years, and marked "Lepsius Pyramid 100" on the maps of the necropolis. Selim Hassan excavated it during the season of 1931–32. It is now clear that it was built by a queen named Khent-kawes, the mother of two kings. The architect designed this tomb in the form of a large sarcophagus standing on a massive base of natural rock, into which the chapel was cut. As in the case of Khufu's pyramid and the Sphinx, he utilized an outcropping of stone that existed already. The rock walls of the chapel were cased with limestone blocks. The entrance to the substructure opened west from the second room of this chapel and led down to a burial chamber which had small side rooms used as magazines. The rock foundation of the great tomb is almost square, measuring about 45.5 meters on a side and 10 meters high. The outer sides were originally recessed but afterward cased with fine limestone. The upper structure measures 27.5 by 21 meters and is 7.5 meters high; it is composed of seven courses of local limestone blocks. The monument, inclosed by a surrounding wall, had a rock-cut boat pit at its southwestern corner, and there may be others under the debris.

Several brick buildings lie in front and east of the monument of Queen Khent-kawes. They served as storerooms and houses for the priests, but have not been fully excavated because they extend under the modern cemetery of the village of Nazlet el Samman.

From inscriptions found on the granite chapel doorway and on the stela, we learn that Queen Khent-kawes was the mother of two kings of Upper and Lower Egypt, and that she herself held a distinguished place in the country. Hassan calls her tomb a pyramid and terms it the "Fourth Pyramid"; he believes that she actually ruled the country.[17] It is, however, impossible to call this building a pyramid—the word describes a specific geometrical form and cannot be applied to every royal tomb, regardless of its design. The inscriptions do not indicate that the lady ruled the country: her name is not written in a cartouche, she does not have the usual royal titles, and she wears the ordinary vulture diadem of kings' wives and princesses rather than a royal crown.

But the tomb is more conspicuous than that of any other queen of the Fourth Dynasty, and has many interesting and unusual features. Khentkawes was most probably a daughter of Menkure. She was certainly of royal blood and possessed the rights of inheritance. Her tomb was inspired by that of Shepseskaf, but she preferred to be buried near the pyramids of her father and her great ancestors. She was, in fact, the link between the Fourth and Fifth Dynasties, and it is not improbable that she was the mother of the first two kings of the Fifth Dynasty, Weserkaf and Sahure.[18] Her inscriptions do not title her "king's wife," and make no mention of her husband. This suggests that he did not belong to the

[17] Selim Hassan, *Excavations at Giza* (Cairo, 1943), IV, 1–68.

[18] The name Khent-kawes became popular after this queen, especially in the royal family. The Khent-kawes of Abusir, who was connected with King Neferirkare, may have been a daughter of hers (L. Borchardt, in *Annales du Service*, XXXVIII [1938], 209–15).

royal family; in view of the marked increase of solar influence in the religion of the succeeding Fifth Dynasty, we may assume that he was a high priest of the sun-god at Heliopolis.

There may be a connection between Queen Khent-kawes and the legend mentioned earlier which attributes the Third Pyramid of Giza to Rhodopis, the "rosy-cheeked." Herodotus did not believe this story, but it was repeated by Diodorus and Strabo, who said that the pyramid was built by the courtesan's lovers. Is this legend due to pure imagination, or to a misunderstanding and an exaggerated story which has a basis in fact? From the text of Africanus we know that Manetho mentioned a queen, reigning at the end of the Sixth Dynasty, who built the Third Pyramid. Her name was Nitocris, and she was the most beautiful woman of her day, with a fair complexion. The only possible explanation for the legend Herodotus retells is that there was a story about a beautiful and important queen who was buried on the Giza plateau. The epithet "rosy-cheeked" created the misunderstanding which led to her identification with Rhodopis, and Manetho's account may err in placing the queen at the end of the Sixth Dynasty instead of the Fourth. Khent-kawes is therefore most likely the queen referred to in these stories, handed down for two thousand years after her death.

8

The Sphinx of Giza

It is impossible to write of the pyramids of Giza, especially the Second Pyramid, without mentioning the Sphinx. There is scarcely a person in the civilized world who is unfamiliar with the form and features of the great man-headed lion that guards the eastern approach to the Giza pyramids (Fig. 92).

The Sphinx is synonymous with mystery. Until 1926 the great statue was buried up to its neck in sand, and visitors speculated about what might lie underneath. Today the archeologist can assure us that the Sphinx, freed from sand and surrounded by ruins, dates from the reign of Khafre, the builder of the Second Pyramid. He will admit, however, that more excavation is needed before we can be certain that the sands hide nothing more.

The story of the Sphinx as it was revealed by excavations, especially those made between 1926 and 1936,[1] is of great interest. There is no doubt that the statue forms part of the pyramid complex of Khafre, but it is a unique feature and no other king can boast of having such a monument. Therefore we may ask how it originated, and why Khafre indulged in this gigantic innovation. The answer lies in its situation.

[1] Porter and Moss, *Topographical Bibliography*, III, 8–9. For the results of the recent excavations of the Sphinx and the references to works on the subject, see Selim Hassan, *The Great Sphinx and Its Secrets* (Cairo, 1953).

The Sphinx occupies a vast, rocky amphitheater at the eastern edge of the plateau, which was nothing more than a great quarry from which workmen cut stone to build the pyramids and private mastabas. They took out the best, hardest stone, so that a mass of softer rock eventually jutted out from the quarry bed. This great mass, lying beside the Valley Temple, impeded the view of the Second Pyramid and its causeway and must have been unsightly. The builders then faced the problem of whether to remove it entirely or transform it. Perhaps its natural shape roughly resembled that of a crouching lion. In any case, Khafre's architect visualized it as a magnificent sphinx, and his skilful masons, translating the vision into reality, transformed the offending eyesore into a sublime monument for their royal master.

Over 20 meters high and 57 meters long, the Sphinx was originally carved from the living rock without additional masonry. Because of the softness of the stone, its body and paws became eroded with time and countless sandstorms, and from time to time later rulers repaired it with stone blocks. The figure faces the rising sun. Its form is simple and the pose majestic; the face, framed by the royal *nemes*-headdress, is an idealized portrait of Khafre himself. Here we must correct the oft-repeated story that Napoleon's soldiers broke off the nose when using

91. *A stela showing the Sphinx and two pyramids drawn in perspective.*

92. *The Sphinx of Giza. Before it are the ruins of its temple; behind it is the Second Pyramid, with the causeway running down to the Valley Temple (on the left).*

it as a target for rifle practice. The story is refuted by the Arab historian El Makrizi (d. 1436):

In our time there was a man whose name was Saim-el-Dahr, one of the Sufis. This man wished to remedy religious matters, and he went to the pyramids and disfigured the face of Abul-Hol [one of the Arabic names of the Sphinx], which has remained in this state from that time to the present. From the time of the disfigurement the sand has invaded the cultivated lands of Giza, and the people attribute this to the disfigurement of Abul-Hol.

As it was first conceived, the Sphinx symbolized the king, and its face was carved in Khafre's likeness. Although no other king imitated

93. *The Sphinx of Giza, showing the granite stela recording the dream of Thutmose IV, and the late granite altar in the foreground.*

Khafre's monument, several pyramid causeways of the Fifth and Sixth Dynasties have reliefs at their lower ends depicting the king in the form of a sphinx trampling on the prostrate enemies of Egypt. It is probable that these reliefs were inspired by the Sphinx of Giza, for it occupies a similar position—the beginning of the causeway—in relation to Khafre's pyramid complex.

By the time of the New Kingdom, the Egyptian conception of the Sphinx had changed. Although its form still symbolized the king (and a female sphinx the queen), the Sphinx of Giza had come to represent the sun-god. As such, it was the center of a special cult and a place for pilgrimage. In spite of this, the ever-encroaching desert sand half-buried it periodically, and even today constant excavation is needed to keep it free.

By the middle of the Eighteenth Dynasty, the Sphinx was apparently buried up to its neck. The desert around the pyramids was filled with wild game, and princes and nobles enjoyed hunting there. According to an ancient document, it happened one day that a young prince named Thutmose, a young son of Amenhotep II, was hunting in the region. At midday he paused for lunch and a nap in the shadow of the Sphinx's head, the only part of the statue then projecting from the sand. As he slept, the prince dreamed that the god spoke to him and complained of the engulfing sand, which hindered his breathing. He promised Thutmose the throne of Egypt if the prince would have the sand cleared away. Thutmose promised and, on awakening, renewed his vow. But he did not tell his dream to anyone. Even though Thutmose had older brothers, the Sphinx kept his part of the bargain, and the prince ascended the throne as Thutmose IV. He had the sand removed, and once more the Sphinx lay revealed. To prevent further encroachments, Thutmose had a series of mud-brick walls built around the monument on the north, west, and south; the bricks bear the stamp of his name. The story of Thutmose's dream and the compact he made with the god were engraved on a slab of granite and set against the breast of the Sphinx, where it still stands (Fig. 93).

The story is probably a piece of propaganda invented by Thutmose to show that his accession was due to divine choice. He had no direct right to the throne, but proclaimed himself king either through influ-

ence or because of conflicts in the royal family. He may have been supported by the priests of Heliopolis and Memphis, who greatly honored
the god Hor-em-akhet (Horus), symbolized by the Sphinx. Thutmose
accordingly wished to show the people that he had been chosen by the
sun-god to rule Egypt. (In this he followed the example of some of his
ancestors, the most famous of whom was Queen Hatshepsut. She
claimed that she was the child of the god Amon-Ra, who had visited
her mother disguised as her husband, King Thutmose I. Hatshepsut's
aim was to convince the people that her claim to the throne far out-
weighed that of her nephew.)

The last excavations around the Sphinx, undertaken by the Antiquities Department under the direction of Selim Hassan, revealed several
interesting stelae and monuments. These indicate that the Sphinx was
the object of royal and private pilgrimages during the New Kingdom.
Most important of all was the discovery of a small temple of the Sphinx,
situated immediately northeast of it. This temple, built of mud brick
with inscribed doorways of fine white limestone, was erected by Amenhotep II, the son of the grand old warrior, Thutmose III. He tells us the
story of the building's foundation on a large white limestone stela set
against the back wall of the temple. As a young child, Amenhotep was
passionately fond of horses and sports. He was happy only when he
could get into his father's stables at Memphis to drive the horses and
learn to train and care for them. One of the courtiers reported the
matter to the Pharaoh, but Thutmose expressed pleasure that his little
son displayed manly traits. Calling the boy to him, he demanded to be
shown what he could do. Proudly the lad demonstrated his skill as a
charioteer, and Thutmose, delighted at the boy's ability and courage,
ordered that he be given the entire Memphis stud. Amenhotep then
relates that one day he harnessed his chariot team in Memphis and drove
to the Giza necropolis, where he spent the day visiting the monuments
and marveling at the wonders of the pyramids and the Sphinx. He
vowed that when he came to the throne, he would erect a temple to the
Sphinx and set in it a stela recording his visit and the pleasant day he
had spent there.

Later kings added to this little temple of Amenhotep II. Seti I, of the
Nineteenth Dynasty, dedicated a limestone stela in a side chapel off the

main hall. On it he is shown hunting wild animals, and the inscription states that he had come to the place where the people came to pray. Seti also added the jambs to the main entrance, one of which was re-inscribed by his grandson, Merenptah.

In addition to the stelae left by kings and princes are a large number dedicated by their subjects. Some of these were tablets showing one or more human ears, sometimes inscribed with a prayer or the donor's name. It is supposed that these ears represented those of the god; the worshiper placed his tablet as near as possible to the divine image, where his prayer was considered to be awaiting the god's attention. Many of the inscriptions request spiritual benefits such as intelligence, understanding, and contentment of heart.

Also of great interest are stelae with representations of the Sphinx. These usually show him crowned, his lion's body covered with hawk's plumage and wearing a wide collar; he lies upon a high pedestal, which is often surmounted by a cornice and provided with doors. These features require explanation, having been represented by contemporary artists who were familiar with the Sphinx's appearance. The crown and body decorations are easy to explain. On top of the Sphinx's head is a deep, square hole (now filled in) which doubtless held the "tongue" of an attached crown. The plumage and collar were perhaps added decorations. The pedestal, however, sent Maspero and other investigators on a useless errand. From early times, even as far back as the Ptolemaic period, tradition held that a secret chamber or tomb existed under the Sphinx, and that a subterranean passage might even connect the statue with the Second Pyramid. Maspero went to much trouble and expense to find this pedestal, which he considered to be the origin of the traditions. He cleaned the front of the monument down to bedrock, but could find no trace of it. The entire structure was cleaned in 1926, and it became obvious that the Sphinx lay upon the leveled floor of the old quarry, forming one piece with it. The mystery of the pedestal remained unsolved. A few years later, however, it was explained by a chance photograph taken during the last excavations. Seen from the east, the Sphinx appears to be lying on top of its temple, and when the latter was complete, with its cornice and doors in place, it would have resembled exactly the high pedestal of the representations. We know that the temple of the Sphinx was completely buried during the New Kingdom, because the foundations of Amenhotep's temple are built bridgewise across one of its corners. In spite of this, artists of the Eighteenth and Nineteenth Dynasties knew that such a building existed and were familiar with its appearance. (This indicates how well we can rely upon the ancient records, and shows that the Egyptians knew more about the history of their ancient monuments than we usually give them credit for.) The New Kingdom representations also show the colossal statue of a king standing before the breast of the Sphinx. All that now remains of it is a large, uneven vertical projection from the chest of the Sphinx, all details of form and features having been eroded away.

The stelae and votive figures of Sphinxes, lions, and falcons found around the Sphinx reveal the names under which it was known and worshiped. Most commonly it was called *Hor-em-akhet*, Horus-in-the-Horizon, or *Hor-akhty*, Horus-of-the-Horizon—both appropriate names, since the ancient necropolis was called *Akhet Khufu*, the Horizon of Khufu. The Sphinx was sometimes called Ḥu and Ḥol, and was also identified with the Canaanite falcon-god, Horoun, whose worship was popular in Egypt during the Nineteenth Dynasty. Egyptians of the New Kingdom again used the Old Kingdom rock tombs in the cliff north of the Sphinx. Some served as burial places, others as repositories for stelae and votive figures donated by followers of the Sphinx cult. In some cases, new tombs were cut at a higher level.

The cult of the Sphinx continued to flourish even after the decline of the Ramesside kings, and graffiti in the neighboring Temple of Isis refer to his priesthood and temple. The great interest taken in the Old Kingdom monuments during the Saite period naturally enhanced the popularity of the Sphinx. Some of the kings left votive figures, and important persons cut their tombs in the vicinity. It is strange that Herodotus did not mention the Sphinx in his account of the Giza pyramids.

The Sphinx must have been free from sand during the Ptolemaic period, because it was found that the statue had begun to lose its shape through erosion. Builders restored its original contours with small blocks of limestone, which can still be seen on the paws, flanks, and tail. A red granite altar was also set up between the paws.

During the Roman period the Sphinx was still a popular place for pilgrimage and sightseeing. The people built a great flight of stairs leading from the plain down into the amphitheater, and monuments nearby, in the classical style, commemorated the visits of important foreign guests. Travelers also scribbled their names and comments on the paws of the Sphinx and on limestone slabs which they left near it. However we may deplore such vandalism, we must forgive the person who scratched the following Greek poem on one of the toes of the Sphinx:

> . . . they are perished also,
> Those walls of Thebes which the Muses built;
> But the wall that belongs to me has no fear of war;
> It knows not either the ravages of war or the sobbing.
> It rejoices always in feasts and banquets,
> And the choruses of young people, united from all parts.
> We hear the flutes, not the trumpet of war,
> And the blood that waters the earth is of the sacrificial bulls,
> Not from the slashed throats of men.
> Our ornaments are the festive clothes, not the arms of war,
> And our hands hold not the scimitar,
> But the fraternal cup of the banquet;
> And all night long while the sacrifices are burning
> We sing hymns to Harmakhis (Hor-em-akhet).
> And our heads are decorated with garlands.[2]

The haunting beauty of these lines re-creates the living reality of the past. The feasts in front of the Sphinx, with young people singing and playing music, can be seen there on any summer night at the time of the full moon. In the peace of the desert, with soft moonlight revealing the calm, majestic features of the Sphinx, one's thoughts turn to peaceful things, and "wars and rumors of wars" seem remote and unreal.

Thousands of years have passed, but the Sphinx still looks to the east, with his faint, mysterious, superior smile. He witnessed Egypt in her great days, and has seen foreign troops on the sacred earth that stretches

[2] Selim Hassan, *The Great Sphinx and Its Secrets*, p. 122.

out from beneath his paws. Times change, and Egypt's history has ebbed and flowed, but Egyptians have always turned to their ancient history for inspiration. They look upon the pyramids as symbols of stability and pride, but they regard the Sphinx as a source of endless wisdom and hope for the future.

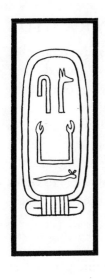

9

The Children

of the Sun-God

The glorious days of the Fourth Dynasty ended in obscurity. The house of Sneferu and Khufu could no longer rule the land. Shepseskaf's reign had in all probability witnessed the gathering of the clouds, for he had not been able to shake off the strong yoke of the priests of Ra. The evidence for this comes from our knowledge of the new reigning house, the Fifth Dynasty, whose kings built their pyramids and temples at Abusir and Abu Gurab, about 5 miles south of the Pyramids of Giza.

A story in the Westcar Papyrus, referred to in an earlier chapter, concerns the origin of the Fifth Dynasty kings and their relationship to the sun-god. According to the tale, King Khufu was told by Dedi, a magician, that a woman named Red-dedet, wife of a priest of Ra, had conceived three children of Ra. "He hath told her," said Dedi, "that they shall exercise this excellent office [the kingship] in this entire land, and that the eldest of them will be High Priest of Heliopolis." This news saddened the king, and Dedi said, "Pray, what is this mood, O King, my Lord? Is it because of the three children? Then I say unto thee: thy son, his son, and then one of them."[1]

[1] According to the prophecy, the first of the new dynasty would come to the throne after the reigns of Khafre and Menkure. Actually there were at least four other kings of the Fourth Dynasty, but apparently it was only the builders of the great pyramids who survived in popular tradition.

The birth of the three children was attended by Isis and several other gods and goddesses. As the children were born, Isis named them Weserref, Sah-Re, and Keku, meaning the first three kings of the Fifth Dynasty—Weserkaf, Sahure, and Kakai (Neferirkare).[2]

This legend, which records the divine birth of the first three kings of the Fifth Dynasty, was not necessarily invented in later times. It might have been recorded at the time of the first king to convince the people that he came to the throne through a divine miracle. His rights would then be indisputable if challenged. The title "Son of Ra" henceforth became a regular feature of the king's name.

THE PYRAMID OF WESERKAF

The first ruler of the Fifth Dynasty chose to build his pyramid at Saqqara, as near the Step Pyramid as possible. (At that time the region offered a great deal of suitable, unoccupied space.) Because of Weserkaf's desire to be close to his great predecessor, Zoser, his architect

[2] For this translation by Blackman, see Erman, *The Literature of the Ancient Egyptians*, pp. 36-47.

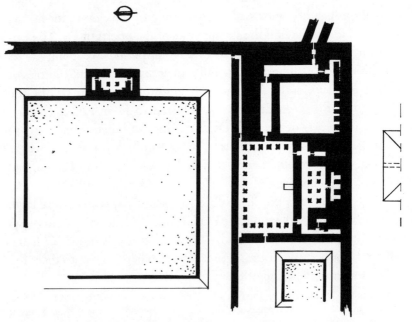

94. *Plan of the pyramid complex of Weserkaf (Firth).*

selected a site near the edge of a ridge of the plateau, about 200 meters from the northeast corner of the Step Pyramid complex.

Nothing in the construction of the pyramid indicates a break with tradition, but the temple provides an innovation: the offering chapel was placed at the eastern side, while the rest of the Mortuary Temple lay at the south (Fig. 94). The excavator of the monument, C. M. Firth, felt that this abnormal arrangement was due to topographical necessities. According to his theory, there was not enough space at the eastern side of the new pyramid to build a Mortuary Temple, so the architect erected only a small limestone chapel and placed the Mortuary Temple proper on the southern side. J.-P. Lauer, the most recent excavator, also holds this view. Herbert Ricke, however, believes that the departure from tradition was intentional and had to do with the sun-worship so prominent in the Fifth Dynasty. The sun travels from east to west in the southern half of the sky, so an altar on the south would never be in the shade.[3] If this theory is correct, we would expect to find the same arrangement in the other temples of the family, or at least in the sun temple of Weserkaf at Abusir. Yet all the Abusir temples had their entrances on the east, and were oriented east-west.

Weserkaf's complex was approached by a basalt-paved causeway and surrounded by a temenos wall. A doorway in the wall led to the Mortuary Temple. When first excavated in 1928, this was found to be in ruinous condition, having been used as a quarry. Several sections were totally destroyed, because Saite nobles had sunk large burial pits within the temple area. From the temenos doorway, two vestibules led to an open court, paved with basalt, which measured 21 by 35 meters. It was originally surrounded on three sides by a portico, supported by red granite pillars 1 meter square. Two doors led from the pillared court to the rest of the temple. Because of the three Saite tombs cut in the floor, several parts, including the room with niches, have disappeared.

In excavating Weserkaf's temple, archeologists found fragments of granite and diorite statues of the king, the most important being a granite head now in the Cairo Museum. It is over three times life size

[3] H. Ricke, *Bemerkungen*, II, 68. For the first report of the excavations at Weserkaf's Sun-Temple, mentioned below, see now H. Stock, "Bericht über die erste Kampagne am Sonnenheiligtum des Userkaf bei Abusir," *Orientalia*, XXV (1956), 74–80.

and was found under the basalt floor in the socket hole of one of the granite pillars (Fig. 95). Excavators also discovered many reliefs and architectural elements which indicated the great care taken in the temple's construction. The beautiful reliefs depict subjects which are more or less familiar in the tombs of the period. Their discovery in 1928 led archeologists to conclude that Weserkaf's reign marked the beginning of the custom of decorating temple walls. But we have seen from the reliefs found in Sneferu's Valley Temple in 1951 that the Egyptians decorated their temple walls at least as early as the beginning of the Fourth Dynasty.

The Southern chapel, lined with red granite and paved with basalt blocks, contained an offering room, with a drain under the floor.[4] The

[4] C. M. Firth, "Excavations of the Department of Antiquities at Sakkara," *Annales du Service*, XXIX (1929), 64–70; J.-P. Lauer, "Le Temple haut de la pyramide du roi Ouserkaf à Saqqarah," *Annales du Service*, LIII (1955), 119–33.

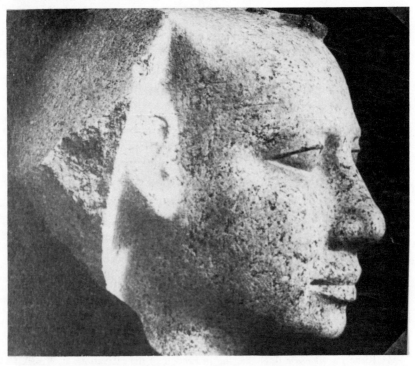

95. *The colossal red granite head of Weserkaf.* (*Cairo Museum.*)

Subsidiary Pyramid is at the western side of the temple, while the queen's pyramid is on the south.

The pyramid itself, known today as "El Haram el-Mekharbesh" (The Scratched Pyramid) was robbed in antiquity. It was entered and examined scientifically during the last century. In construction, it follows the traditions of the Fourth Dynasty. The core, built of large limestone blocks, had a casing of fine white limestone. The pyramid is small compared to those of the previous dynasty. Originally, each side measured 70.37 meters and the height 44.53 meters. When Perring and Vyse examined it in 1837, the length of the base was 63.84 meters and the height 32.83 meters. The passage, opening from the middle of the northern side, has walls and ceiling of great blocks of red and black granite. The heavy granite portcullises originally blocking the corridor were avoided by the thieves, who tunneled through the softer limestone masonry above them. Nothing of any importance was found inside the main pyramid or the queen's pyramid.

THE PYRAMID OF SAHURE

After a reign of eleven years, Weserkaf was succeeded on the throne by Sahure. The latter built his pyramid at Abusir, 3 miles north of Saqqara. This site became the royal cemetery of several Fifth Dynasty kings.

Sahure's monument is the northernmost of the pyramids at this site,[5] and was approached by a causeway about 200 meters long. At the lower end is a Valley Temple of somewhat unusual design (Fig. 96). It has two entrances opening onto a large, well-built landing-stage. One entrance, which faces east, is provided with a portico upheld by eight columns. The other entrance faces south and has a portico with four columns. The main structure of the Valley Temple measures about 40 meters from north to south and 30 meters from east to west. Each of the two entrances leads to a hall, which had palmiform granite pillars and walls richly decorated with painted reliefs. The hall was 5.42 meters high. The temple is now ruined, but the lower part of the causeway (235 meters long) is fairly well preserved. From it we have an interesting

[5] The principal publication is L. Borchardt, *Das Grabdenkmal des Königs Sahure* (2 vols.; Leipzig, 1910, 1913).

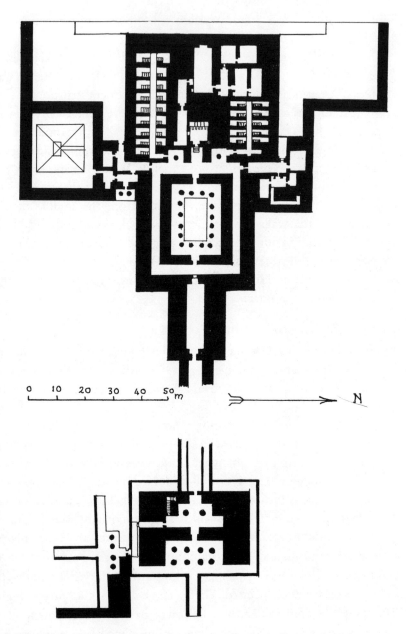

96. *Plan of the pyramid complex of Sahure at Abusir. (After Borchardt.)*

series of reliefs depicting events of the king's reign and religious subjects.

At the upper end of the causeway is the Mortuary Temple, entered by a corridor whose walls are over 3 meters high. It leads to an imposing central court, which was once surrounded by sixteen red granite columns of the palmiform order. The pavement was of black basalt, and the walls of fine limestone adorned with colored reliefs. One of the scenes, now in the Cairo Museum, depicts King Sahure defeating the Libyans. He is seen grasping the Libyan chief by the hair, about to brain the cowering wretch with his stone-headed mace. A Libyan woman, doubtless the chieftain's wife, and two of his sons raise their arms to the Pharaoh to implore his mercy. So far as we know, these details appear here for the first time, but rapidly became traditional. Later kings repeated the theme of the defeat of the Libyans, even to the names of the chieftain's family. (Thus we cannot always accept such scenes as depicting historical events.)

Surrounding the colonnaded court is a wide corridor, which also has basalt paving and limestone walls decorated with reliefs. Most of the scenes here show the king hunting and offering to the gods. These reliefs survived the general destruction of the temple because of a curious accident. In one, the king is seen presenting offerings to the cat-headed goddess Bastet, who later seems to have become confused with the lioness-headed Sekhmet. Sekhmet, as the wife of Ptah, had her cult center in nearby Memphis. At the time of the New Kingdom, the corridor with the relief of Bastet was roofed and walled and transformed into a sanctuary for a local cult of Sekhmet, where she was worshiped under the name of "Sekhmet of Sahure."

West of the court, beyond a surrounding corridor, lay several chambers and storerooms. Directly behind the court were the five niches. North of these were two groups of five storerooms, one above the other, connected by stairways. South of the niches was a similarly arranged group of storerooms, seventeen in all. Both groups of storerooms were approached from two square recesses in the western side of the corridor, the roofs of which were upheld by papyrus-bud columns of red granite.

A corridor from the southern end of the niche chamber led to the sanctuary and five cult chambers beyond it. The former, about 13.72 meters long and 4.5 meters wide, was probably paved with alabaster, and its western end was occupied by a false door of granite, before which stood an alabaster altar. The northern, southern, and eastern walls had a granite dado below the fine white limestone relief that showed the gods of Egypt bringing provisions to the king.

A curious and interesting feature of this temple is its drainage system. Rain falling on the roof was carried off by lion-headed gargoyles, which projected well beyond the eaves, and fell into open channels cut in the pavement. Within the temple were five copper-lined basins fitted with lead plugs. (Two were in rooms near the sanctuary, one in the sanctuary itself, one in the corridor, and a fifth in the group of ten storerooms.) Copper pipes from these basins carried off water and other liquids used in the cult ceremonies. They connected with an underground drainage system, also of copper pipes, which passed under the temple paving and down the entire length of the causeway, at the southern side of which was an outlet.

South of the colonnaded court is a small entrance opening east onto a portico with two columns. Beyond is a corridor which leads to the court of the Subsidiary Pyramid.

King Sahure's pyramid has suffered greatly, both inside and out, and

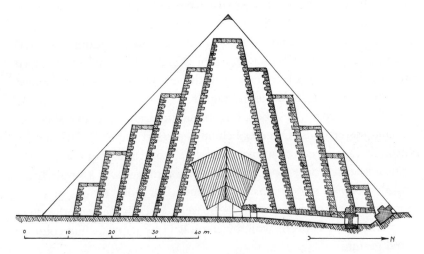

97. *Section of the pyramid of Sahure at Abusir. (After Borchardt.)*

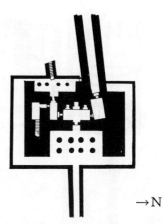

98. *Plan of the Valley Temple of Neferirkare at Abusir. (After Borchardt.)*

→ N

scarcely any of the white limestone casing has survived. The building must originally have stood about 48 meters high on a base of 78 meters; the angle of its slope was about 50°36'. The masonry is of the poorest quality, and consists of accretions of coarse local limestone, filled with sand and rubble. There were apparently six accretions, decreasing in size from the nucleus (Fig. 97). The steps were finally filled in with the same poor mixture of sand and rubble, and the whole monument cased with fine limestone.

The entrance opens at ground level, a little east of dead center in the northern face. It is walled and roofed with black granite and leads to an antechamber about 8 meters long, the southern end of which is closed by a granite portcullis operated vertically. Behind this is a corridor (now inaccessible) which is roofed and walled with fine limestone. The passage slopes gently upward for about 25 meters to the burial chamber, the floor of which is level with the base of the pyramid. The pointed roof consists of three layers of massive limestone blocks, the ends of which rest against and support each other. The blocks increase in size as they ascend. This type of roofing is typical of the burial rooms of Fifth Dynasty pyramids.

THE PYRAMID OF NEFERIRKARE

The pyramid complex of King Neferirkare, who succeeded Sahure, lies some distance from the latter's pyramid, and is separated from it

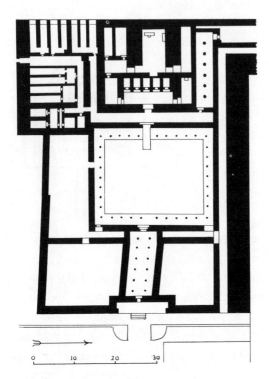

99. *Plan of the Mortuary Temple of Neferirkare at Abusir. (After Borchardt.)*

by that of King Neuserre, who built in the intervening space.[6] It appears as though Neferirkare had intended to model his pyramid complex on that of his predecessor, on a larger scale. However, he did not live to complete his plan; his successor finished the work in mud brick and modified the layout.

Neferirkare's Valley Temple, like that of Sahure, has two entrances, an eastern one with a portico of eight columns and a western one with a portico of four columns. Both entrances lead into four small rooms, the northernmost of which opens on the lower end of the causeway. In spite of the Valley Temple's now complete ruin, blocks of granite, basalt, and fine white limestone attest to its former splendor.

The causeway had a dado of black basalt, an unusual feature; some of the slabs still remain in place. The white limestone walls above it were adorned with colored reliefs.

[6] L. Borchardt, *Das Grabdenkmal des Königs Nefer-ir-kere'* (Leipzig, 1909).

The Mortuary Temple consisted of an entrance passage leading to a central colonnaded court (Fig. 99). The wooden columns, with lotiform capitals, were mounted on limestone bases, which still exist. In the inner western section of the building are the five niches, the storerooms, the anterooms, and the sanctuary. In the last stood a large false door of red granite. A German expedition found several beautiful ceremonial vases in the debris of the temple. They were made of gilded wood inlaid with colored faience and were intended to simulate gold vessels inlaid with semiprecious stones.

Neferirkare's pyramid is the largest of the Abusir group, and original-ly stood 70 meters high and 106 meters square; its slope had an angle of about 53°. The structure was built in six accretions composed of small blocks of coarse local limestone. These accretions and the core itself were cased with large blocks of fine white limestone, as was almost certainly the outer surface of the monument. The few remaining blocks of red granite indicate that the lowest course of the exterior was cased with this material.

The entrance to the pyramid, on the north, is now inaccessible. The burial chamber has a pointed roof composed of massive blocks of lime-stone, as is the passage leading to it.

King Neuserre later diverted the upper end of Neferirkare's causeway to his own pyramid complex, so that the mortuary priests of his prede-cessor had to group their mud-brick houses against the walls of the Mortuary Temple instead of living in the usual pyramid city near the Valley Temple.

THE PYRAMID OF NEFEREFRE

Neferefre, who succeeded Neferirkare, seems to have had a brief reign. He began a pyramid slightly southwest of his predecessor's, but appar-ently it was never completed. At the present time it consists of a low square of masonry, 60 meters on each face, with a flat top. About eight courses of local limestone remain, five of them visible above the sur-rounding sand. In the center of the northern face an entrance opens on the passage leading to a large cavity in the center of the pyramid. This is the unlined, unfinished burial chamber. Apparently the temples and causeway attached to this pyramid were never completed.

THE PYRAMID OF NEUSERRE

King Neuserre built his pyramid between those of Sahure and Neferirkare and appropriated to his own use the probably unfinished Valley
Temple and causeway of the latter. In doing this, he diverted the upper
half of the existing causeway, giving it a sharp angle to the northwest,
so that it enters his own Mortuary Temple at the southeastern corner of
the temenos wall (Fig. 100).[7]

Neuserre's Mortuary Temple has an unusual L-shaped plan, with the
outer and inner sections of the building on two different axes. This
deviation may be due to the presence of already existing tombs which

[7] L. Borchardt, *Das Grabdenkmal des Königs Ne-user-re* (Leipzig, 1907).

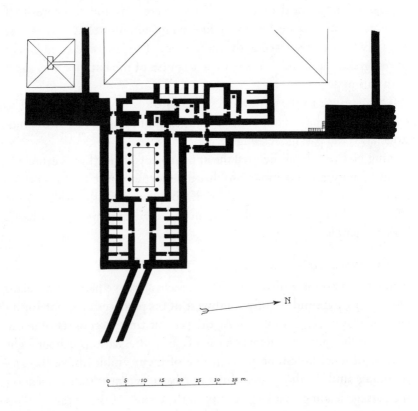

100. *Plan of the pyramid complex of Neuserre.* (*After Borchardt.*)

the king did not wish to disturb, or to unsuitable terrain. The causeway leads into a wide corridor, flanked north and south by storerooms. Its western end opens into a large central colonnaded court with sixteen red granite papyriform columns; the floor is paved with black basalt. In the center of the western wall, a doorway opens into a corridor which leads to five niches on the west, the pyramid court to the north and south, and two corridors running east, which in turn communicate with the storerooms flanking the entrance passage. North of the niche chamber is a small, square room, the roof of which is upheld by a single column. Beyond are a small antechamber, the sanctuary, and several other rooms.

The small Subsidiary Pyramid stands at the southeastern corner of the pyramid, inclosed within its temenos wall. It measures about 11 meters high and 15 meters square. A passage from the center of the northern face leads to the usual transverse chamber.

The pyramid of King Neuserre was originally about 52 meters high and 80 meters square, with an angle of approximately 51°50′. The interior masonry consists of coarse local limestone, intermixed with sand and rubble. It has five inner facings, each with a slope of 70°. The original casing of fine limestone has been removed. The entrance on the

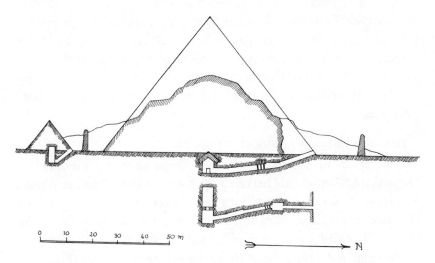

101. *Plan and section of the pyramid of Neuserre at Abusir. (After Borchardt.)*

102. *The pyramid of Dedkare Isesi as seen from cultivation.*

northern side is surrounded by blocks of granite and is now inaccessible
(Fig. 101). It leads to a short passage, then a vestibule, and again a longer
passage, closed by three portcullises operated vertically. At the end is
an antechamber, from which a short corridor leads to the burial chamber. The latter has the pointed roof characteristic of Fifth Dynasty
pyramids.

THE PYRAMID OF DEDKARE ISESI

The pyramids of some Fifth Dynasty kings, including Menkawhor,
Shepseskare, Wenis, and Dedkare Isesi, have not been found at Abusir.
The last-named monarch had long been known to Egyptologists, but
his place of burial was unknown until recently, when Abdel Salam
Hussein identified it as the pyramid called "El Shawwaf" (The Sentinel)
on the edge of the plateau just above the village of Saqqara (Fig. 102).
This pyramid, commanding one of the finest views over the fields of
Memphis, had always been an enigma. Archeologists investigated it

partially at the end of the last century, but abandoned work on it when they found that its interior was uninscribed. It was not until 1946, when Hussein excavated the pyramid's Mortuary Temple, that Egyptologists realized that this pyramid complex belonged to King Dedkare Isesi.

Unfortunately, the temple had been destroyed during the succeeding centuries, and its floor used as a burial ground by the second half of the Eighteenth Dynasty. The site revealed many beautiful reliefs, however, as well as several of the architectural elements of the temple. Among the latter are statues of foreign prisoners and of lions, bulls, rams, and sphinxes. Everything was found scattered pell-mell, and it was impossible to tell whether anything, except for a few pieces from door jambs and columns, lay near its original place. The remains did indicate that the plan of the temple resembled those of other Fifth Dynasty temples.

My excavations in the winter of 1952–53 resulted in the discovery of several tombs dating from the end of the Sixth Dynasty. These lay just east of the Mortuary Temple. One, belonging to a certain Pepi-ankh Sethu, has a painted burial chamber in an excellent state of preservation, whose walls bear colored representations of food offerings and funerary equipment. A more important find north of the Mortuary Temple was a small mound which proved to be the pyramid of Isesi's queen. East of it lay a Mortuary Temple, larger than any other queen's temple of the Old Kingdom. Many reliefs came to light, but both pyramid and temple had shared the same fate as Isesi's monuments.

The causeway leading to Dedkare Isesi's Valley Temple is well marked, and some of the granite blocks of the latter may be seen among the houses at the edge of the cultivation. The Valley Temple has not yet been excavated, and the whole complex requires more work before the final plan can be given.

THE PYRAMID OF WENIS

The pyramid of King Wenis, who has been regarded both as the last Fifth Dynasty king and the first ruler of the Sixth Dynasty, occupies a distinguished place among the pyramids. In 1880 Maspero discovered the famous Pyramid Texts, hitherto unknown, inscribed on the inside walls of the pyramid of Pepi I. Shortly afterward similar inscriptions were found in other pyramids. The oldest version of these texts is that in the pyramid of Wenis; continuous excavations for eighty years have not revealed an earlier pyramid so inscribed. The interior of Wenis' pyramid is well preserved and easy to visit. It is an important monument, and should be seen by every visitor to Saqqara.

There are several arguments in favor of considering Wenis as the first king of the Sixth Dynasty, rather than the last of the Fifth. No pyramid prior to his was inscribed with the Pyramid Texts, while all those of the Sixth Dynasty, even the queens', were so inscribed. It is also significant that King Teti of the following dynasty completed the inscriptions of his predecessor. Wenis' name occurred in the Mortuary Temple of Dedkare Isesi's wife, and the casing of Wenis' pyramid contains inscribed and decorated blocks apparently taken from the Mortuary Temple of Dedkare Isesi. It is possible, however, that these were old blocks re-used by Prince Khaemwase in his restoration of the pyramid, because Dedkare Isesi's temple had already been destroyed during the second half of the Eighteenth Dynasty. Another curious feature of the pyramid complex of Wenis is the position of the subsidiary pyramid, which is located south of the Mortuary Temple, a little west of dead center, rather than in the usual position south of the main pyramid.

The large Valley Temple of Wenis lies on both sides of the modern road that leads from the cultivation to the plateau of Saqqara. It was partially excavated a few years before World War II, but the work has not yet been completed. Its ruins revealed several palmiform columns of fine red granite.

The causeway, over 660 meters long, begins at the southwestern side of the Valley Temple and angles twice because of the steep ascent. The lower end has not yet been fully excavated, but we know that the causeway was walled, roofed, and paved with fine white limestone. The roof was decorated with stars carved in relief and painted yellow against a blue background. The walls had scenes in delicate low relief. Some of the subjects are traditional, including offering-bearers and ceremonial and hunting scenes. Others are unique, as far as we know. One such scene shows a fleet of ships bringing various architectural elements from the quarries at Aswan to Saqqara. Among these may be seen pairs of palmiform columns, laid end to end. Measurements given in the accompanying inscription tempt us to conclude that the relief actually represents the granite columns which today lie in the ruins of the Valley Temple.[8] One puzzling scene shows a group of famine-stricken persons, apparently foreigners.

The Mortuary Temple is ruined, but enough remains to allow the plan to be traced (Fig. 103). It was partly excavated in 1900–1901 by Barsanti,[9] and again more thoroughly in 1929, under the direction of C. M. Firth.[10] In general, the plan and construction closely resemble the corresponding temple of Sahure at Abusir, but there are several differences in the arrangement of the corridors and storerooms in the inner temple. The main entrance gateway of red granite was left unfinished at the death of Wenis, and was completed by King Teti of the Sixth Dynasty, who inscribed his own name on one of the jambs. The colonnaded court had sixteen palmiform columns, at least two of which were of brown sandstone from the quarries north of Cairo called, now as in ancient times, "The Red Mountain." The other columns of the same type were of red granite. The floor of the court, as well as that of some of the corridors, was paved with alabaster. In general plan, the temple

[8] Selim Hassan, in *Annales du Service*, XXXVIII (1938), 519–20.

[9] A. Barsanti, in *Annales du Service*, II (1901), 244–57.

[10] C. M. Firth, in *Annales du Service*, XXX (1930), 186.

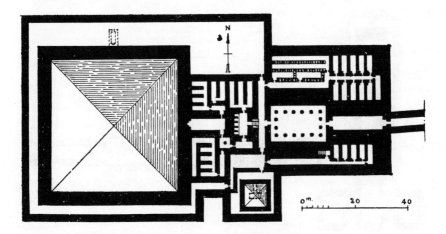

103. *Plan of the Mortuary Temple of Wenis at Saqqara.*

is symmetrical, and may be said to form a link between the Mortuary Temples of the Fifth and those of the Sixth Dynasties.

The pyramid of Wenis is 67 meters square; it is about 19 meters high, but originally stood about 44 meters. It is in such a ruined condition that we are not sure about the method of its construction. Certainly the whole superstructure is a solid mass, without accretions, and the passages and chambers were cut in the natural rock. Much of the lower limestone casing remains in place, especially on the northern and eastern sides. On the southern side, carved in large, bold hieroglyphs, is a text recording Khaemwese's restorations.

The entrance is at ground level, almost in the center of the northern face. It is cut in the rock outside the pyramid, and its ceiling just reaches the base line of the monument. The entrance was originally closed with a limestone plug, but is now open and accessible to the public. Inside, a sloping passage 14.35 meters long descends at an angle of 22° and ends in a vestibule (Fig. 104). Three portcullis slabs of granite block a horizontal passage 18 meters long, which leads to an antechamber with a pointed roof. From the eastern side of the antechamber, a short passage leads to three small recesses. On the west, a similar short passage leads to the burial chamber. This has a pointed roof decorated with stars carved in relief against a blue background. At the far end stands a sarcophagus of highly polished black granite. The walls of the burial

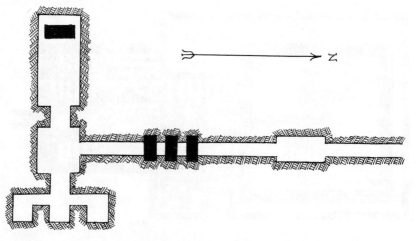

104. *Plan of the substructure of the pyramid of Wenis at Saqqara.*

chamber surrounding the sarcophagus are of polished alabaster and are carved to represent the conventional "palace-façade," which is painted green and black. All the other walls of the substructure (except those of the granite descending passage) are of fine white limestone. Those of the rest of the burial room, the antechamber, the short passages, and the inner end of the main passage are covered from top to bottom with sections from the Pyramid Texts. The hieroglyphic inscriptions, carved intaglio and colored blue, are finely cut and in an excellent state of preservation. They include portions of the texts which do not occur in later pyramids and have a distinctive literary style not lacking in poetic beauty.

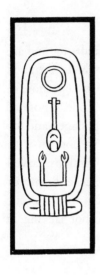

10

The Decline

It is difficult to see why the Fifth Dynasty should have come to an end. Dedkare Isesi had a long and stable reign, and, judging from the monuments he left, the country was enjoying a period of prosperity. Wenis had an even longer reign, thirty years, during which Egypt witnessed a revolution in literature, religious reforms, and art.

According to Manetho, Teti was the first king of the Sixth Dynasty. Whether it was Teti or Wenis who founded the new dynasty, we cannot discern a marked change at the end of the Fifth Dynasty, and the new line of kings may possibly have been related to the royal line of the previous dynasty. The pyramids and temples of the Sixth Dynasty kings exhibit traces of a decline in construction techniques but do follow the main traditions.

Although the Sixth Dynasty kings were not as powerful as their predecessors, their names are associated with a policy of foreign trade and conquest, which they pursued with enthusiasm. As early as the Fifth Dynasty, the kings had sent expeditions outside Egypt for both commercial and military purposes. There were skirmishes against the Libyans in the west and against Syria and Palestine in the east. An Egyptian fleet in the Mediterranean occasionally visited the harbors of nearby countries, and royal expeditions also went south to Nubia and the

Sudan, as well as to the Land of Punt (Somaliland and southern Arabia). The kings of the Sixth Dynasty paid particular attention to the south and ordered the governors of Aswan to lead expeditions to penetrate the heart of Africa. The biographies of these men, which they inscribed in their tombs in the western cliffs opposite Aswan, tell the stories of their great adventures and of how the kings rewarded them for their services. Some of these pioneers of African exploration lost their lives in fulfilling the commands of their masters in Memphis, and paid in blood for the ebony, incense, gold, ostrich feathers, medical herbs, and other wares from the south. Occasionally they brought back a rarity much appreciated by the kings—a little black pigmy, skilled in performing a special kind of religious dance.

In spite of these activities, signs of decadence began to appear in the Egyptian court and the nation itself during the long period of the Sixth Dynasty. The kings were no longer absolute rulers and the unquestioned divine lords of the whole land. The governors of the provinces now had considerable power, and their offices, originally bestowed on them by royal favor, had become hereditary.

From earliest times, the ambition of every high official was to be buried in the necropolis surrounding the tomb of his royal master. Beginning with the Fifth Dynasty, however, we see a gradual change. The local governing families began to build their tombs in their own provinces, cutting them out of the rock. These local governors did not consider themselves independent rulers, but loyal subjects of the king, with their men at his disposal if he needed them. We should remember, however, that Egypt was no longer the powerful country it had been in the Fifth Dynasty. Misgovernment had sapped the internal prosperity of the land, and the kings tried to strengthen their weak position by marrying the daughters of the rich, powerful governors.

THE PYRAMID OF TETI

The area which King Teti chose for his pyramid is a commanding site quite close to the eastern edge of the plateau overlooking the broad green plains of the Nile Valley. The Valley Temple, if it still exists, has not been excavated. The causeway, which must have been either very long or very steep, has disappeared entirely, except for a small portion at its western end, near the pyramid. It might have been built of mud brick, which would explain its disappearance.

Little remains of the large Mortuary Temple. As in Wenis' temple, the entrance passage is flanked by storerooms and leads into a central colonnaded court, the columns of which were apparently of wood. At the far end of the court a few steps led up to the five niches, with more storerooms on the north and west.

Still farther west, against the face of the pyramid, was the sanctuary. It contained a sandstone false door, the base of which is still *in situ*. Among the ruins of the temple may be seen many limestone blocks from the ceiling, all decorated on their undersides with the usual five-pointed stars in yellow on a blue ground. One important and interesting find was a plaster death mask, which, according to Quibell, is most likely of Teti himself, in view of its location. There are indications that the floor of the court was paved with alabaster. Again, as in the case of the pyramid complex of Wenis, Teti's Subsidiary Pyramid lies south of the Mortuary Temple rather than south of the main pyramid.

We are fairly sure that the destruction of the temple took place during the Second Intermediate Period, because we know that the cult of Teti, like that of the kings of the Fourth and Sixth Dynasties, was still flourishing during the Middle Kingdom. The ruins of the temple revealed part of a limestone statue of a certain Teti-em-saf, who, in addition to being chief ritualist of the pyramid of Teti, was connected with the temple of the god Ptah, both the northern and southern pyramids of Sneferu, the pyramid of Khufu, and temples erected by several Twelfth Dynasty kings.[1] The temple had been destroyed by the time of the New Kingdom, and its remains were buried in the sand. It still retained the tradition of sanctity, having become a burial ground for commoners in the Eighteenth Dynasty. By the time of the Nineteenth Dynasty, it had become an important cemetery, and continued as such for a long time.

Teti's pyramid was large but is now woefully dilapidated because of its poor construction. The core and accretions are of small blocks of coarse local limestone and rubble faced with local limestone. The outer casing, of which Quibell found some blocks still in place on the eastern

[1] J. E. Quibell, *Excavations at Sakkara* (1907-8), pp. 113-14, Plate 57.

face, was of the traditional fine white limestone. At present the pyramid is about 20 meters high and 65 meters square.

The entrance is at ground level, approximately in the center of the northern face. Against it was built a small offering chapel containing a basalt false door. This must have been completed after the interment of Teti because the false door, regarded as the door for the Ka of the king, would have completely blocked the entrance. The passage, 15 meters long, led to a vestibule, a horizontal passage closed by granite portcullises, and an antechamber. On the eastern side of the antechamber was a recess and on the west the burial chamber, which still contains the basalt sarcophagus. These rooms all have pointed roofs decorated with five-pointed stars, and their walls are inscribed from the Pyramid Texts.

THE PYRAMID OF QUEEN IPUT I

Queen Iput I was the wife of King Teti and the mother of his successor, Pepi I. Her pyramid complex lies about 100 meters north of her husband's Mortuary Temple. It was first excavated by the Antiquities Department under Loret's direction in 1897–99, and later by Quibell in 1907–8.[2]

Apparently there was no Valley Temple or causeway, and the small Mortuary Temple is ruined. In the western wall of the sanctuary was a large false door of limestone, of which only fragments remain. In front of it stood a large offering table of red granite inscribed with the queen's titles and name. This was apparently dedicated to her by her son, Pepi I, because the name of his pyramid complex—*Men-nefer-Pepi*—occurs in the inscriptions.[3]

Iput's pyramid was small, and today measures only about 4.5 meters high and 15.5 meters square. It has a steep angle of 65°. Loret failed to find the entrance on the northern side and made a second attempt in the eastern face, behind the limestone false door in the sanctuary. This attempt also failed, because the pyramid did not have the usual type of entrance passage. The burial room actually lay at the bottom of a large, deep shaft, the usual arrangement in a private tomb. At some later period, the rubble core of the pyramid had been dug out and a large, com-

[2] C. M. Firth and B. Gunn, *The Teti Pyramid Cemeteries*, I, 11–14.

[3] *Ibid.*, Vol. II, Plates 55 and 2.

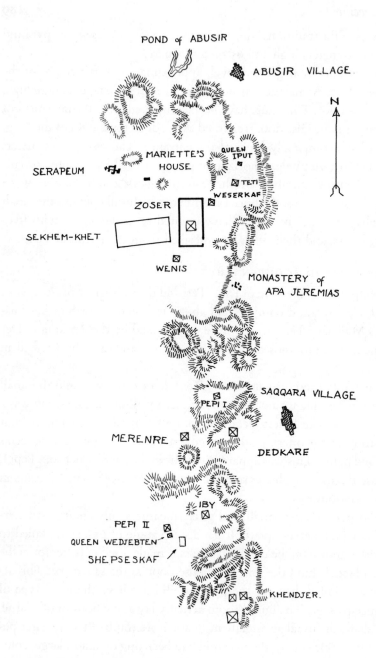

POND of ABUSIR

ABUSIR VILLAGE.

N

MARIETTE'S HOUSE

QUEEN IPUT

SERAPEUM

TETI

WESERKAF

ZOSER

SEKHEM-KHET

WENIS

MONASTERY of APA JEREMIAS

SAQQARA VILLAGE

PEPI I

MERENRE

DEDKARE

IBY

PEPI II

QUEEN WEDJEBTEN

SHEPSESKAF

KHENDJER.

105. *Map of the necropolis of Saqqara.*

munal burial chamber constructed in it. This latter chamber was roofed by a mud-brick vault. After excavators had removed the floor and eastern wall of this later room, they discovered the original shaft.

The burial chamber contained a limestone sarcophagus with its lid still cemented in position. However, thieves had robbed it by cutting a hole through one of the sides. Inside the sarcophagus was a cedar coffin which still held the queen's skeleton. Apparently the thieves were hasty or careless, because they overlooked several fragments of the queen's necklace as well as a gold bracelet which remained in place on her right arm. The burial room had been filled with limestone chips to the level of the sarcophagus. Mingled with these were several model vessels of alabaster and several model tools and vessels of copper. All of these had been covered with gold leaf and several were inscribed with Iput's name and titles. There were also pottery vases of finely polished red ware and small cups made from rock crystal, limestone, and marble.

Behind the sarcophagus was a set of five canopic jars of coarse red pottery. The number five is unusual, the common number being four. The queen's skeleton was examined by Derry, who reported that she was middle-aged at the time of her death, and that she had relatively large eyes and a narrow nose.

Almost in the center of the northern face of the pyramid, at ground level, was a fine red granite false door. This occupied the place where the entrance to the pyramid would normally have been. It is inscribed with the name and titles of the queen, and the central niche is carved to represent double doors of wood fastened by a bolt.[4]

THE PYRAMID OF PEPI I

After the death of Teti, the royal family of the Sixth Dynasty changed the site of their burial ground. They moved southward, and Pepi I erected his pyramid complex near that of Dedkare Isesi at Saqqara South (Fig. 105).

The pyramid complex of Pepi I has never been completely excavated. The remains of the Valley Temple are not visible, but must lie near the end of the causeway, which can be seen clearly under the sand from the edge of the cultivation almost to the eastern face of the pyramid. The

[4] *Ibid.*, Vol. II, Plates 55 and 1.

Mortuary Temple is also unexcavated, although there is little doubt that parts of it remain.

The pyramid itself is almost completely ruined and at present stands only about 12 meters high and about 70 meters square. The core masonry, once cased with fine limestone, is little more than a heap of rubble. A northern entrance opens into a descending passage, vestibule, horizontal passage, antechamber, and burial chamber. In the latter were a basalt sarcophagus and granite canopic chest, which contained the remains of three of the original four alabaster jars.

In spite of its uninspiring appearance and neglect by archeologists, the pyramid of Pepi I has two great claims to distinction: For one, it gave its name to the ancient city of Memphis. The name of the pyramid, *Men-nefer-Pepi*, was extended to the pyramid city and then to a quarter of the old capital, previously named *Het-ka-Ptah*, *Ineb-hedj*, and *Ankh-tawi*. *Men-nefer-Pepi*, abbreviated as *Men-nefer*, was successively pronounced Menfer, Memfer, and finally Memfi, a name still used for a small village a few miles south of the pyramids of Giza. Thus it became the Memphis of the classical authors. The pyramid's second claim to fame is that it was the first pyramid to reveal to the modern world the supremely important Pyramid Texts.

THE PYRAMID OF MERENRE

The pyramid of Merenre, the successor to Pepi I, lies a short distance southwest of Dedkare Isesi's complex. Neither the Valley Temple, causeway, nor Mortuary Temple has been excavated. The pyramid itself, now ruined, was originally about 95 meters square. It has not been examined in recent years, but in 1881 was opened by Mariette and entered by Maspero, when the latter investigated the pyramids of Saqqara in connection with the discovery of the Pyramid Texts.[5] Maspero found that the interior arrangement resembled that in Wenis' pyramid and in those of the Sixth Dynasty kings. The burial chamber contained a fine sarcophagus of black granite with a mummified body which may be that of King Merenre.

We are fortunate to have contemporary information about this sarcophagus. The biographical inscriptions of Weny, one of the great

---

[5] Maspero, in *Recueil de travaux*, IX, 177–91.

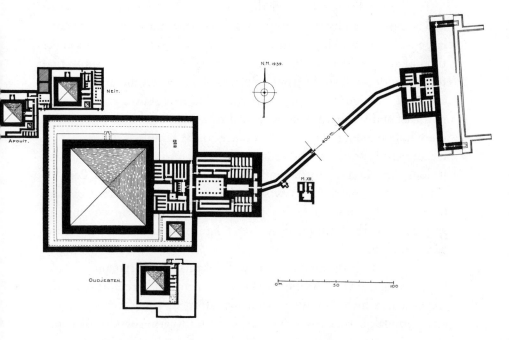

106. *The pyramid complex of Pepi II. (After Jéquier.)*

nobles of the Sixth Dynasty, relate that he had been dispatched to Ibhet, near Aswan, to fetch stone for its manufacture, as well as for the pyramidion (the piece at the top) and the false door. He made a second expedition to the quarries of Hatnub in Middle Egypt in order to bring alabaster for the offering tables in the king's pyramid complex.[6]

THE PYRAMID OF PEPI II

The pyramid complex of Pepi II was thoroughly excavated and recorded by Jéquier in 1926–36 for the Antiquities Department.[7] His careful research revealed a fairly well-preserved pyramid complex in a late, highly developed form (Fig. 106). Although many of the monuments comprising it are ruined, the complex is still well enough preserved to permit actual as well as theoretical reconstruction.

[6] "Inscription of Weny," lines 38–44.

[7] For the publication on this pyramid, see G. Jéquier, *Le Monument funéraires de Pepi II* (3 vols.; Cairo, 1936–40).

The Valley Temple lies near the edge of the cultivation. It faces east and is approached by two ramps at the northern and southern ends of a large platform, which probably served as a landing stage for boats in the time of the inundation. Enough remains of the temple to show that the masonry platform in front of it was bordered on the north, south, and west by high, thick masonry walls. Narrow staircases within the northern and southern walls ascended to a parapet, which surrounded the whole building. The main entrance to the temple is in the eastern façade, a little north of dead center, and opens into a hypostyle hall with its long axis running north-south. It is interesting to note that Pepi reverted to the Fourth Dynasty style, for the roof is supported by rectangular pillars instead of the palmiform or papyriform columns in vogue during the Fifth Dynasty. (Rectangular pillars also appear in the Mortuary Temple.)

Although little of the limestone walls of this temple remain in place, Jéquier found several of the blocks from them, and reconstructed the scenes with which they were originally adorned. These were generally conventional. It is noteworthy that in the transverse corridor of Pepi's Valley Temple, sculptors repeated the scene of the slaying of the Libyans which had earlier appeared in Sahure's pyramid complex. They even copied the names of the Libyan chief and his family.

The causeway ascends the plateau in a southwesterly direction and forms at least two angles in its course. There is a small entrance near the final angle at the western end, to allow priests to enter the Mortuary Temple without walking all the way from the Valley Temple up the causeway. This entrance is furnished with a porter's lodge. The causeway is badly ruined, but, here too, Jéquier found enough blocks from the walls to reconstruct the fine bas-reliefs that once adorned them.

The causeway meets the Mortuary Temple in the center of its eastern façade. The narrow entrance to the temple opens into a transverse corridor, at the northern and southern ends of which are small rooms, each with a staircase leading up to the temple roof. Beyond is the usual corridor, flanked on each side by storerooms, and then the central court with seven more rooms on each side.

So far the Mortuary Temple of Pepi II does not deviate very much from what we have seen of its predecessors, although it has smaller chambers and storerooms. However, the foregoing parts of the temple are separated from the rest by the temenos wall of the pyramid inclosure. A door in the center of the court's far wall—actually the eastern temenos wall of the pyramid—opens on a transverse corridor, each end of which leads into the pyramid inclosure. A short flight of steps in the center of the far wall of this corridor leads to a room containing the five niches. These niches had double wooden doors, and one of them contains remains of the pedestal of a limestone statue. The sanctuary is reached through a narrow antechamber and an almost square vestibule with a single large column. The three rooms were decorated with reliefs, those of the sanctuary appropriately including scenes of the slaughter of sacrificial animals.

As the plan indicates, the temple contained many rooms, and although the pyramid itself was of relatively poor construction, the temple and its reliefs were carefully executed. The pyramid complex served as the model for that of Senusert I of the Twelfth Dynasty.

The Subsidiary Pyramid of Pepi II follows the later tradition in its location south of the inner part of the Mortuary Temple, close to the southeastern face of the main pyramid.

Pepi's pyramid is built of small blocks of coarse local limestone, but its construction is somewhat better than average for the period. Some of the large casing blocks of white limestone are still in place on the western side. The pyramid originally stood 52 meters high and 76 meters square, with an angle of about 53°.

The entrance is at ground level on the northern side. There are traces of the small offering chapel which stood against this entrance, but it was dismantled at a later stage of building and the decorated stones of its walls re-used. In internal structure, the pyramid closely resembles that of Pepi I. All the passages and chambers of the pyramid were cut in the natural rock of the plateau. The passage, 16 meters long, descends at an angle of 25°. About midway down its length was a portcullis, the granite fitting for which is still in place, although the stone itself has been displaced. The vestibule at the end has stars on the ceiling and selections from the Pyramid Texts inscribed on the walls. It contained remains of alabaster jars, as well as a gold implement which may have been used in one of the funeral ceremonies. Beyond the vestibule is a horizontal passage about 38 meters long. It was blocked by three granite portcullises, operated vertically, and ended in an antechamber. The pointed roof of the latter is decorated with stars and the walls are inscribed with Pyramid Texts, which unfortunately are not as completely preserved as those in the rest of the pyramid.

From the western end of the antechamber a short passage leads to a large, very fine burial chamber. It, too, has a pointed, star-spangled roof and walls (except for those surrounding the sarcophagus) inscribed with the Pyramid Texts. In the western end of the room is a magnificent sarcophagus of polished black granite, on one side of which an inscription records the titles and name of the king. The surrounding walls are decorated in the "palace-façade" style. The lid of the canopic chest was also found here.

One curious feature of this pyramid requires comment. In addition to the usual temenos wall inclosing the courtyard and the inner part of the Mortuary Temple, there was a high, thick girdle wall against the pyramid itself, interrupted only by the Mortuary Temple on the east. We can see that this girdle wall was an afterthought and not part of the original plan, because it was built against the lower courses of the pyramid casing, and the builders had to dismantle the northern offering chapel to make room for it. It has been suggested that the wall may have been built to add stability to the pyramid, which is said to have been shaken in an earthquake.[8]

Attached to the pyramid complex of Pepi II are the pyramids of three of his queens—Neit, Iput II, and Wedjebten—the first two north of the king's pyramid and the last south of it. They are similar in construction, and all are inscribed on the interior with the Pyramid Texts. We may discuss as an example the best preserved, that of Queen Neit.[9]

THE PYRAMID OF QUEEN NEIT

The pyramid complex of Queen Neit lies exactly opposite the northwestern corner of the pyramid of Pepi II and is inclosed by a rectangular temenos wall. The main entrance, in the eastern corner of the southern

[8] I. E. S. Edwards, *The Pyramids of Egypt*, p. 163.

[9] For the publication on this pyramid and those of the other queens of Pepi II, see Jéquier, *Les Pyramides des reines Neit et Apouit* (Cairo, 1933); *La Pyramide d'Oudjebten* (Cairo, 1928).

temenos wall, is reached through a narrow passage lying between this wall and the northern temenos of the complex of Pepi II.

The vestibule walls of Neit's Mortuary Temple were decorated with reliefs; those remaining show several throne daises adorned with lions. Beyond the vestibule, to the north, is a colonnaded hall with a portico extending along the southern, western, and northern sides. It was supported by nine square limestone pillars, three of which remain. To the north are five storerooms and beyond them a doorway into the inner temple. Here a rectangular cult chamber is followed by three niches. Behind these is a narrow, doorless room, which doubtless served as a statue chamber.

South of the niches lies the sanctuary. Its western wall was once occupied by a large false door, before which stood a high offering table, perhaps of alabaster. This has disappeared, but a flight of three monolithic steps leading up to it remains, as does a large stone bench trimmed with a cavetto cornice. This served as a kind of sideboard from which the officiating priest took offerings one by one to place upon the offering table when performing the rites of the funerary cult. South of the sanctuary is another room with a doorway leading to the court of the queen's pyramid and that of her Subsidiary Pyramid. The latter, 5.25 meters square, is in a good state of preservation and retains much of its original casing. The descending passage, opening from the north, is very narrow. The debris covering the floor of this Subsidiary Pyramid yielded pottery vessels as well as fragments of alabaster inscribed with the offering formula and the name of Queen Neit. Excavators found several wooden model boats in the space between the Subsidiary Pyramid and the queen's pyramid.

Queen Neit's pyramid is about 21 meters square and now only about 4 meters high. Much of its casing remains in place, and from it we can determine its angle as 60°. The entrance, in the center of the northern face, was concealed by a false door and an offering table, both of which stood in a small chapel. The passage leads down at an angle of 25° to a vestibule. At its far end is a portcullis, part of which still remains in place. The walls of the antechamber beyond this are inscribed with the Pyramid Texts. The antechamber leads straight into the burial chamber. Here the flat roof is decorated with stars; Pyramid Text inscriptions cover all the walls except that behind the sarcophagus, which is carved to represent the palace façade. The room contained a granite sarcophagus and a granite canopic chest with hollows in the base to receive the four canopic jars. The ceiling decoration and wall inscriptions are very crudely executed, compared to those of the pyramid of Pepi II or even with the ones in Neit's Mortuary Temple.

Pepi II came to the throne at the age of ten. From the beginning of his reign he was surrounded by officials who governed the country in his name. Unfortunately for Egypt, he lived to a great age; his reign of over ninety years was the longest in history. During the last decades of this period, misgovernment reached its zenith, and those who surrounded the king thought only of how they could profit from the situation. Peasants were robbed of their property and heavily taxed. Canals were neglected, and the fields no longer yielded their usual crops. Soldiers had become a source of terror to the civilian population. From the papyri of Ipuwer and Neferty, preserved in Leiden and Leningrad, we know that advisers tried to open the ruler's eyes to the facts. During their years of misery, the people looked impatiently to their gods and implored their help and protection, but finally lost confidence in divine aid. When the great revolt came, the people spared neither palace nor temple, avenging themselves equally upon ruler and gods.

During this period in Egyptian history, no power could stop the people from robbing tombs of gold and valuables. The pyramids were great landmarks and were known to contain the bodies of dead rulers surrounded by treasures of gold and jewelry; there is hardly any doubt that the majority of the pyramids were robbed at this time of great confusion. A papyrus describes the situation thus:

The southern ship [Upper Egypt] is adrift. The towns are destroyed, and Upper Egypt has become an empty waste. The Red Land [desert and foreign land] is spread abroad throughout the country. Nomes are destroyed. The stranger people from without come into Egypt. Gold and jewels are hung about the necks of slave-girls, but noble ladies walk through the land, and mistresses of houses say, "Would that we might have something that we might eat." The children of princes, men dash them against the walls. The children that have been earnestly desired, they are laid upon the high ground.

The hot-headed man saith, "If I knew where God is, then I would make offering to Him!" Grain hath perished everywhere. People are stripped of clothing, perfume and oil. Everyone saith, "There is no more." The store-house is bare, and he who kept it is stretched out upon the ground. Behold, he that was buried as a hawk [the king] lieth on a bier. What the pyramid hid will become empty. It is come to this, that the land is despoiled of the kingship by a few senseless people. They that possessed clothes are now in rags. He who wove not for himself now possesseth fine linen. The poor of the land have become rich; he that possessed something is one that hath nothing. He that had no bread now possesseth a barn; but that wherewith his store-house is provided is the property of another. No office is any longer in its right place; they are a frightened land without a herdsman. The land is diminished and its governors are multiplied. The field is bare and its imposts are great; little is the grain and great is the grain measure, and it is measured to overflowing.[10]

This period of anarchy after the fall of the Sixth Dynasty is called the First Intermediate Period, and includes the Seventh, Eighth, and Ninth Dynasties. Representatives of several great families assumed the traditional title of King of Upper and Lower Egypt, but it was an empty honor. Several families ruled in the south, others in Middle Egypt, and still others in the Delta. It is remarkable that several of these rulers built pyramids, the traditional tombs of the great kings. Most of them, however, did not reign long enough or lacked the power and means to attempt such enterprises.

One of the most powerful of these petty kingships, that of Heracle-opolis (in the modern Beni Suef Province of Middle Egypt), is known to us as the Ninth and Tenth Dynasties. It gradually annexed the neighboring territories and maintained a flourishing court. The cemeteries of this period have been found at the edge of the desert, but the tombs of the kings have not yet been located. We cannot say whether they built pyramids or were content with ordinary tombs.

Some of the pyramids of the First Intermediate Period have been identified. Others are known to us only from contemporary inscriptions, which record the priests and officials attached to them. The actual buildings have seemingly disappeared, although it is unlikely that they were totally destroyed without leaving a single trace. Probably they are

[10] For this translation and similar works, see Erman, *The Literature of the Ancient Egyptians* (trans. Blackman).

either among the unidentified pyramids or still await the day when the excavator's spade will reveal their secrets.

One of these "missing" pyramids is mentioned on the false door of Queen Ankhnes-Pepi, which Jéquier found near the pyramid of Pepi II at Saqqara. The inscription mentions a pyramid called *Ded-ankh-Nefer-kare*. Queen Ankhnes-Pepi was a wife of Pepi II, and the inscription says that she was the mother of King Neferkare. Jéquier suggests that the title "Mother of the King" may be understood as "Grandmother," and that the Neferkare in question may be one of the kings of that name of the Seventh or Eighth Dynasty. He searched in vain around the pyramid complex of Pepi II in the hope of finding this pyramid, and concluded that the king's reign had been short and his monument left unfinished. This may be true, but it is equally possible that the structure may lie only a few meters away from the very place where Jéquier stopped work.

Another undiscovered pyramid which was certainly completed, used for burial, and maintained by its own priests and officials, was that of King Merikare. It probably stands near Teti's pyramid at Saqqara, as this is the region whence came the monuments of its priests and officials. Firth and Gunn suggest that this may be the small pyramid lying south of Teti's Mortuary Temple, the blocks of which appear to have been taken from an earlier pyramid.[11] This suggestion is not valid, however, as the situation, plan, and general construction of the pyramid in question prove it to be the Subsidiary Pyramid of Teti's pyramid complex. On the northern side of Teti's pyramid, however, there is a heap of quarry rubbish which contains blocks of white limestone pyramid casing and a shaft, 40 meters deep, ending in water. Even the workmen's huts, as well as their grain bins, have survived. The quarry debris indicates a demolished monument, but the shaft may be only a well. So the "Mystery of Merikare" remains unsolved.

The Sixth Dynasty was followed by a Seventh, but the anarchy which prevailed in the whole land seems to have found its way into the ancient records. Manetho says in his history that the Seventh Dynasty had seventy rulers, who reigned in succession or together for seventy days. This is no doubt incredible, but it reflects the attitudes of later historians to-

[11] Firth and Gunn, *The Teti Pyramid Cemeteries,* I, 8.

ward this period. Under such circumstances we cannot expect the rulers to have built pyramids. Many of the names of the Seventh Dynasty kings have come down to us, but none is connected with any pyramid or important monument.

The rulers of the Eighth Dynasty which followed tried to restore order, but none of them had power over the whole land, although they ruled from Memphis and assumed the title of King of Upper and Lower Egypt. Some of them did build pyramids, and two have been found in the Memphite necropolis.

THE PYRAMID OF IBY

The pyramid of King Iby, dating from the Eighth Dynasty, lies southwest of the Valley Temple of Pepi II at Saqqara South (Fig. 107). Apparently it had no Valley Temple or causeway, and its Mortuary Temple, on the east side as usual, is a meager structure of mud brick.[12] The temple entrance on the north gave on a vestibule, behind which were a fairly large chamber, an antechamber on the southwest, and

[12] Jéquier, *La Pyramide d'Aba* (Cairo, 1935).

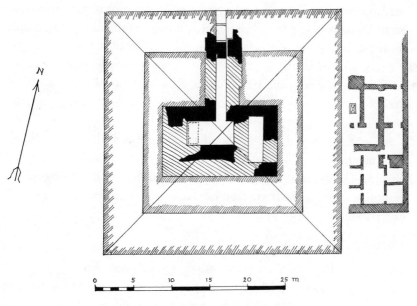

107. *The plan of the pyramid and temple of Iby at Saqqara South. (After Jéquier.)*

finally the sanctuary. A limestone libation basin is set in the floor of this room near the base of a false door. Excavators also found here a fine, round offering table supported on a low pedestal. Jéquier, who excavated this pyramid in 1930, felt that this brick chapel was only a temporary structure.

Iby's pyramid now measures about 21 meters square, but was originally about 31.5 meters square. Its height cannot be determined with certainty, but Jéquier, judging from its general appearance, believed that it had approximately the same dimensions as the pyramid of Queen Neit.

The core of the pyramid seems to have been constructed as one mass rather than in accretions. It was built of small limestone blocks set with mortar made from Nile mud. This shoddy construction was faced with a double casing of white limestone 5 meters thick. All of the superstructure has disappeared, except for the foundation.

The entrance, approximately in the center of the northern face, opens on a passage which descends at an angle of 25° and leads directly into the burial chamber. (This plan, with the absence of a vestibule, antechamber, and horizontal passage, is reminiscent of the queens' pyramids of the Sixth Dynasty.) The burial chamber is almost totally destroyed, but the ruins yielded many of the limestone blocks that lined the walls. They are inscribed with the Pyramid Texts, and are of special interest as a reflection of the religious beliefs of the First Intermediate Period. While the texts duplicate some earlier inscriptions, they also contain much that is new.

Near this pyramid Jéquier found several stelae of the Ramesside period, most of them in excellent condition. They belonged to persons of the same family, or at least the same social group. It is interesting to note that most of them either are surmounted by a pyramid or have the form of an obelisk.

THE PYRAMID OF KHUI

The pyramids of the First Intermediate Period were built in the provinces, as well as in the Memphis necropolis. One example, ascribed to King Khui, stands at Dara in the Libyan Desert opposite Manfalut. The pyramid was excavated in 1911 by Ahmed Kamal, who did not recog-

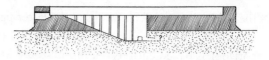

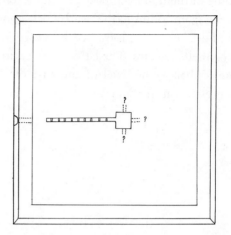

108. *Plan and section of the
pyramid of Khui.*

nize its true significance and referred to it as a royal mastaba, despite the
fact that it is square rather than rectangular. A block found in a brick
tomb south of the pyramid showed part of an offering scene and a
cartouche with the name of King Khui. This fragment, which may possibly have come from the Mortuary Temple of the pyramid, led Kamal
to attribute the pyramid to Khui.

Although constructed of mud brick, this pyramid is relatively large.
In its present dilapidated state, each side measures 130 meters, with a
height of only 4 meters (Fig. 108).[13] The entrance, which has a curved
roof, is on the north. A passage 2.45 meters wide descends with a gentle
slope for 6 meters and then runs horizontally for another 3 meters. Here
it narrows to 1.75 meters and again descends for 48.4 meters, after which
it continues horizontally for a final 12 meters until it meets the door of

[13] Ahmed Kamal, in *Annales du Service*, XII (1912), 128 ff.; R. Weill, "Fouilles à
Dara (Moyenne Égypte), campagne de 1947–1948," *Comptes Rendus* (Académie des
inscriptions et belles-lettres, Paris, 1948), pp. 177–80; R. Weill, "Dara (Moyenne Égypte,
Markaz de Manfalout)," *Chronique d'Égypte*, XXIII (1948), 37–45; R. Weill, "Dara
campagne de 1947–1948," *Chronique d'Égypte*, XXIV (1949), 35–48; J. Vercoutter,
"Dara: Mission française 1950–1951," *Chronique d'Égypte*, XXVII (1952), 98–111; R.
Weill, *Dara: Campagnes de 1946–1948* (Cairo, 1958).

the burial chamber. The walls in the latter part of the passage have but-
tresses, or pilasters, which Kamal thought were for added strength. The
corridor is paved entirely with limestone, some of it from tombs of an
earlier period. Judging by their style and the personal names found on
some of them, they appear to belong to the Sixth Dynasty and to have
come from tombs in the nearby necropolis. The limestone doorway to
the burial chamber is framed by a torus molding and opens into a room
2.94 meters square. The latter, built entirely of limestone, is situated 8.8
meters below the level of the base of the pyramid and has a square
depression in the floor for a canopic chest.

II

The Revival

During the Ninth and Tenth Dynasties, when Heracleopolis ruled Middle Egypt, another ambitious dynasty had arisen at Thebes. The two rivals clashed and, after several minor wars, the Thebans won. The princes of the Eleventh Dynasty of Thebes united the land, and Egypt entered one of her most glorious periods, known as the Middle Kingdom. The names of five Mentuhoteps are known to us among the rulers of the Eleventh Dynasty, which began about 2134 B.C. and ended around 1991 B.C.

The earlier princes of the Theban family had built their tombs, each surmounted by a small pyramid, at the foot of the Theban cliffs, on a site now known as El Tarif. When all Egypt recognized the Theban Dynasty, however, and the kings became the sole rulers of the land, a new form of royal tomb developed; it is represented by a sole surviving example at Deir el-Bahri.

When the days of the Eleventh Dynasty came to an end and a new house ruled the land as the Twelfth Dynasty, its rulers left Thebes to build a new residence. These kings did not follow the design of the royal tombs adopted by their predecessors, but built true pyramids like those of the Old Kingdom which stood near their new capital. These pyramids and their temples were influenced, however, by those of the Eleventh Dynasty.

109. *A reconstruction of the temple-pyramid of Nebhepetre-Mentuhotep.*

THE TEMPLE-PYRAMID OF NEBHEPETRE-MENTUHOTEP

The vast tomb of King Nebhepetre-Mentuhotep of the Eleventh Dynasty was cut in the rock of Deir el-Bahri and surmounted by a temple which included a pyramid (Fig. 109).[1] This unusual monument presents a striking architectural effect, and speaks eloquently for the ability of the unknown architect who designed it in complete harmony with the surrounding landscape. Undoubtedly the setting, with the desert and the towering cliffs of Deir el-Bahri as a background, influenced the design. On the top of the western cliffs stands a curiously formed natural

[1] This building was excavated in 1903–7 on behalf of the Egypt Exploration Fund by Naville (*The XIth Dynasty Temple at Deir el Bahari* [3 vols.; London, 1907–13]), and subsequently by H. E. Winlock for the Metropolitan Museum of Art in New York (*Bulletin of the Metropolitan Museum of Art* [December, 1922], pp. 21 ff., and subsequent numbers of the same journal).

pyramid, called "El Ḳarn" (the horn) in Arabic. It was known to the ancient Egyptians as the "Holy Mountain" or "Peak of the West," and was sacred to the goddess Mertseger, "She who loves silence."

The funerary monument was approached through a Valley Temple on the edge of the cultivation along an open causeway that ran westward for 1,200 meters. Statues of the king as the god Osiris were set against the walls of the causeway at 10-meter intervals. The western end of the causeway terminated in a large courtyard bounded on the north, south, and east by high walls, and on the west by the raised platform of the temple-pyramid.

In the courtyard were a number of sunken circular pits, where tamarisk trees were once planted. Flanking both sides of the ramp at the end of the causeway was a row of four sycamores. In the cool shade of each sycamore tree rested a seated statue of the king and a small altar for offerings.

The building is basically a large T-shaped platform cut from the solid rock, with the crosspiece on the east and the upright running back to a cutting in the western cliffs. The base of the platform was faced with fine limestone and decorated with reliefs depicting the king's prowess in war. The reliefs were protected by a colonnade upheld by two rows of square pillars.

In the center of the raised platform rose a great rectangular pedestal, or podium, on top of which stood the pyramid, a solid structure of masonry without passages or chambers. The pedestal was masked by a covered building supported on all sides by square pillars. Surrounding this building, in turn, was a covered colonnade, open on the outside, with three rows of octagonal pillars on the front and sides and two rows at the back. On the shaft of the T stood a square building, behind which was a colonnaded court. (Here, in the center of the courtyard floor, was the concealed opening of the tomb.) To the rear was a hypostyle hall, its roof upheld by eighty octagonal pillars. The western end of this hall reached the face of the cliff, where a niche was excavated to contain a statue of the king.

Apparently the original design for this amazing building had been more modest. Builders had completed six burial shafts and chapels for ladies of the royal household just west of the podium, and the women had actually been buried there. But when the plan was changed and the temple-pyramid extended farther west, the wall separating the pyramid from the court covered the reliefs on the women's chapels, and the pavement effectively hid the shafts—a situation which contributed to their safety. From the tombs of several of these royal ladies came the wonderful limestone sarcophagi with vivid reliefs that can now be seen in the Cairo Museum.

The passage leading to the king's burial chamber descended westward and ended far away under the cliff in a granite-lined room. Here stood a shrine built of granite and alabaster, which must have contained the mummy of the king, resting in a painted wooden coffin. When excavators opened the shrine, they found no trace of the king's body or of the coffin; the room contained only two small wooden model boats, several bows, a few broken scepters, and several funerary cones (conical objects inscribed with the king's names and titles).

Near the southeastern corner of the great court, in front of the temple-pyramid, lies a false burial of King Nebhepetre-Mentuhotep. This apparently corresponds to the Southern Tomb of Zoser and the Subsidiary Pyramids of the Old Kingdom pyramids. The discovery of this burial was remarkable. In 1900, Howard Carter, then Inspector-General of the Antiquities Department, was riding over the plain of Deir el-Bahri near Mentuhotep's temple-pyramid when the ground gave way beneath his horse's feet. On examining the hole, Carter noticed traces of masonry and concluded that it must be the opening of a tomb. He decided to excavate, and after a little while found that it was indeed an entrance passage, the door of which proved to have its original mud-brick sealing intact. The "tomb" proved to contain a large statue of the king in painted limestone and the remains of funerary equipment, but no burial. The statue was wrapped in many folds of linen and placed on its side—in other words, treated as a substitute for the actual mummy.[2]

Another find in connection with this pyramid complex was even more dramatic. In the spring of 1923 the expedition of the Metropolitan Museum discovered a tomb with a burial chamber under the king's

[2] H. Carter, *Report on the Tomb of Menthuhotep I*, in *Annales du Service*, II (1901), 201–5.

temple. It had obviously been prepared for members of the royal family or high officials of the court, but it contained the bodies of sixty men, all prepared for burial in the simplest manner possible. Examination proved that they were soldiers slain in battle, many of them with arrows in their wounds. These must have been some of the king's troops slain in a battle of supreme importance. Perhaps it was the decisive battle against the Heracleopolitans which gave Nebhepetre-Mentuhotep the mastery of all Egypt. The simple wrappings prove that these were common soldiers rather than officers. The king so honored their supreme sacrifice that he ordered their burial in the precincts of his own temple-pyramid, so that they might share in his future life.[3]

Mentuhotep's architect took as his model the Peak of the West, but there is little doubt that Senmut, the great architect of Queen Hatshepsut, took Mentuhotep's monument as the model for the beautiful temple he built for his royal mistress. Unfortunately, he seems to have used the older monument not only as a model but also as a quarry, and thus all that remains today are the rock foundations, fragments of the many columns of the portico and hypostyle hall, and the base of the pyramid.

We should remember that Mentuhotep's pyramid was part of his great temple and, unlike earlier pyramids, not a structure used as a tomb with chambers and passages within or below it.

The dynasty of the Mentuhoteps was replaced about 1991 B.C. by the new royal house of the Twelfth Dynasty, whose kings were named Amenemhet and Senusert. This family, which was of southern origin on one side, must have had a strong influence in Thebes. It is possible that the first king, Amenemhet I, previously held the office of vizier under the last of the Mentuhoteps, but we do not yet know how the change in the dynasty came about.

The kings of the new dynasty were powerful, capable, and farsighted. Sensing that the seat of government had to be at the apex of the Delta, where the "Two Lands" meet, they transferred their capital to a new site a few miles southwest of Memphis, which they named Ithtawi.

[3] H. E. Winlock, *Bulletin of the Metropolitan Museum of Art*, February, 1928, pp. 12–16.

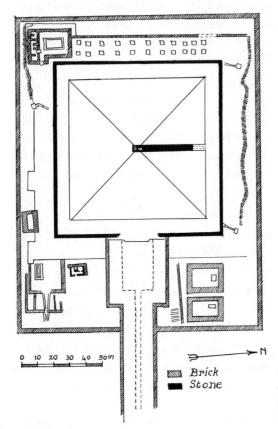

0 10 20 30 40 50 m
→ N

////// Brick
■■■■ Stone

110. *Plan of the pyramid of*
Amenemhet I at Lisht.
(Bulletin of the Metropolitan
Museum of Art, New York,
December, 1922, p. 5.)

They built their palace in a site commanding not only the Nile Valley
but also the Faiyum. The latter was largely an area of undrained swamp
bordering Lake Moeris until the new royal family energetically transformed it into one of the most fertile areas in Egypt by means of vast
irrigation works and drainage systems.

The Amenemhets and Senuserts of the Twelfth Dynasty also abandoned the southern necropolis at western Thebes and built their tombs,
in the ancient pyramidal form, either on the eastern or western edge of
the strip of desert which separates the Nile Valley from the Faiyum.
Thus their pyramids are either in the vicinity of the mighty monuments
of Sneferu at Dahshur or on the edge of the Faiyum Basin.

THE PYRAMID OF AMENEMHET I

The pyramid complex of the first ruler of the Twelfth Dynasty, at Lisht, presents several interesting features.[4] While following the main principles of the Old Kingdom royal burials, it seems to have been influenced by Mentuhotep's temple-pyramid at Deir el-Bahri. Thus we have a complex, built upon the rising ground with its buildings at two different levels, which incorporates the tombs of members of the royal family and of favored courtiers. The pyramid complex was excavated in part by the Egyptian Expedition of the New York Metropolitan Museum of Art.

The Valley Temple of Amenemhet I has not been discovered, but there must have been one, because excavators have found parts of the causeway leading to it. A pit near the latter revealed a remarkable limestone head from a royal statue, now in the Metropolitan Museum.

The ruins of the Mortuary Temple may still be seen against the eastern side of the pyramid (Fig. 110). It was on a lower level than the base of the pyramid itself, although the builders apparently planned at first to have the two buildings on the same plane. After they changed the plan, they used blocks from the original building in constructing the new temple. In both the original and later plans, the temple stood inside the temenos wall of the pyramid complex.

The temple itself, of which little remains beyond the pavement and some scattered blocks, was decorated with reliefs clearly copied from those of the Old Kingdom. As in the Old Kingdom, the ceiling was ornamented with stars. Foundation deposits found under the pavement consisted of six bricks, each containing a plaque bearing the name of the king and of his pyramid. There were two plaques each of copper, limestone, and faience. Other deposits included an ox skull, alabaster vases, and red pottery dishes, broken perhaps intentionally. The name on the plaques is "The Abodes of Sehetepibre are shining," although on other monuments the name of the pyramid is "Lofty is the Goodness of Amenemhet." Hayes suggests that the first name might be that of the

[4] This pyramid, as well as that of Senusert I at the same site, was excavated under the direction of A. M. Lythgoe, A. C. Mace, H. E. Winlock, and A. Lansing. Preliminary reports were published in the issues of and supplements to the *Bulletin of the Metropolitan Museum of Art*, beginning in 1907.

pyramid or its capstone, and the second that of the Mortuary Temple or
the pyramid district.[5] This is not in accordance with our knowledge of
the earlier pyramids, where the name of the pyramid is identical on
every part of its complex, including the queen's pyramid and the rest of
the royal necropolis. It may be that the name of Amenemhet's pyramid
was changed.

Among the blocks found at the site were two false doors, one of limestone and the other of granite; both are inscribed with the titulary and
names of Amenemhet I. The granite false door probably came from an
offering chapel which originally existed in front of the entrance to the
pyramid at the north side. With the limestone false door was found a
fine granite offering table, its sides decorated with a procession of figures
personifying the nomes of Egypt.

North of the temple are the remains of a construction ramp and two
private tombs which formed part of the original design. The westernmost of these mastabas has subsidiary burial chambers arranged in a
most unusual manner: at intervals down the 16-meter shaft are three
groups of burial chambers. Each group has six rooms placed in a star-
shaped pattern; the main burial was reached through a sloping passage
which is now flooded.

South of the temple is the tomb of the Vizier Antefoker and a most
interesting mastaba, or Subsidiary Pyramid. West of the pyramid, within the temenos wall, is a group of burials belonging to members of the
royal family and their dependents.

The pyramid of Amenemhet I has been aptly described as a museum
of Old Kingdom art, for its core masonry, as well as the pavement surrounding it, includes sculptured blocks taken from the Old Kingdom
monuments of Giza and Saqqara. Some of these blocks are thought to
have been taken from the Valley Temples of Khufu and Khafre. Little
remains of the fine white limestone casing.

At present the pyramid is about 20 meters high. It was originally 84
meters square and 58 meters high with a slope of approximately 54°.
Under the southwestern corner was a foundation deposit, which consisted of articles similar to those found near the Mortuary Temple. The
entrance is in the northern side, as in the Old Kingdom pyramids, and

[5] W. C. Hayes, *The Scepter of Egypt*, Part I, p. 175.

was lined with great slabs of granite, which remain *in situ*. Inside, the passage slopes gently down to an upper room, in the floor of which is a vertical shaft to the burial chamber. Unfortunately this room is now below the level of the subsoil water, and is permanently flooded.

In view of the fact that this pyramid contains inscribed stones dating from the Old Kingdom, I am convinced that more would be gained by dismantling it than by leaving it in its present state. The blocks from temples and tombs of preceding dynasties would be a mine of valuable information for scholars. Dismantling the pyramid would also tell us much about how it was constructed.

THE PYRAMID OF SENUSERT I

During the last ten years of the reign of Amenemhet I, Senusert I acted as co-regent with his father. Evidently an attempt had been made to murder the king, and he found it prudent to shift a great part of the burden and responsibility of government to his eldest son, who was chosen to inherit the throne. We do not know much about Senusert I during these early years, but from a famous papyrus called the "Story of Sinuhe," we learn that during his co-regency the prince was active in restoring order at the frontiers of his realm. When the news of his father's death reached him, he was encamped with his army in the Western Desert. He gave orders that the news should be suppressed and sped by night to reach the capital, where in due time he was proclaimed the ruler.

Senusert I was an able and energetic ruler who continued to increase the power of Egypt. In his days Egyptian influence penetrated to the countries lying east and west of the Nile Valley, as well as to the islands of the Mediterranean. Senusert ruled forty-five years—ten years as co-regent with his father, Amenemhet I, and three years in co-regency with his son, Amenemhet II. He was buried in the pyramid he had built beside that of his father at Lisht.

The pyramid complex of Senusert I lies south of that of Amenemhet I. No Valley Temple has been found, but the presence of a causeway makes its existence a certainty. The causeway was built of fine white limestone. The lower parts of the walls were painted to imitate red granite while the upper parts were adorned with colored reliefs, frag-

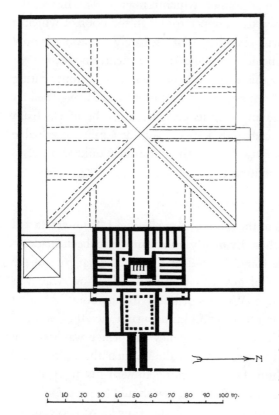

111. *Plan of the pyramid of Senusert I at Lisht. (Excavations of the Metropolitan Museum of Art, New York.)*

ments of which show fishing scenes and groups of foreign war prisoners. Niches 10 meters apart held Osiris statues of the king, possibly copied from the causeway of Mentuhotep at Deir el-Bahri.

The Mortuary Temple is preserved well enough to reveal its plan and is similar to the Mortuary Temples of the late Old Kingdom (Fig. 108). Its walls were decorated with colored reliefs, many of which are now in the Cairo Museum. The temple, like that of Amenemhet I, contained a granite offering table decorated with figures symbolizing the nomes of Egypt.

A curious find came to light in the corner immediately north of the temple at the eastern face of the pyramid. Here, in a depression in the ground, were found ten life-size limestone statues of Senusert I, now in the Cairo Museum. They show the king seated on a throne, clad in the royal kilt and the *nemes* headdress. They are in excellent condition, but it is difficult to determine their original position in the temple.

South of the temple is a small Subsidiary Pyramid surrounded by its own temenos wall. This pyramid had two layers of casing, some of which still remains in place on the western side.

The pyramid originally measured 61 meters high and 105 meters square, with an angle of about 49°. The remarkable core construction consists of eight massive stone walls, running from the center to each corner and the middle of each side, and four pairs of shorter, but equally strong, walls that branch off the main ones near the corners (Fig. 111). These walls formed a series of irregularly shaped rooms, with outer walls of fine white limestone. The chambers were filled in with a mass of rubble and sand. Near the southwestern corner was a foundation deposit consisting of plaques, pottery, and the head of an ox. The plaques give the name of the pyramid as "Senusert Surveys the Two Lands." Other records, including the Story of Sinuhe[6] and an endowment stela found at Memphis,[7] give the name as "Protected are the Places of Senusert." Therefore, as with the pyramid of Amenemhet II, there are two names for one pyramid.

In the center of the northern face of the main pyramid was a small offering chapel covering the entrance, which is still accessible. The descending passage is lined and roofed with finely dressed slabs of red granite. It slopes to the burial chamber—now inaccessible because of subsoil water.

An interesting feature of this pyramid complex is the presence of two temenos walls. The outer wall, of mud brick, inclosed the nine pyramids of the royal ladies. Each of these small pyramids is built of coarse limestone, with a casing of fine limestone. Each has its Mortuary Temple on the east, a small offering chapel over its northern entrance, and its own temenos wall. As in Old Kingdom complexes, the angle of these pyramids is steeper than that of the king's.

The inner temenos wall, built of fine white limestone, inclosed the inner part of the Mortuary Temple and the king's pyramid. It originally stood about 5 meters high and had relief panels 5 meters apart. (Some of

[6] A. H. Gardiner, *Notes on the Story of Sinuhe*, p. 9, n. 2.

[7] W. M. F. Petrie, *Memphis*, Vol. I, Plate V.

these have been set up in the Cairo and Metropolitan museums, but the bases of many remain in place on the southern and western sides of the pyramid.)

An interesting description of this pyramid complex occurs on the stela of a certain Mereri, who was involved in its construction. It reads: "The King ordered me to execute for him an eternal seat, greater in name than Rostaw [Giza] and more excellent in appointments than any place in the excellent district of the Gods. Its columns pierced heaven; the lake which was dug reached the river; the gates, towering heavenward, were of limestone of Troja [Tura]. Osiris, First of the Westerners, rejoiced over all the monuments of my Lord. I myself rejoiced, and my heart was glad at that which I had executed."[8]

THE PYRAMID OF KING AMENEMHET II

Senusert's successor, Amenemhet II, abandoned Lisht as a royal cemetery, and instead built his pyramid southeast of the Northern Pyramid of Sneferu at Dahshur, nearer the edge of the plateau.

The Valley Temple has not yet been discovered, but a causeway 800 meters long extends from the edge of the cultivation directly westward to the pyramid. The Mortuary Temple is ruined, but fragments of inscribed and sculptured limestone found there bear the name of Amenemhet II and served to identify the owner of the monument.

The pyramid itself was thoroughly plundered in ancient times, and is now so ruined that its exact dimensions are not clear, although it seems to have been about 50 meters square. De Morgan excavated it in 1894–95, and reached the interior.[9] He found that the core was divided by several walls into square and diagonal compartments, which were filled with sand. Not a single casing stone was found, so it is quite impossible to determine the angle of the slope.

The entrance, now inaccessible, is in the northern side, following the usual tradition. It opens into a sloping passage which descends to a horizontal gallery closed by two portcullises, one operated vertically and the other transversely. The gallery leads to the burial chamber, at the western side of which is a sandstone sarcophagus sunk in the floor.

[8] J. H. Breasted, *Ancient Records*, Vol. I, par. 509.
[9] J. de Morgan, *Fouilles à Dahchour en 1894–1895*.

Immediately west of the pyramid, inclosed within the temenos wall, are the tombs of the queen and four of the princesses.

About 125 meters southeast of the pyramid of Amenemhet II is a square mass of white limestone rubble, from which a causeway runs eastward to the cultivation. This is without doubt the remains of a destroyed pyramid. A thorough examination would certainly uncover the substructure and might possibly reveal the identity of its builder.

THE PYRAMID OF SENUSERT II

After the reign of Amenemhet II, the kings of the Twelfth Dynasty once again changed their place of burial. The pyramid of Senusert II is at El Lahun in the mouth of a wide desert wadi leading to the Faiyum. Although actually in the Nile Valley, the pyramid was so situated that it also commanded a view of the then newly developed province of the Faiyum.

A ruined Valley Temple lies about 1,600 meters from the pyramid, opposite the center of its eastern face. It stands on the very edge of the desert and is surrounded by the mud-brick houses of an ancient town. Petrie thought that this town had been built for the workmen, but it probably housed the priests and officials of the pyramid. The temple suffered much in ancient days, and all that now remains are limestone chips covering the ground; several fragments bear traces of carving and brilliant coloring. There must also have been statuary, as indicated by part of a leg of basalt and fragments of a black granite statue and a red granite shrine. In the center of the area was a pit containing foundation deposits. Excavators also found important papyrus manuscripts here. From the eastern side of this Valley Temple a causeway about 100 meters long extends to the edge of the cultivation, but another causeway, which probably connects the Valley Temple with the Mortuary Temple and the pyramid, has not yet been excavated.

Senusert's Mortuary Temple is built at the center of the eastern face of the pyramid. It must have been a splendid monument in its day, as it seems to have been constructed largely of red granite, its incised reliefs and inscriptions filled with green pigment. The site has also yielded fragments of gray granite that seem to have been part of an altar. The temple was probably demolished under Ramses II. His cartouche has been found there, and Senusert's name appears on a reworked block in the temple of Ramses II at Ahnas el Medineh.

Having been constructed largely of mud brick with only a thin casing of white limestone, the pyramid itself is now in dismal condition, being little more than a high mound with a square base. It originally measured 48 meters high and 106 meters square, with an angle of 42°35'.

The pyramid lies upon a natural rise in the ground, and the outcrop of rock which forms its core represents about 12 meters of the total height. On this rocky core sat a square structure divided diagonally by two cross walls. All the walls consisted of large blocks of limestone; the spaces in between were filled with bricks and the pyramid completed in the same material. Finally the whole monument was cased with white limestone, of which almost no trace remains. Graffiti found at the site point again to Ramses II as the king under whom the pyramid was demolished.

Senusert II evidently determined to protect his grave from robbery, so he abandoned the time-honored tradition of a northern entrance. The rock-cut substructure was entered instead from the south by means of two vertical shafts cut outside the building. The main shaft was concealed under the pavement of a tomb of one of the royal princesses, and the secondary shaft lay under the pavement of the pyramid court. The principal shaft, about 25 meters deep, gives on a long passage which slopes upward to a vestibule. Beyond this, it continues in a northerly direction to an antechamber and finally to the burial room. The latter is lined with blocks of red granite and has an arched roof. It measures about 5 meters long, a little over 3 meters wide, and 3 meters high at the highest part. In the western end stood a red granite sarcophagus and an alabaster offering table bearing the name of Senusert II. Nothing remained of the burial except a gold cobra from the front of a crown. (This find of Petrie's is now in the Cairo Museum.) An opening in the short passage connecting the antechamber with the burial chamber leads to a passage which runs south, turns west at right angles, takes successive turns to the north, east, and south, and finally joins the burial chamber at its northwestern corner. Its purpose is not clear, but Petrie believed that it was designed to baffle thieves.

Northeast of the pyramid of Senusert II is a small pyramid built of mud brick and now much ruined. It originally stood about 18 meters high and 27.6 meters square and had a slope of 54°15'. Under each of the corners were small, square holes containing foundation deposits. Part of a name on a vase suggests that the building held the burial of a wife or daughter of Senusert II. The interior of this pyramid has not yet been reached.

To the south, east, and west of the large pyramid were groves of trees, planted in round pits. This is in the tradition of the Eleventh Dynasty temple-pyramid of Mentuhotep at Deir el-Bahri. The trees have not been identified, but we do know that they numbered forty-two on each of the sides so far examined (the eastern and southern); they may have been commemorative trees planted to represent each of the forty-two judges of the Hall of Truth.

A mud-brick temenos wall surrounds both the large and small pyramids. Within the same inclosure, about 70 meters north of the northwestern corner of the pyramid, is a ruined building which may have had to do with the Sed Feast. Also inside the inclosure are several tombs, which almost certainly belong to members of the royal family. All these tombs were plundered in antiquity, but Petrie's 1920 expedition decided to clean them. A great surprise awaited them.

The tomb of one of the princesses contained a rose granite sarcophagus and several canopic jars (the former brought to the Cairo Museum in 1936). The tomb had been completely plundered, but a plastered patch was noticed on one of the walls. On examination, it proved to cover a small recess containing a wooden box filled with jewelry. The box was decayed, but its contents were in an almost perfect state of preservation.[10] This famous collection of jewelry can now be seen in the Metropolitan and Cairo museums. (Archeologists presumed that this represented the princess' entire collection of jewels and that there had been none on the mummy, but this was certainly not the case. When I cleared the tomb in 1936, I found many beads inside the sarcophagus and mingled with the sand on the floor of the chamber. These included five of gold and a few others of turquoise and carnelian.)

Eight large mastabas lay north of the pyramid. Other tombs in the neighborhood include that of Inpy, Senusert's architect.

[10] Guy Brunton, *Lahun I: The Treasure* (London, 1920).

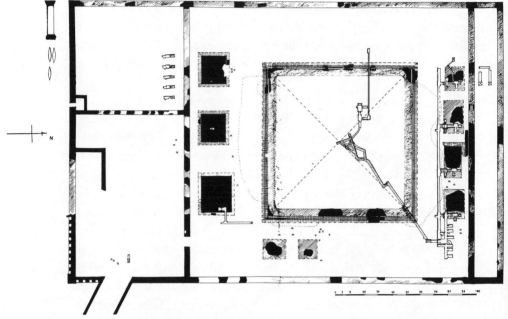

112. *Plan of the pyramid of Senusert III at Dahshur. (After De Morgan.)*

THE PYRAMID OF SENUSERT III

Senusert III was the greatest of the kings of the Middle Kingdom, the famous Sesostris of the classical writers. His activities extended Egypt's southern frontiers far into the Sudan and spread Egyptian culture to the neighboring countries of western Asia and the Mediterranean region. He chose to build his great brick pyramid at Dahshur, on one of the spurs overlooking the capital not far from the pyramid of his grandfather, Amenemhet II.

The Valley Temple has not yet been excavated, but its causeway can be traced from the edge of the cultivation; it runs northwest and joins the temenos wall of the pyramid a little south of the Mortuary Temple. This temple is a complete ruin, but Perring and Vyse in 1839 found several sculptured blocks bearing the name of Senusert III. It was excavated in 1894 by De Morgan, who also found the name of the king inscribed on stone fragments.[11]

[11] J. de Morgan, *Fouilles à Dahchour, mais-juin 1894*, pp. 47. ff.

The pyramid, now ruined, was built of mud brick and cased with limestone. On the outside of the brick core, builders constructed a series of steps, each wide enough to hold a limestone block. These casing blocks were then set in place, and each stone was bonded to its neighbor by dovetail cramps. Several stones thus bonded together may be seen lying east of the pyramid. Perring and Vyse concluded that this pyramid had been built on sifted sand, with which the desert had been leveled.

The pyramid was entered through a pit far to the west of the actual building; this was found by De Morgan and is now inaccessible. Again the builders abandoned the traditional northern entrance in order to hide its location (Fig. 112). The burial chamber is built of enormous blocks of red granite; its roof is pointed on the outer side but vaulted within. At its western end stood a red granite sarcophagus decorated with vertical paneling.

A gallery under the northwestern corner of the pyramid connects with the tombs of several women of the royal family. It was here that De Morgan discovered the famous collection of jewelry now in the Cairo Museum. In these ornaments, the most perfect specimens of ancient jewelry so far known, the art of the goldsmith reached its zenith, never to be surpassed in the greatest days of the Egyptian empire.

Immediately south of the temenos at the western end, De Morgan made another great discovery—three large boats of cedar, each 10 meters long and in good condition. He also found fragments of at least five others, some of them buried in a tunnel-like brick structure. It is generally stated that these were the boats used to transport the king's funeral cortege across the Nile. Recent discoveries, however, indicate that the boats represent a continuation of Old Kingdom traditions and that they were cult objects placed there, like the boats of Khufu and Khafre, to fulfil a special religious purpose. With these boats was a large wooden sledge, which had been used to transport them from the water to their burial place. Two of the boats are now in the Cairo Museum, and a third is housed in the Chicago Natural History Museum.

It is almost certain that Senusert III was buried in his pyramid at Dahshur, surrounded by his family and courtiers. In Abydos the remains of a small pyramid and temple might belong to him. This is a cenotaph built in the sacred area of Osiris, where the mummy of the king might have rested for some time before its final burial.

THE PYRAMID OF AMENEMHET III AT HAWARA

As we have seen, it is not at all unusual to find two tombs for the same king. One of them would be in the Memphis necropolis, while the other would be in the south, in or near Abydos. One baffling exception to this was provided by King Sneferu, who had two great pyramids within a mile of each other at Dahshur. King Amenemhet III also departed from custom when he built one pyramid at Hawara in the Faiyum—in which he was probably buried—and another one at Dahshur, only a few miles south of his father's.

Amenemhet built one of his pyramids at Hawara because he was closely concerned with the fortunes of the Faiyum, the district which his foresightedness had developed. Like the pyramid of Senusert II at Lahun, that of Hawara commands a view of the Faiyum as well as the Nile Valley.

As far as we know, there was no Valley Temple or causeway for the pyramid of Hawara. Immediately south of it, however, is the site of the famous Labyrinth, at least part of which was the temple of Amenemhet III. It was apparently completed by his daughter Sobek-Neferu, who came to the throne as the last ruler of the Twelfth Dynasty. This immense building must have been about 305 meters long and 244 meters wide, large enough to hold the great temples of Karnak and Luxor. It has been used extensively as a quarry since Roman times, and today not a single wall remains standing. The site is indicated by the concrete beds of the foundations and by the vast mass of white limestone and granite chips covering the entire surface of the ground.

When seen by Herodotus, the Labyrinth was still in all its glory, though no doubt it had been restored and enlarged by the Saite kings. The historian says that it surpassed the pyramids, for it had twelve walled courts, six facing north and six facing south. It was said to contain 3,000 rooms, 1,500 above ground and 1,500 below. Herodotus tells us that he personally inspected the rooms above ground, but was not allowed to see the others. He was told that they were the burial places of the sacred crocodiles and of the kings who had originally built the Labyrinth. At

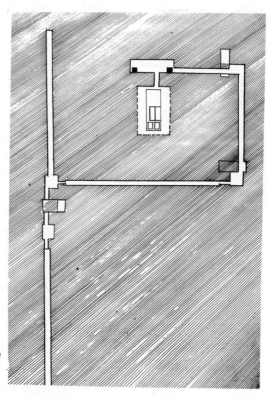

113. *Plan of the passage and chambers of the pyramid of Amenemhet III at Hawara. (After Petrie.)*

the back of the Labyrinth there appears to have been a great granite shrine, containing two figures of the king.

Herodotus also mentions the pyramid of Hawara, which he says adjoined the Labyrinth. It measured 73 meters in height and had large figures carved on it. Although Herodotus does not mention Amenemhet III as the builder of the pyramid, it is clear that his memory was revered there in Ptolemaic times, because people living in the vicinity then were named after him. He is mentioned in an inscription recording a restoration made by a certain Ptolemy and Cleopatra.

The pyramid of Hawara is most interesting, displaying a great amount of ingenuity in the way the architect sought to outwit tomb-robbers.[12] It resembles the pyramid of Senusert II at Lahun, with a mud-brick core, brick filling between cross walls, and a casing of white lime-

[12] W. M. F. Petrie, *Kahun, Gurob, and Hawara* (London, 1890), Plates 2–4.

stone. The interior rooms and corridors, however, are unique (Fig. 113).

Originally the pyramid measured about 100 meters square and about 58 meters high, with a slope of 48°45′. From the entrance, on the south, a flight of stairs led down to a vestibule. This was seemingly a dead end, but actually the roofing slab was made to slide back and reveal the opening to another room, from which led a passage filled with blocks of stone. This was a trick to mislead intruders, and apparently it worked, for an ancient thief patiently tunneled through the blocks to find nothing at the end! The real passage led to another apparently blind chamber. Here again a sliding portcullis revealed a passage leading to a dead end; from this a trap door opened on a passage which led past one side of the burial chamber. Two false burial shafts descended from the floor of this passage to keep the thieves busy, and the other side of the passage was filled in with masonry blocks to lead tunnelers away from the burial. In spite of all this, a persevering plunderer found the cross trench which really led to the burial room. His troubles were not at an end, for this room, which was hollowed out of a single block of hard yellow quartzite, had no door. It could be entered only by moving or breaking one particular roofing block, a single slab of stone that weighed forty-five tons. Thieves did mine through the block, reached the burial, and took all they wanted. Apparently they avenged themselves for the trouble they had undergone by burning the entire contents of the chamber, including the body of the king. Burned fragments of diorite and lapis lazuli inlay testify to the magnificence of his funeral equipment.

The monolithic burial chamber measures about 7 meters long and 2.5 meters wide on its inner sides. The walls are about .55 meters thick, so the stone must weigh about 110 tons. The quartzite room was sunk into a rock-cut pit under the pyramid and roofed with limestone slabs about 2 meters thick; over this was a brick archway and, above this, the superstructure of the pyramid itself.

The burial chamber contains the quartzite sarcophagus of Amenemhet III, quite plain but for a panel design on the foot and a curved lid. Between the sarcophagus and the wall stood a second coffin, built of quartzite blocks and likewise covered with a lid. Two identical quartzite

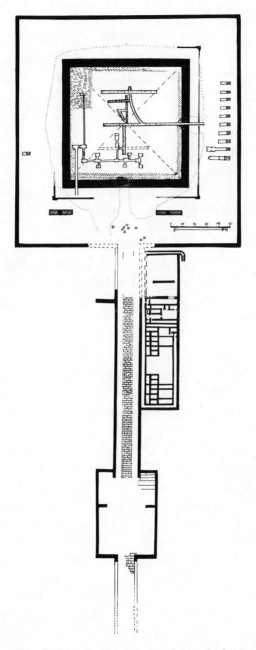

114. *Plan of the pyramid of Amenemhet III at Dahshur. (After De Morgan.)*

canopic chests stood at the head of the sarcophagi. There were no inscriptions on any of these objects.

When investigated by Petrie, the chamber was half full of water, and
its examination was a work of the greatest difficulty and discomfort.
From the water Petrie recovered fragments of alabaster vases bearing
one of the names of Amenemhet III, while in the final passage stood a
beautiful alabaster altar and several alabaster dishes in the form of ducks.
They are inscribed "King's Daughter, Ptah-neferu."

Southeast of the pyramid, on the other side of a modern canal, are the
remains of an inclosure wall which surrounded a mud-brick mound,
removed in comparatively recent times. Several huge blocks of stone,
averaging fifteen tons in weight, lie scattered over the area. It was examined in 1956 and proved to be the tomb of Amenemhet's daughter
Ptah-neferu. Her name appears on large silver vases discovered under the
water that had seeped into the chamber and on the huge pink granite
sarcophagus. Her sarcophagus also yielded beautiful jewelry, including a
handsome necklace of gold and precious stones; all these objects are now
in the Cairo Museum.

THE PYRAMID OF AMENEMHET III AT DAHSHUR

The pyramid which Amenemhet III built for himself at Dahshur lies
between the Bent Pyramid of Sneferu and the modern village of Min-
shat Dahshur. It is near the cultivation and is the southernmost of the
Dahshur group.

The Valley Temple has not yet been found, but its presence is indicated by a long, wide causeway. This was originally paved with limestone slabs and walled with mud brick. It was about 600 meters long and
18.5 meters wide, including the walls. At the upper end of this causeway, just east of the pyramid, are a number of mud-brick buildings,
doubtless the offices of the pyramid administrators and houses for the
priests. Here also are the remains of the Mortuary Temple, of which
little now remains (Fig. 114).

The pyramid itself is a commanding feature of the Dahshur landscape.
Standing tall and dark on the edge of the plateau, it appears much higher
than it really is and is far enough away from its mighty neighbor, the
Bent Pyramid, to avoid being dwarfed by it. The mud-brick core of the

pyramid is all that can be seen. It was originally about 100 meters square, but its height is not known. The base is littered with chips of the white limestone casing stones that once covered it. Perring found one of the casing blocks intact, with an angle of 57°20'. Not only was this pyramid used as a quarry, but even the mud bricks were taken by local villagers as building material for their houses. Fortunately they overlooked the beautiful dark gray granite pyramidion which originally crowned the summit of this imposing monument. It bears the name of King Amenemhet III and is now in the Cairo Museum. Its discovery served to fix the ownership of the pyramid beyond any doubt.

The entrance to the pyramid is on the east side, near the southeast corner. The interior arrangement of passages and vestibules, all lined with limestone, resembles that of Hawara. They lead eventually to the burial chamber, which lies some distance east of the center of the building. The chamber contains a magnificent red granite sarcophagus.

The pyramid, temple, and other buildings are all inclosed in a temenos wall measuring 184 meters on each side.

There is no doubt that the king was buried in his pyramid at Hawara and that this pyramid, in the necropolis of the Old Kingdom Pharaohs, was a cenotaph. As a reason why the king chose a location so far away from Abydos, the customary site for cenotaphs, I offer the following hypothesis: from the monuments discovered in the vicinity, especially those found during my 1952 excavations there, we know that Sneferu was deified during the Twelfth Dynasty. Amenemhet III may have considered that Dahshur, the burial place of Sneferu, was a sacred area and thus a substitute for Abydos. I offer this theory with reservations; the existence of two burials for the same king is one of the problems of archeology which has not been completely solved.

The reasons for the collapse of the Twelfth Dynasty are obscure. The country was enjoying a period of peace and prosperity under the strong rule of Amenemhet III. After his death, the clouds suddenly gathered. His son Amenemhet IV, his successor and co-regent during the latter years of his reign, had only a brief rule, and Queen Sobek-Neferu occupied the throne for about three years after his death. However, the kings of the Thirteenth Dynasty carried on the tradition of building pyramids.

Their monuments stand near Saqqara, because their capital continued to be in the north. The best-known of these pyramids is that of King Khendjer.

THE PYRAMID OF KHENDJER

One mile south of the Mastabet Fara'un at Saqqara South is a group of three pyramids, only one of which has been identified. This is the north-ernmost of the group, and was built by Khendjer of the Thirteenth Dynasty (Fig. 115).

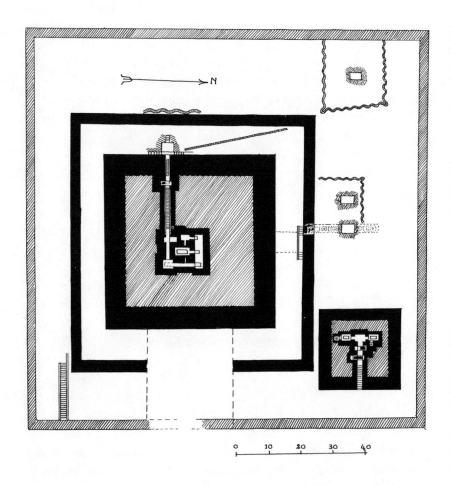

115. *Plan of the pyramid of Khendjer at Saqqara South.* (*After Jéquier.*)

No Valley Temple is known, nor has a causeway been discovered. It has, however, a Mortuary Temple on the eastern side and a small offering chapel on the north. In the latter structure excavators found the fragments, now reassembled, of a fine pyramidion of highly polished black granite. It is inscribed and decorated on all four faces; the eastern side has an interesting scene of the two solar boats of the day and night sun, with the appropriate form of the sun-god in each. Parts of a false door and a statuette of the king himself were also found. At the northeast corner of the pyramid was a foundation deposit consisting of four rough earthenware vases.

The pyramid of Khendjer is inclosed within two temenos walls. The mud-brick outer wall measures 125 meters square, and the inner wall, of fine white limestone, measures about 75 meters square.

The pyramid itself, excavated by Jéquier in 1929,[13] followed the general plan of the Middle Kingdom in regard to its superstructure, consisting of a core of mud brick with fine white limestone casing. This superstructure is now nearly destroyed, but seems to have originally stood about 37.35 meters high, with a slope of 55°; it was about 55 meters square. Apparently the casing was removed during the reign of Ramses II, as one of his architects named Nashui left an inscription in the temple recording the operation. It is strange that Ramses II should be responsible for the demolition of this ancient monument, while less than a mile away his son, Prince Khaemwese, was restoring the Mastabet Fara'un, as well as the pyramid of Wenis at Saqqara!

The entrance to this pyramid, now inaccessible, is on the west. It was walled and roofed with white limestone and opened on a splendid flight of fourteen steps. A short landing was blocked by a portcullis made of a huge block of quartzite and operated transversely. Beyond is another flight of stairs, this time of twenty-nine steps, and a second portcullis. Next comes an elaborate arrangement of passages and chambers, leading finally to a burial chamber situated nearly in the center of the building. The room is hewn out of a single block of quartzite which must weigh about sixty tons. It is roofed with two large slabs of stone, above which was constructed a pointed roof.

Near the northeast corner of Khendjer's pyramid, between its inner

[13] G. Jéquier, *Deux pyramides du moyen empire* (Cairo, 1933).

and outer temenos walls, is a small mud-brick pyramid cased with white limestone. This structure was originally about 25 meters square. When Jéquier excavated it in 1929–31, he found a few courses of the super-structure and one or two casing stones, but not a trace of a Mortuary Temple. The entrance was in the center of the eastern face and had white limestone walls, roof, and floor. It is now blocked with sand, but once led to a passage 15 meters long, beginning with a flight of twenty-one steps. At the bottom is a passage constructed on two dif-ferent levels, each section closed off from the other by means of a port-cullis made of a massive quartzite slab. This corridor terminates in an antechamber, from the north of which a passage leads to a burial cham-ber completely filled by a quartzite sarcophagus. The lid of this coffin is supported on five piles of ancient masonry. It was left in this state await-ing the burial of the owner of the pyramid—a burial which never took place.

South of the antechamber a corridor led to a similar chamber, also completely filled by a quartzite sarcophagus. Here also the lid was sup-ported on ancient piles of masonry, six in number. In each chamber an empty and unused canopic chest lay near the sarcophagus.

AN UNFINISHED PYRAMID

At a short distance southwest of Khendjer's pyramid lie the remains of a large unfinished pyramid. No trace can be seen of a causeway, a Valley Temple, or even a Mortuary Temple, although excavations may reveal them. In its present state, this pyramid is about 95 meters square but only a little over 3 meters high. The superstructure is of mud brick, sur-rounded by the backing stones of the casing, which was probably of white limestone. The foundation deposits discovered in these backing stones, at the corners of the pyramid, consisted of rough earthenware jars and small copper models of tools and implements.

Two pyramidions were found near the entrance, which is in the east-ern face of the monument. Made of black granite, they are unfinished and uninscribed. One of them is truncated, as though it were intended to have a point made of some other material. It is difficult to see why one pyramid should need two pyramidions, each of about the same size. Perhaps one of them was made for a queen's pyramid.

The interior arrangement of this pyramid is very complicated (Fig. 116). Like the two monuments just described, it has an entrance opening on a flight of steps, at the bottom of which a transverse portcullis bars the way. After this is a vestibule and another passage, which makes a right-angle turn to the south and continues for 12 meters. Then comes another vestibule, followed by a flight of five stairs, then another right-angle turn to the west. After traversing more passages and staircases and two more quartzite portcullises, the visitor at last arrives at two ante-chambers and two burial chambers. The larger room has a pointed roof, above which is a small arch. It contains a quartzite sarcophagus, the lid supported on four piles of masonry—indicating that the owner of the

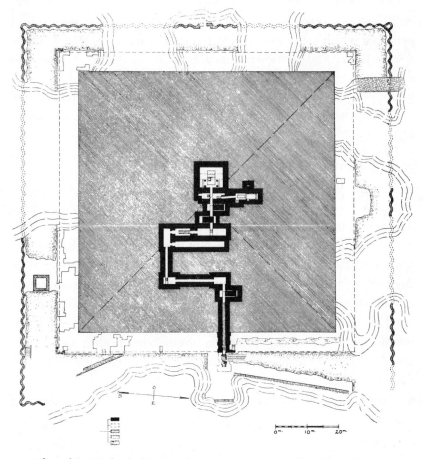

116. *Plan of the Unfinished Pyramid at Saqqara South. (After Jéquier.)*

pyramid had never been buried there. The smaller burial chamber also has a pointed roof and an unused quartzite sarcophagus.

A curious feature of the inside walls of this pyramid is the series of short, vertical lines of black paint arranged parallel with each other about 10 to 15 centimeters apart. We do not know whether they are a form of decoration.

Surrounding the pyramid is a temenos wall of mud brick. It is built on a curious serpentine plan, a feature peculiar to the Middle Kingdom. This particular wall is perhaps the best specimen which has been preserved.

THE PYRAMIDS OF MAZGHUNA

At Mazghuna, between Dahshur and Lisht, there are two very ruined pyramids which are usually considered to date from the Middle Kingdom. Mackay and Petrie examined both in 1910–11.[14] We have no definite evidence of their ownership. It has been suggested that they belong to King Amenemhet IV and Queen Sobek-Neferu of the Twelfth Dynasty, but I believe that they date rather from the Thirteenth Dynasty.

The northern pyramid offers no trace of a Valley Temple, causeway, temenos wall, or Mortuary Temple, and the superstructure of the pyramid itself is now only a shapeless mound a little over 1 meter high. It appears to have been built of limestone. The real entrance has never been discovered, but a flight of ten steps descends at an angle of 27° from north to south. At the end of these steps is a vestibule, and after a right-angle turn to the west, a flight of thirty-one steps, descending at an angle of 13°30′. Both these stairways are flanked by narrow ramps. At the bottom of the second is a transverse portcullis of quartzite. Beyond are more portcullises, passages, and vestibules, and eventually the burial chamber. The sarcophagus is of quartzite. Both it and the exposed surfaces of the quartzite portcullises were painted red with black dashes to imitate red granite.

The southern pyramid of Mazghuna is now merely a low mound of

---

[14] W. M. F. Petrie, Wainwright, and Mackay, *The Labyrinth, Gerzeh, and Maz-ghuneh* (London, 1912).

limestone chips. No remains of a Valley Temple or causeway were found near it, but there was a small Mortuary Temple of mud brick at its eastern side. The pyramid, which was originally about 55 meters square, consisted of a mud-brick core and fine white limestone casing. Of this superstructure, only one or two courses of the brick core still remain. The casing is represented by a foundation trench and chips of limestone covering the surface of the site. Since not a single casing stone was found intact, it was impossible to gauge the original height and slope of the monument.

A flight of stairs descends from the entrance, which lies in the middle of the south side. At the bottom is a transverse portcullis of red granite. This is followed by a second flight of stairs and a second red granite portcullis. Three passages, all at right angles to each other, lead to the burial room, which originally had a pointed roof. This chamber contained a red granite sarcophagus and, in the floor south of it, a square hole for the canopic chest.

The pyramid is surrounded by a mud-brick temenos wall, of the curious undulating type characteristic of the period. There was one gap in the middle of the eastern side—probably for the Mortuary Temple—and another at the eastern end of the south side, representing the original entrance to the pyramid inclosure and the termination of the causeway, if one ever existed.

It is possible that neither of these pyramids was ever completed. In any case, the area has not been thoroughly examined, and cemeteries may be discovered which will reveal the identity of the pyramid owners.

After the Thirteenth Dynasty, Egypt entered a dark period in her history. She could no longer guard her frontiers, and one invasion after another of her eastern borders destroyed the central authority. The eastern Delta was occupied by a foreign enemy called the Hyksos. Possibly of Indo-European origin, they came from the east and had earlier settled in Syria and Palestine and intermarried with Semites for many generations. None of the royal tombs of the Hyksos period have been found, but they were probably not pyramids.

In the following period, the New Kingdom, the important tombs throughout the country were either cut in the rock or built of masonry. Many, however, were surmounted by a small pyramid. This tradition began in the Middle Kingdom, as we know from the tombs of Abydos discovered by Mariette (Fig. 117).[15]

During the Seventeenth Dynasty, the tombs of the princes of Thebes were surmounted by brick pyramids. They are mentioned in the Abbott Papyrus, which describes inquiries made during the Twenty-first Dynasty concerning the robbery of several earlier royal and private tombs. As an example, the papyrus mentions the pyramid of King Antef-aa at Diraa Abul Naga and a stela there which showed the king accompanied by his four dogs. (Mariette discovered the very same stela in position beside the ruins of the tomb, and the fragments are now in the Cairo Museum.) The tombs of Diraa Abul Naga indicate that the tradition of building large pyramids had disappeared. In their place princes and nobles built relatively small tombs in pyramidal form.

A major change in the form of the royal tomb took place at the beginning of the Eighteenth Dynasty. This Theban dynasty was founded by Ahmose, the last of the three rulers who had fought the Hyksos. Both

[15] A. Mariette, *Abydos* (2 vols.; Paris, 1869–80).

117. *Tombs at Abydos surmounted by a small brick pyramid.*

he and his successor, Amenhotep I, built their tombs in the tradition of their immediate predecessors. But the reign of the following king, Thutmose I, saw an important innovation.

Thutmose's architect, Ineni, relates in the biography on the walls of his tomb that the king commissioned him to find a suitable place for the royal tomb. For two months Ineni searched in the hills of western Thebes, "no one seeing, no one hearing," until he found a place which may be the modern Valley of the Kings. There, Ineni ordered the excavation of the first royal tomb to be cut in that valley, a rock-cut crypt that was to be hidden forever. It is probable that the great natural pyramidal peak of the Theban hills, which overlooks the Valley of the Kings, was to serve as a substitute for a pyramid.

Other precautions were also taken to hide the tombs of the kings. The essential funerary temple at the eastern side of the tomb was no longer built in the immediate vicinity of the tomb, where it would indicate the location of the burial. Instead it was constructed at the edge of the cultivation some distance away—still to the east, but separated from the valley by a wall of high cliffs.

The Egyptians had learned a lesson from the times of disorder. They realized that the towering pyramids of former times indicated to tomb-robbers where buried treasure lay; consequently thieves had broken into almost all the pyramids of the Old and Middle Kingdoms, stolen the contents, and destroyed the mummies.

118. *A contemporary drawing of a private Theban pyramid-tomb.*

Although the kings of Egypt abandoned pyramids as their burial places, the pyramid tradition was deeply ingrained in the minds of the people, and private individuals still adhered to it. Some surmounted their simple tombs with brick pyramids topped by a stone pyramidion (Fig. 118). Others placed stelae with pyramidal tops in their tombs.

12

The Epilogue

in the South

Although the royal tradition of a pyramid burial died out in Egypt at the end of the Middle Kingdom, it was destined to be revived once again in the Nile Valley, though neither in the Delta nor in Upper Egypt. This occurred rather in the northern Sudan under the kings of Napata during the Twenty-fifth Dynasty (about 700 B.C.)

Cultural relations between Egypt and the Sudan existed from the beginning of Egyptian history. All the great events in the north had their echo in the south, and in times of prosperity the Egyptian kings sent missions to the Sudan. From time to time African tribes attacked the southern frontiers of Egypt, and the Pharaohs had to send military expeditions to curb the aggressors and restore order. From the time of the early Eighteenth Dynasty, however, Egypt and the Sudan were closely allied. Egyptian temples were built in every part of the northern Sudan and almost as far south as modern Khartoum. The Sudanese worshiped Egyptian gods and followed Egyptian traditions.

The tribute from the south depicted on the walls of private tombs at western Thebes indicates that life in some Sudanese towns was not primitive and that some local industries might have reached a high level. For example, paintings in the tomb of Huy, governor of Cush during the reign of King Tutankhamen, represent part of the tribute from the

237

southern people in the form of goldsmiths' work, chariots, arms, and ornaments. The influence of Egyptian civilization is quite clear in another scene, which shows the procession of a Cushite queen in her ox-drawn chariot. Other works of art in the same tomb display pyramidal forms, an influence that must have come from the north.

The priests of Thebes gained the upper hand in Egyptian politics at the end of the Twentieth Egyptian Dynasty, when the High Priest of Amon-Ra, Herihor, declared himself king in Egypt. Undoubtedly, priests in the Sudan were likewise extending their power. Since the Eighteenth Dynasty, the conical hill of Gabal Barkal near the Fourth Cataract was a sacred place, and temples to the god Amon-Ra were built at its foot. The town of Napata, which rose at the base of the sacred mountain, became the seat of the Viceroy of Cush and the capital of the district. Not far away from the great temple of Amon-Ra stood the palaces of the high priests who officiated there. It is no wonder that when Egypt was in danger and the priest-kings of Thebes had to surrender to their enemies, they took refuge among their southern counterparts. When Egypt was finally humiliated by a foreign invasion, the Napatan priests declared themselves the rulers not only of Cush but also of Thebes and regarded the temples of Amon-Ra at Karnak as their spiritual home. Needless to say, the royal house of Napata worshiped Amon-Ra, spoke the Egyptian language, built monuments in the Egyptian style, and inscribed them with Egyptian hieroglyphs.

The first name recorded in the royal house which came to rule all Egypt was that of Alara. He was followed on the throne by his son Kashta. The latter began to have designs on the north, but the decisive step was taken by his successor, the great Piankhi. For the first twenty years of his reign, he remained at Napata and was content with his friendly relations with the Thebans. But Egypt was no longer a united country. One of the kings of the Delta kingdom, Tefnakht, began to wage war against the princes of Upper Egypt. When he launched an attack against Thebes, the Thebans sent report after report to Piankhi asking his help, and he dispatched an army which met the invaders in Middle Egypt.

The Sudanese army eventually defeated the northerners but failed to occupy their stronghold at El Ashmunein, ruled by an ally of Tefnakht.

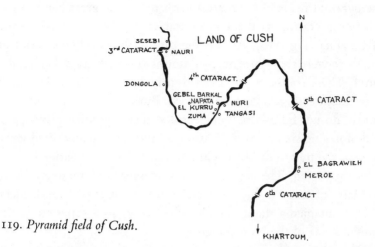

119. *Pyramid field of Cush.*

The latter retreated northward, where he proceeded to raise another army. When this news reached Napata, Piankhi was furious and decided to go himself at the head of a new army. After many fierce battles, Piankhi and his army overcame all resistance. (The interesting details of these battles appear on the famous Victory Stela, which the king dedicated in the Temple of Amon-Ra at Napata and which is now in the Cairo Museum.)

Although Piankhi was a great warrior and a humane and chivalrous conqueror, he lacked political and administrative ability. After defeating his rival, he suddenly decided to leave Egypt and return to Napata. During the remainder of his life he showed no inclination to return to Egypt. While he was in the north, however, he was impressed by the pyramids, and he was buried in such a tomb in emulation of the great Pharaohs of the past. In building his pyramid, he did not try to copy the colossal and majestic monuments west of Memphis, but instead modeled it on those in the Theban necropolis, opposite the great Temple of Amon-Ra. Similar pyramids crowned the tombs of the New Kingdom in Nubia itself.[1]

The many pyramids in the Sudan were not confined, as in Egypt, to reigning kings and their queens. Many belonged to princes and other members of the royal family.

[1] L. Woolley, "The Eckley B. Coxe Expedition," Pennsylvania University *Museum Journal*, I (1910), 42–48; Porter and Moss, *Topographical Bibliography*, VII, 78.

The pyramid fields of Cush are all situated in the great bend of the Nile between Napata, at the Third Cataract, and Meroë, north of the Sixth Cataract (Fig. 119). As was the case in the royal cemeteries of Egypt, there were two types of royal tombs, the mastaba and, later, the pyramid. These southern pyramids display variations in style. Some have a smooth casing; others are stepped. But the stepped pyramids in the Sudan do not follow the same form as their Egyptian prototypes. Instead of having six or fewer great stages, they have many small steps. In general, the pyramids of the Cushite cemeteries are relatively small and steeply angled. The superstructures, of sandstone masonry, were solid. Many of them had a small niche in the upper part; each niche probably contained a statue, similar to what we sometimes see in the pyramidal stelae of the New Kingdom.

The oldest pyramid in the Sudan is that of Piankhi (*ca.* 720 B.C.), which was built at Kurru, about 8 kilometers downstream from the ancient capital of Napata. Some of Piankhi's descendants preferred the site of Nuri, on the opposite side of the Nile, where they built pyramids for themselves, their queens, and their princes and princesses.

When the Ptolemaic Dynasty began its rule in Egypt in the fourth century B.C. and started consolidating and expanding, the kings of Ethiopia transferred their capital farther south to Meroë, near the modern town of Shendi, 209 kilometers north of Khartoum. Meroë was the capital from about 300 B.C. until A.D. 350, when the Axomites (Abyssinians) invaded and put an end to the kingdom. But, during this long period of more than 650 years, continuing rivalry between the members of the royal house resulted in twice changing the capital from Meroë to Napata, which explains the presence of many late pyramids near the latter city.

THE PYRAMIDS OF EL KURRU

The pyramids of El Kurru, on the western bank of the Nile, include the tombs of Piankhi and the immediate members of his family.[2] These monuments follow more or less the same plan in construction. Each had a superstructure built around a core of mud, sand, and small, rough

[2] For a description of the pyramids and the objects found in them, see Dows Dunham, *El Kurru* (Cambridge, Mass., 1950).

pieces of stone, covered with a smooth or stepped sandstone casing. The superstructure was a solid mass with the burial chamber in the natural rock below, approached by a flight of stairs cut in the rock from an entrance outside the pyramid. (This arrangement reminds us of the early archaic tombs of Egypt.) Some of the rooms in the substructure had vaulted ceilings, and each burial chamber had a large rock-cut bier to support the sarcophagus. The chapel, always on the southeast of the pyramid, was small but often pretentious in form, having high and imposing pylons sculptured with portraits of the ruler in warlike poses. Religious scenes adorned the chapel walls.

Piankhi's tomb, the most important of those at El Kurru from the historical point of view, exemplifies most of these traits. The chapel and all the superstructure have been completely destroyed. The angle of its sloping sides was probably about 68°. The entrance, beyond the chapel façade, opens on a rock-cut trench with a flight of nineteen steps leading down to a vaulted doorway. The lower part of the door is cut in the rock, but the upper part, including the vault, is built of stone blocks. The burial chamber measures 5.05 by 3.15 meters, and was roofed with a corbelled masonry ceiling. Almost in the center of the room is a rock-cut bier, which, following the local custom, has the corners cut to allow the legs of a wooden bedstead to stand over it. Apparently this bier was in reality only a support for the sarcophagus, which once rested on the wooden bedstead, as we see in Egyptian reliefs and paintings. The great weight of the mummy and its coffin was thus carried by a stone slab.

Reisner's 1918 expedition found the pyramid to have been completely plundered but did discover the remains of several objects in the debris. Scraps of gold foil, fragments of alabaster, ornaments of lapis lazuli and multicolored faience from inlaid work, alabaster and pottery vessels, and bronze and silver vases testify to the splendor of Piankhi's funeral equipment. There were also several finely formed amulets in the style characteristic of this civilization and many small statuettes known as *ushabti* figures. (Each of these was supposed to "answer" for the deceased when he was called to work; there was an ushabti for every day of the year, as well as overseers.) The chief treasure was a splendid bronze libation stand with attached vessels. This was found twisted and buckled but has since been skilfully straightened.

There are two groups of cemeteries near El Kurru. One, to the south, lies at Zuma, on the eastern bank of the Nile. Local residents have removed the casing to build their own tombs and foundations for their water wheels. The cores of these pyramids are largely of mud brick, but here and there are the ruins of a well-built step pyramid. A similar necropolis exists at Tankasi, opposite Zuma on the western bank of the Nile.[3]

THE PYRAMIDS OF GABAL BARKAL

The peculiar flat-topped mountain known today as Gabal Barkal was believed in ancient times to be the residence of the great god Amon-Ra, and several splendid temples to him were built in the vicinity. The ancients called the mountain *Du-w'ab* ("The Pure Mountain") and built several groups of pyramids on the plain at its foot. Others stood on the lowest foothills of the mountain itself. The pyramids on the plain vary in size from 7.25 meters to 19.82 meters square and from 10.67 meters to 18.3 meters high. They were built of sandstone, and their construction resembled more or less the style of the pyramids of El Kurru. At the southeastern face of each pyramid and built against it was a chapel, sometimes fronted by a pylon bearing reliefs (Fig. 120). Most of these monuments have been destroyed since the time of the French traveler F. Cailliaud, who recorded them in 1820.

The substructures of these pyramids differ from those of El Kurru. Several examined by Budge in 1897 had the approach to the burial

[3] This is based on the descriptions of early visitors to these sites. My friend and colleague Mr. John Cooney drew my attention to the fact that they are earth mounds and that the excavations of the Sudan Antiquities Service in 1953 had shown no connection with pyramids.

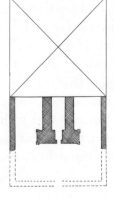

120. *Plan of a pyramid and its chapel at Gabal Barkal.*

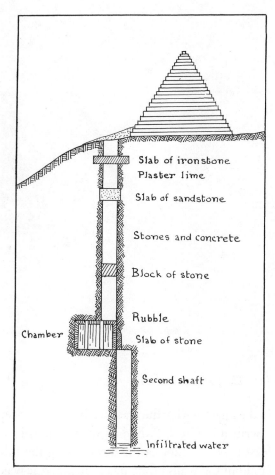

Slab of ironstone

Plaster lime

Slab of sandstone

Stones and concrete

Block of stone

Rubble

Chamber

Slab of stone

Second shaft

Infiltrated water

121. *Section of a pyramid and its substructure (excavated by Budge in 1887).*

chamber through a vertical shaft instead of a staircase. Figure 121 shows a typical example. Immediately west of the pyramid a vertical shaft opened in the ground. At a little distance down this shaft was a thick slab of ironstone set in a bed of lime, and under it a solid layer of lime-plaster, concrete, stone slabs, and rubble. About 18.3 meters below the first ironstone slab were three blocks of stone, which proved to be the roof of a rectangular room. Neither the walls nor the two square pillars supporting the roof were inscribed. From the southeastern side of the chamber, a narrow passage led into another rectangular room, also with square pillars. Both chambers were nearly filled with fine yellow sand.

122. *The pyramids of Nuri.*

In the inner one lay the bleached bones of a sheep and part of an amphora inscribed in Greek "Rhodian wine"—possibly the remains of a funeral feast held in honor of the dead during the filling of the shaft. On examining the walls of the inner chamber, it was found that one of them sounded hollow when struck. The removal of a slab revealed a small vaulted chamber, which contained the opening of another vertical shaft. The shaft had straight sides to a depth of 12.2 meters, then began to widen. At the depth of another meter, workmen were standing in water, so excavators had to abandon the work without reaching the burial chamber.[4]

THE PYRAMIDS OF NURI

The pyramids of Nuri, on the western bank of the Nile, are much better built than most Sudanese pyramids. Their core masonry consists of

[4] E. A. W. Budge, *The Egyptian Sudan*, I, 169–74.

blocks of hewn sandstone, well laid in regular courses, as though they might have been copied from the great pyramids of Egypt (Fig. 122). Some are stepped; others have smooth casings. Their excellent construction led Budge to conclude that they were the oldest in the Sudan,[5] but subsequent investigation proved that this was not the case.

There are over sixty pyramids, the largest being that of King Taharka, a famous king who is mentioned in the Bible.[6] He was the son of King Piankhi and defended Egypt's boundaries against the rising power of the Assyrians. Taharka's pyramid has a most impressive substructure. A flight of stairs leads down to a passage, at the end of which lies a large burial chamber. The roof is supported by six rectangular, rock-cut pillars, which divide the chamber into three aisles. In the central one is the stone slab which supported the sarcophagus upon its wooden bedstead. A corridor around the room is reached by a short flight of steps at the end of the burial chamber.

[5] *Ibid.*, p. 120.
[6] II Kings 19:2.

123. *The pyramids of Meroë as they appeared in 1820.*

Some of the pyramids of Nuri have a torus molding at the corners of the superstructure. Others have a stepped casing with the angle-stones dressed smooth, a treatment which produces a very pleasing effect. All had chapels at the southeastern side, and when seen by Cailliaud, were in good condition.

THE PYRAMIDS OF MEROË

The southernmost pyramids of the Sudan are four groups known as the pyramids of Meroë, which belonged to the kings and queens of the ancient kingdom known as the Island of Meroë (Fig. 123). Several of these were destroyed by Joseph Ferlini while "excavating" in the 1830's, and our knowledge of them comes from his reports.

Ferlini was an Italian physician, who in 1830 entered the service of the Egyptian government as an army medical officer. While serving in the Sudan, he observed the ancient monuments there and became convinced that the pyramids concealed rich treasures. After leaving government service, Ferlini set out on a treasure hunt with his partner, an Albanian merchant named Antoine Stefani. They dug in various ancient sites in

124. *A pyramid of Meroë destroyed by Dr. Joseph Ferlini in 1834.*

the Sudan and at last turned their attention to the pyramids of Meroë. Unfortunately, their idea of "excavating" was simply to pull down the superstructure of any pyramid they wished to examine. Having recruited over three hundred men whom they heartily distrusted and feared, they set to work on their campaign.

While Ferlini demolished one pyramid, Stefani worked on another. The fine pyramid shown in Figure 124, built for a queen, was one of their victims. Ferlini sent his men to the top of it with instructions to tear it down stone by stone. After a while he saw his trusted servant lying down and reaching into a cavity in the monument. The local laborers tried to drive the servant away and take whatever was in the hole, but Ferlini and his partner drove them off. On investigating, Ferlini claimed that they found a chamber in the superstructure, about 2.13 meters long and 1.52 meters wide. In the center of this room was a "masso" (probably the stone slab to support the sarcophagus) covered with a white cloth, which fell to pieces at a touch. Under this cloth was a wooden bier, beneath which were vases. On the floor were amulets, figures of gods, a metal kohl-pot, several tools, and necklaces of gold, paste, glass, and stones. Ferlini gathered up the valuable objects, placed them in leather bags, and returned to camp.

Stefani wanted to return at once to their headquarters, as he feared the laborers would murder them in order to steal the treasure. His partner refused and buried the objects in the sand under his tent. The following morning he returned to the pyramid, which he continued to demolish. In the center he found a small chamber or niche with two bronze vases, showing Greek influence, in an excellent state of preservation. Ferlini finally dismantled the entire superstructure and at ground level found large slabs of black stone. The chapel then came in for his attention, but he contented himself by breaking off a small portion of the doorway in order to carry away the cartouche of the pyramid's owner. Eventually he hit upon the entrance to the substructure, which lay outside the chapel, and, believing that he was on the verge of an important discovery, he began to dismiss his workers. The men refused to leave, and a servant reported that they were planning to kill the excavators, so they escaped that night, taking the objects they had found.

Such is the main outline of Ferlini's narrative. His statement that he found the treasure in a chamber in the pyramid's superstructure is very much open to doubt. The cores of these pyramids were too poorly built of loose rubble to have contained a chamber such as he describes, and it is unlikely that the queen who built the tomb would have entrusted her treasures to so accessible a place. No other pyramid has proved to contain such a chamber in the superstructure, though many have small niches which may have contained a statue. It is possible that the treasure had been collected earlier from several different pyramids and hidden in the cavity where Ferlini found it. Budge believed that Ferlini bought the objects at Kus or a similar place, where rich Graeco-Roman burials were often found, and that the narrative which he published was nothing more than a mixture of his own experience and tales told by native treasure-hunters.[7] Subsequent excavations in the Sudan show that the objects discovered by Ferlini were undoubtedly of Sudanese origin, so we can believe him on this point. But it is well known that dealers in antiquities never divulge the real provenance of the objects they offer for sale, because they always hope to go back to the same place and find more.

The pyramids of Meroë are in three groups, north, south, and west. The superstructures of many are still preserved, but most of them are reduced to heaps of debris. They follow the same design of the pyramids of El Kurru and Nuri, with the base between 8 and 14 meters square and the angle between 65° and 70°. The height varied but averaged between 12 and 20 meters.

All the pyramids of Meroë were of stone except for those built during the decadent period of the Meroitic kingdom, beginning about 200 A.D. These later pyramids were built of mud brick coated with a white layer of plaster.

These pyramids were scientifically investigated by the Boston Expedition under the direction of G. Reisner during the latter years of World War I and the years following.

After the fall of the Meroitic kingdom in 250 A.D., a new religion and new ideals found their way into the Nile Valley, and the Egyptians ceased building pyramids there. But, long before they stopped building

[7] Budge, The Egyptian Sudan, I, 297–98.

pyramids, the form had found its way into many cultures outside Egypt, in far-distant places in Asia, Europe, and Africa. Pyramids were also built in pre-Columbian America, although they were probably not inspired or influenced by ancient Egypt. (They differed in several respects from those of Egypt. Most of them did not contain burials but were surmounted by altars where sacrifices were made.)

We are still far from knowing how the Egyptians built their pyramids, or how they successfully mastered the many difficulties in transporting the huge stone blocks they used. There is still much to be done before we can even know how many pyramids exist or fully describe many that have been partially excavated. More than this, archeologists cannot say that they know the purpose of the passages and chambers inside the pyramids and temples. Nor can they tell whether the fundamental changes in pyramid construction were accidental or had a definite purpose. One thing is certain: the more we learn about the pyramids, the more we admire the science and skill of the ancient Egyptian masons and artists. Let us hope that future excavations and the advancement of many branches of science will help solve the problems concerning their work.

Kings' Pyramids,

with Base Measurements

The unit of measurement used in building the pyramids was the Egyptian cubit, which was divided into seven palms and twenty-eight digits. The standard was the royal cubit equal to 20.6 inches. The angle was usually between 50° and 55° in the kings' pyramids and greater in those of the queens. The reasons for the choice of angle are probably structural; the subject has recently been discussed by J.-P. Lauer "Sur le choix de l'angle de pente dans les pyramides d'Égypte," *Bulletin de l'Institut d'Égypte*, XXXVII (1956), 57–66. In the following list, the base measurements of the pyramids are given in feet, to the closest foot, in order to afford a basis for comparing their relative sizes.

ARCHAIC PERIOD

Dynasties I and II (3200–2780 B.C.)

Mastaba tombs. No pyramids yet assigned to this period

Dynasty III (2780–2680 B.C.)

Zoser	Saqqara	Step Pyramid	411′ × 358′
Sekhem-khet	Saqqara	Unfinished Step Pyramid	400′
Kah-ba	Zawiet el Aryan	Layer Pyramid	276′

| Neb-ka | Zawiet el Aryan | Unfinished Pyramid (superstructure razed) | 590′ × 656′ |
| Hu (Huni) | Meydum | | 473′ |

The Three Unidentified (Royal?) Pyramids

No. 1	Seila	74′ +
No. 2	Zawiet el Amwat	. . . .
No. 3	El Kola	61′

OLD KINGDOM

Dynasty IV (2680–2560 B.C.)

Sneferu	Dahshur	South Stone Pyramid (Bent Pyramid)	619′
Sneferu	Dahshur	North Stone Pyramid	722′
Khufu	Giza	The Great Pyramid	756′
Rededef	Abu Rawwash		320′
Khafre	Giza	The Second Pyramid	708′
Menkure	Giza	The Third Pyramid	356′

Dynasty V (2560–2420 B.C.)

Weserkaf	Saqqara	231′
Sahure	Abusir	257′
Neferirkare	Abusir	360′
Neferefre	Abusir	197′
Neuserre	Abusir	274′
Isesi	Between Saqqara and Saqqara South	270′
Wenis	Saqqara	220′

Dynasty VI (2420–2280 B.C.)

Teti	Saqqara	210′
Pepi I	Between Saqqara and Saqqara South	250′
Merenre	Between Saqqara and Saqqara South	263′
Pepi II	Saqqara South	245′

First Intermediate Period

Dynasty VIII (2280–2242 B.C.)

Iby	Saqqara South	103′

Dynasties IX–X? (ca. 2242–2052 B.C.)

Khui	Dara, Middle Egypt	Structure M	*ca.* 245′

Middle Kingdom

Dynasty XI (ca. 2234–1991 B.C.)

Nebhepetre-Mentuhotep III	Deir el-Bahri	70′

Dynasty XII (1991–1778 B.C.)

Amenemhet I	Lisht	276′
Senusert I	Lisht	352′
Amenemhet II	Dahshur	263′
Senusert II	El Lahun	347′
Senusert III	Dahshur	350′
Amenemhet III	Hawara	334′
Amenemhet III	Dahshur	342′

Dynasty XIII (1778–1625 B.C.)

Khendjer (I)	Between Saqqara South and Dahshur		172′
Unidentified king	South of that of Khendjer		300′
Unidentified king	Mazghuna	North Pyramid	Measurement not possible
Unidentified king	Mazghuna	South Pyramid	182′

New Kingdom

Pyramid tombs replaced by tombs cut in rock cliffs

Post New Kingdom

Dynasty XXV (751–656 B.C.)

Piankhi	El Kurru, Sudan	26′

Recent Investigations

During the last six years, since the second impression of this book, some new data on the pyramids has come to light. This has been the result either of new archeological work or of new publications.[1] This section is a brief summary of the new data from recent investigations.

THE GREAT PYRAMID

The Antiquities Department of Egypt has given special attention to the monuments of the Giza plateau since 1965; the work has been under the supervision of Aly Hassan, the inspector of the pyramids.

Until two and a half years ago, only the Great Pyramid was lighted in its interior and its passages equipped with rails and steps so that it

---

[1] Since 1962, although dozens of papers and several books have been published in which the pyramids are mentioned or discussed, only a very few of them have contributed anything new. A reference must be made, however, to the publications of V. Maragioglio and C. Rinaldi, which began in 1962 with their book *Notizie sulle piramidi di Zedefra, Zedkara, Isesi, Teti* (Turin, 1962). Their series of publications L'architettura delle Piramidi Menfite, which contains a description, new plans, and architectural studies of the pyramids and their temples, is a welcome contribution to the studies of the pyramids; Part 4 was published in 1965. The text is in Italian and English.

In 1965, Herbert Ricke published the first volume on his excavations of the Sun-Temple of King Weserkaf under the title, *Das Sonnenheiligtum des Königs Userkaf* ("Beiträge zur ägyptischen Bauforschung und Altertumskunde," Vol. VII [Cairo, 1965]).

could be visited; now the other two pyramids are also lighted and are accessible to visitors.

There have also been other improvements to the Great Pyramid. Visitors once entered this pyramid through the hole cut during the reign of El Mamun, in the ninth century A.D. Now the original entrance, at a higher level than the later, forced one, has been cleaned, and the debris which partly filled the original passage has been removed. The unfinished burial chamber, which many visitors used to complain of being unable to visit, has been cleaned and lighted and is now accessible to all visitors (see above, p. 117).

THE SECOND PYRAMID OF GIZA

Since January, 1965, the Antiquities Department has been removing the accumulated debris against the western and northern faces of the Second Pyramid, and at the same time, thoroughly cleaning its interior. The two entrances are now accessible, its passages and chambers are illuminated, rails and steps have been installed for the benefit of the visitor, the burial chamber has been cleaned, and the ancient sarcophagus is now in its original place. These improvements were completed in January, 1966.

From the archeological point of view, nothing new has been added to our knowledge of the interior of the pyramid, but the removal of the outside debris accumulated against the northern face has shown that the lowest course of the pyramid casing was of rose granite and that many of its blocks are still *in situ*.

A few rock-cut tombs to the west of the pyramid were found. The most important one belongs to a Washptah. At a distance of twelve meters from the pyramid base, in a passage six meters long, a limestone statue of a court official called Seshem-nefer-ptah was found. The owner of the tomb as well as the owner of the statue were high court officials and belong, in all probability, to the period between the middle of the Fourth Dynasty and the middle of the Fifth.

Since April, 1967, the southern half of the burial chamber of this pyramid has been occupied by apparatus of a unique project for "X-raying" the pyramids, the Joint UAR–USA Pyramid Project (see below).

THE TEMPLE EAST OF THE SPHINX

Since the spring of 1966, the Swiss Archaeological Institute in Cairo, under the supervision of its director, Dr. Herbert Ricke, has been studying the temple which lies in front of the Sphinx. The ruins of this temple have been excavated several times since the middle of the last century, but until now, no reliable plan has been published. Ricke's careful and thorough studies and the needed cleaning have not yet come to an end, and all Egyptologists are eagerly awaiting his report. It is generally accepted that these ruins date from the Old Kingdom and must have been connected with the Sphinx in some way. It was apparently abandoned at an early date and was buried under the sand during the New Kingdom (see pp. 163–64).

Ricke's recent investigations have shown without doubt that the building dates from the Fourth Dynasty but was started after the completion of the Sphinx, most likely, in the reign of Khafre or at the latest in the reign of Menkure. The rectangular building has two entrances on its east side but has no exit at the back connecting it with the Sphinx. To this date it cannot be said with certainty what its function was. There is no evidence to connect it definitely with the Sphinx or to a special cult, but it can be said that in all probability this temple was related to the cult of Khafre and his great statue, the Sphinx. Future work might give us the answer to all these questions.

THE THIRD PYRAMID

In May, 1968, the Antiquities Department decided to prepare the Pyramid of Menkure, as it had the Pyramid of Khafre, and entrusted the work to its inspector of the pyramids, Aly Hassan. Now its interior is clean and illuminated and can be easily visited.

Upon removing the great heaps of debris against the north face, near the entrance, archeologists had more than one surprise. Since 1839, when the entrance of this pyramid was found by Perring and Vyse, many visitors, especially Egyptologists, have visited the interior, but none ever suspected that at a distance of half a meter from the entrance (below and to the east) there was a hieroglyphic text on the granite casing of the pyramid.

The text is composed of at least five lines in sunken relief. The western part of it has deteriorated badly and only a few signs are visible, but the eastern half of the text, i.e., the part which is furthest from the entrance, is in better condition. It gives us the date on which the king was buried in his eternal abode, his tomb, though, unfortunately, the year is missing. The stone has weathered badly in the place where the year ought to be, but from the preserved part we know that his burial took place on the twenty-third day of the fourth month of the winter season. This month begins roughly in the middle of February, and thus we can say that Menkure was buried in his pyramid in March. His death must have occurred some months earlier since mummifying the body and preparing the funerary furniture took several months (see above, pp. 16–17). The length of Menkure's reign is generally accepted as not less than 21 years and not more than 28; and this deteriorated hieroglyphic text was our best chance to discover the exact date.

Four cartouches containing royal names can be distinguished, with some difficulty because they are very badly preserved. The names in two of them are beyond recognition, and a third is not certain. The preserved cartouche contains the name "Menkure." We can expect that one of the three other cartouches is that of his son Shepseskaf, because it was he who suceeded Menkure to the throne, performed all the ceremonies of the burial and completed Menkure's unfinished monuments, including the pyramid and its temples (see above, p. 139).

Around the entrance we can see eight courses of granite blocks remaining from the ancient casing; three of these courses are above the entrance, which is cut in the fifth from the base. The granite casing blocks were left rough; the ancient masons smoothed only the part which contains the entrance and the text. Menkure, however, died before his pyramid was finished.

In June, 1968, almost in front of the entrance, remains of brick walls and a great number of small chips of stone were found. The work is not yet complete, but in my opinion we have here in all probability the remains of a chapel in which stood an offering table. Several examples of these chapels, which stood before the entrances of the pyramids at the north side, are known to us; a good example was found in front of the entrance to the Bent Pyramid of Sneferu at Dahshur (Ahmed Fakhry, *The Monuments of Sneferu at Dahshur*, I [Cairo, 1959], 41 ff.).

X-RAYING THE PYRAMIDS

Since the summer months of 1966, the world has followed with great enthusiasm a project for probing the interior of the pyramids using the advanced techniques of high energy cosmic-ray physics. The purpose of this experiment is to determine if there are still undiscovered galleries or chambers in the body of some of the pyramids, or if there is nothing more than what the archeologists already know. Until now no results have been announced because the recording of the data needs more time, but let us start the story from its beginning.

In the winter months of 1964, the distinguished American physicist, Dr. Luis W. Alvarez, Professor of Physics at Lawrence Radiation Laboratory of the University of California, Berkeley, visited Egypt and took an interest in its monuments. When he returned to the United States, he wanted to know more about the monuments he had visited. Soon after, on a trip to the Arctic region, he spent one of the long cold evenings in the company of a book on Egyptian monuments which he had brought with him. When he compared the drawings of several pyramids he wondered why the Bent Pyramid of Sneferu at Dahshur and the Great Pyramid of Giza, built by his son Khufu, had galleries and chambers in their cores, whereas the Second Pyramid built for Khafre, the son of Khufu, had none; it has only a gallery leading to a chamber at the ground level. Is the whole core of the pyramid solid, with no galleries or chambers? Egyptologists are not at all disturbed by this and are more or less convinced that nothing else is to be found, because the pyramid was built to serve as a tomb for its owner, and here in the Second Pyramid we have the burial chamber which contains the sarcophagus. They explain the presence of the several galleries and chambers as the result of changing the plan during the construction; they refer to the Northern Pyramid of Sneferu and the pyramid of Meydum and to the other pyramids of the Fourth Dynasty to prove their point of view.

But Alvarez' scientific mind hesitated to accept this without discussion; the problem could be solved another way. Why not use high energy muons (mu mesons) in probing the pyramids? Muons shower the earth continually and pass through most all matter they contact. For example, they hit and pass through the human hand about once per second and through the human body about one hundred times per second. Some of these muons have enough energy to pass through the limestone mass of the pyramids. The less limestone the muons go through, the greater the number of muons that reach the base. In other words, if there was a chamber within the pyramid, more muons would be detected at the bottom than if the pyramid were solid.

In 1955, cosmic rays were used to determine the mass of rock overlying a deep tunnel in the Snowy Mountains of Australia; and if this could be done with the rather primitive equipment available in 1955, there was no doubt that with more recent, sophisticated electronic equipment and the newly developed spark chambers any void in the core of the pyramid could be found. The progress achieved in this branch of physics offers even more; it can give us the measurements of the void, and its exact place in the core of the pyramid. The range of error would not exceed three or four feet, and the direction would be certain.

Alvarez decided to carry out his project, and the more he worked on it, the more certain he became that it could be done. From the very beginning he was firmly convinced that international cooperation in scientific matters is greatly desired and that it must be a joint project between the USA and the UAR represented by American and Egyptian scientists. The cooperative project is now being conducted under an agreement between the two governments signed in June, 1966.

Scientists from the Lawrence Radiation Laboratory at Berkeley, headed by Dr. Luis Alvarez, in cooperation with the Department of Physics at Ein Shams University in Cairo, headed by Dr. F. El Bedewi, are conducting the experiment. All of the apparatus and the necessary equipment was shipped from Berkeley to Cairo.

The majority of Egyptologists were reserved toward the project and could not hide their doubt that any galleries or chambers would be found. Some, however, including myself, argued that no one can claim to know everything about the pyramids and their construction, especially the pyramids of the Fourth Dynasty. I am completely convinced that, in spite of my five years' work in the Bent Pyramid of Sneferu at Dahshur, there is still an undiscovered gallery or chamber (see above, pp. 93–94).

It was decided by the Executive Committee of the project that a test should be made to convince archeologists of the validity of the method. If the "pictures" could show the casing left near the top of the pyramid, and also the corners of the pyramid, this should be proof enough. The apparatus was installed in the burial chamber of the Second Pyramid, everything was in order, and the Egyptian and American scientists were about to begin recording the data, when war broke out on June 5, 1967, and the work was stopped. In March, 1968, it was resumed, and one of the American scientists, Lauren F. Yazolino, returned to work with his Egyptian colleagues. They are now waiting with impatience for the arrival in August of a computer for preparing the necessary analysis of the data taken.

Details about the equipment built at Berkeley are available in the First Report on this project[2] but for the layman the following points, taken from a release distributed by the Lawrence Radiation Laboratory when the equipment was about to be shipped to Egypt,[3] can explain in simple language how the experiment is performed.

The experimental method involves the use of cosmic ray muons, unstable particles of the electron family, as "X-rays". As the muons pass through matter they lose energy, and are ultimately stopped. The spark chambers will record the cosmic ray muons energetic enough to reach the detection system from all directions.

The detection apparatus consists of two associated systems. The two spark chambers form one system. They are arranged in a horizontal position, parallel to each other, about a foot apart. Each is about an inch thick, 3 feet wide and 6 feet long. The chambers are hollow, have two layers of wires, and are filled with neon gas in which a passing particle causes a spark.

The spark chambers operate only when "told" to do so by the second system, consisting of three layers of plastic scintillation counters. A layer of scintillators is placed above the top spark chamber and two others below the lower chamber.

Between the lower chamber and the bottom rack of scintillators is a 4 foot thickness of iron (total weight, about 45 tons).

[2] *First Report of the Joint UAR–USA Pyramid Project* (Berkeley, August, 1966), which includes an "Archaeological Introduction" by Ahmed Fakhry, a paper on "Pyramids and Cosmic Rays" by Luis W. Alvarez, a paper on "Electrical and Mechanical Construction" by Jared A. Anderson, and an Appendix "Some Solutions to Data-Handling Problems Associated with the Magnetostrictive Spark Chamber" by F. A. Kirsten, K. L. Lee, and J. Couragan.

[3] Release by the Office of Public Information of the University of California, Berkeley-Lawrence Radiation Laboratory (February 22, 1967).

The racks of scintillators are arranged, with the iron, in such a way as to be sure that a particle passing through all three scintillators is a muon that will be useful for the experiment. The iron filters out weak particles that wobble through all three detectors without indicating their true direction and fool the experimenters.

Passage through all three scintillator arrays, occurring in a few billionths of a second, triggers the spark chambers, which retain the energy impulse of the particle after it has passed through the third scintillator below the iron.

A spark occurs in each chamber; electronic equipment determines the point in each chamber at which the particle passed, and relays the information to the recording laboratory.

The two points determine the angle of passage and the direction from which the particle came.

Muons which have passed through a void in the limestone—such as a hidden chamber—will be relatively more frequent and more energetic than those passing through solid rock. Thus, more of them should reach the spark chambers to be recorded, and the hidden void should show up in the detectors as a comparatively higher rate of incoming particles.

With the two spark chambers about a foot apart from each other the scientists believe it will be possible to detect any hidden chamber and to pinpoint its location to within a few yards. Tunnelers could then bore directly to the chambers to explore further.

The spark chambers will operate around the clock for several months. Computer analysis of the data will be made at the Ein Shams Computing Center in Cairo.

We have to wait a few months more to know the results. However, regardless of the results, positive or negative, the experiment will have been a great contribution to the study of this pyramid and will end speculations once and for all. This is a great opportunity for science to render a service to archeology without any harm coming to either the pyramid or the archeologist. The same equipment, as well as the great experience gained, can be used in the future to probe other pyramids of Egypt and monuments of similar architectural construction in other civilizations.

This project, which puts the techniques of high energy physics in the service of archeological research, represents a new chapter in the history of archeology.

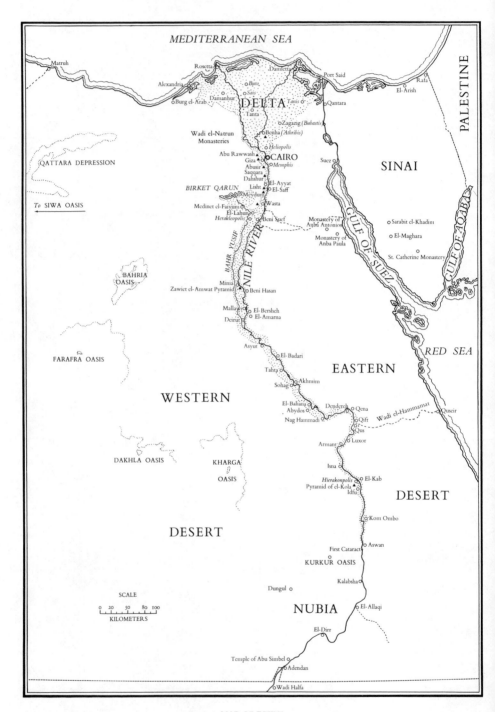

MAP OF EGYPT

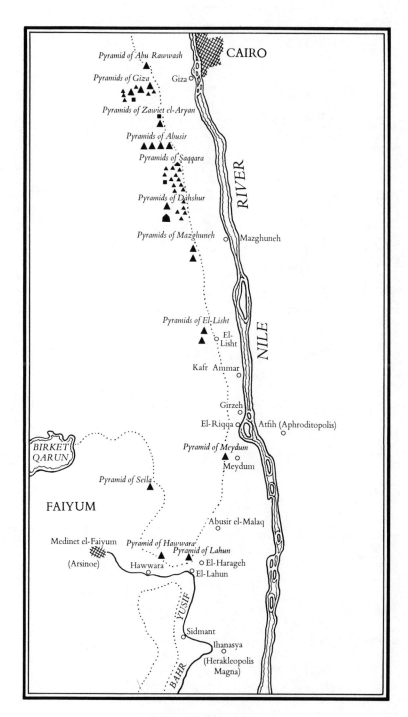

Pyramid of Abu Rawwash
CAIRO
Pyramids of Giza   Giza
Pyramids of Zawiet el-Aryan
Pyramids of Abusir
Pyramids of Saqqara
Pyramids of Dâhshur
Pyramids of Mazghuneh   Mazghuneh

RIVER

NILE

Pyramids of El-Lisht
El-Lisht
Kafr Ammar
Girzeh
El-Riqqa   Atfih (Aphroditopolis)

BIRKET QARUN
Pyramid of Meydum
Meydum

Pyramid of Seila

FAIYUM

Abusir el-Malaq

Medinet el-Faiyum   Pyramid of Hawwara
(Arsinoe)   Hawwara   Pyramid of Lahun
El-Harageh
El-Lahun

YUSIF

Sidmant
Ihanasya
(Herakleopolis Magna)

BAHR

MAP OF PYRAMID FIELDS

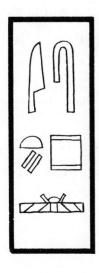

Index

267